Language Socialization in Classrooms

Classrooms are dynamic spaces of teaching and learning, where language and culture are intertwined in remarkable ways. The theory of language socialization explores how sociocultural practices help to shape language learning and development. This collection is the first of its kind to bring together research on this fascinating concept. It presents 10 case studies, based on linguistic and ethnographic research conducted in classrooms located within communities in North America, Europe, and India, spanning learners from preschool, to primary and secondary school, to university. Following an introduction that discusses the theory and core concepts of language socialization, the volume is divided into three central themes: socializing values, dispositions, and stances; socializing identities; and language socialization and ideology. Both new and more experienced researchers will appreciate its fresh insights into how language socialization is carried out across the globe.

MATTHEW J. BURDELSKI is Professor of Applied Japanese Linguistics at Osaka University, Japan. Focusing on Japanese and US classrooms and communities, his research utilizes language socialization and conversation analysis to investigate adult–child and children's multimodal interactions in teaching, learning, acquiring, and using Japanese as a first, second, and heritage language.

KATHRYN M. HOWARD is Associate Dean and Director of Clinical Experiences and Partnerships at California State University, Channel Islands. Her work focuses on how multilingual children develop a range of linguistic resources from multiple languages in formal (classrooms) and informal educational contexts to display or enact social identities and to engage in complex social relationships.

Language Socialization in Classrooms

Culture, Interaction, and Language Development

Edited by

Matthew J. Burdelski
Osaka University

Kathryn M. Howard
California State University, Channel Islands

CAMBRIDGE
UNIVERSITY PRESS

University Printing House, Cambridge CB2 8BS, United Kingdom

One Liberty Plaza, 20th Floor, New York, NY 10006, USA

477 Williamstown Road, Port Melbourne, VIC 3207, Australia

314–321, 3rd Floor, Plot 3, Splendor Forum, Jasola District Centre,
New Delhi – 110025, India

79 Anson Road, #06–04/06, Singapore 079906

Cambridge University Press is part of the University of Cambridge.

It furthers the University's mission by disseminating knowledge in the pursuit of
education, learning, and research at the highest international levels of excellence.

www.cambridge.org
Information on this title: www.cambridge.org/9781107187832
DOI: 10.1017/9781316946237

© Cambridge University Press 2020

First published 2020

A catalogue record for this publication is available from the British Library.

Library of Congress Cataloging-in-Publication Data
Names: Burdelski, Matthew J., 1967– editor. | Howard, Kathryn M., 1966– editor.
Title: Language socialization in classrooms : culture, interaction, and language
development / Matthew J. Burdelski, Kathryn M. Howard.
Description: Cambridge ; New York, NY : Cambridge University Press, 2020. |
Includes bibliographical references and index.
Identifiers: LCCN 2019038916 (print) | LCCN 2019038917 (ebook) |
ISBN 9781107187832 (hardback) | ISBN 9781316638354 (paperback) |
ISBN 9781316946237 (epub)
Subjects: LCSH: Language and education–Case studies. | Socialization–Case studies. |
Language and culture–Case studies. | Language and languages–Study and
teaching–Social aspects–Case studies. | Classroom environment–Case studies. |
Sociolinguistics.
Classification: LCC P40.5.S57 L37 2020 (print) | LCC P40.5.S57 (ebook) |
DDC 306.44–dc23
LC record available at https://lccn.loc.gov/2019038916
LC ebook record available at https://lccn.loc.gov/2019038917

ISBN 978-1-107-18783-2 Hardback

We dedicate this volume to
Alexandra "Misty" Jaffe (1960–2018),
an extraordinary scholar, mentor, and colleague.

Contents

Figures

Tables

Contributors

USREE BHATTACHARYA is Assistant Professor in the Department of Language and Literacy Education, College of Education, University of Georgia.

MATTHEW J. BURDELSKI is Professor of Japanese Linguistics in the Faculty of Letters at Osaka University.

ASTA CEKAITE is Professor of Child Studies, Department of Thematic Studies, Linköping University.

PATRICIA A. DUFF is Professor of Language and Literacy Education at the University of British Columbia.

DEBRA A. FRIEDMAN is Associate Professor of Second Language Studies at Indiana University, Bloomington.

INMACULADA M. GARCÍA-SÁNCHEZ is Associate Professor of Anthropology and Director of Undergraduate Studies at Temple University.

KATHRYN M. HOWARD is Associate Dean of the School of Education at California State University, Channel Islands.

ALEXANDRA JAFFE was Professor of Linguistics and Anthropology at California State University, Long Beach.

MARTHA SIF KARREBÆK is Associate Professor, Department of Nordic Studies and Linguistics at the University of Copenhagen.

WENDY KLEIN is Associate Professor of Linguistics and Anthropology at California State University, Long Beach.

ANDREA LEONE-PIZZIGHELLA is Director of the TESOL Essentials Series at the University of Pennsylvania.

EKATERINA MOORE is Assistant Professor of Clinical Education, Rossier School of Education, University of Southern California.

BETSY RYMES is Professor and Chair, Educational Linguistics Division, Graduate School of Education, University of Pennsylvania.

LAURA STERPONI is Associate Professor of Language, Literacy and Culture, Graduate School of Education, University of California, Berkeley.

Acknowledgments

The editors would like to express our gratitude to the following people for providing feedback on the content of this volume at various stages of its development: Karin Aronsson, Netta Avineri, Patricia Baquedano-López, Patsy Duff, Cyndi Dunn, Debra Friedman, Paul Garrett, Wendy Klein, Adrienne Lo, Ben Rampton, and Betsy Rymes. We would also like to thank the anonymous reviewers for providing comments that helped shaped this volume, and the staff at Cambridge University Press, especially Helen Barton and Adam Hooper, who guided us through the process.

Transcription Conventions

Symbol	Name	Use
[text] / [[text]]	Brackets	Start and end points of overlapping speech.
=	Equals sign	Break and subsequent continuation of a single interrupted utterance.
(# of seconds)	Timed pause	Number in parentheses indicates the time, in seconds, of a pause in speech.
(.)	Micropause	Brief pause, usually less than 0.2 seconds.
.	Period	Falling pitch.
?	Question mark	Rising pitch.
,	Comma	Temporary rise or fall in intonation.
-	Hyphen	Abrupt halt or interruption in utterance.
>text<	Greater than/less than symbols	Enclosed speech was delivered more rapidly than usual for the speaker.
<text>	Less than/greater than symbols	Enclosed speech was delivered more slowly than usual for the speaker.
°	Degree symbol	Whisper or reduced volume speech.
CAPS	Capitalized text	Shouted or increased volume speech.
word	Underlined text	Speaker is emphasizing or stressing the speech.
:::	Colon(s)	Prolongation of an utterance.
hhh	Letter h	Audible exhalation or laughter.
.hhh	High dot	Audible inhalation.
(text)	Parentheses	Speech that is unclear or in doubt in the transcript.
((text)) / ((*text*))	Double parentheses	Annotation of nonverbal activity, or transcriber comment.
!	Exclamation point	Emphasis at the end of an utterance.

Additional transcription symbols, if any, are provided in individual chapters.

Based on Jeffersonian transcription notations (with some modifications); see Jefferson, G. (1984), Transcription notation. In J. Atkinson and J. Heritage (eds.), *Structures of Social Interaction*. New York, NY: Cambridge University Press.

1   Introduction

Language Socialization in Classrooms

Matthew J. Burdelski and Kathryn M. Howard

1.1   Introduction

In societies across the globe, an immense amount of energy and resources is poured into educational enterprises aimed at teaching and learning in various classroom settings. These endeavors instill students with academic knowledge and promote their acquisition of skills in creating new and competent members. Yet, there is a profoundly cultural organization of learning in classrooms. Classrooms are complex and dynamic spaces where teaching and learning are mediated by specific languages, communicative resources and practices, and culturally informed activities. Thus, as students participate in classroom discourse and activities they not only develop knowledge and skills, but also are socialized into a "habitus" (Bourdieu, 1991), or a set of ideas, beliefs, preferences, and practices that afford and enable, as well as constrain and limit, their actions in the social world. As the formation of knowledge/skills and personhood/subjectivity are intertwined, these dimensions of human activity and the ways in which they mediate learning and development over time are the focal concern of scholarship in the field of language socialization (e.g., Ochs and Schieffelin, 1984; Schieffelin and Ochs, 1986). Although social theory has long assumed that schools are fundamental sites of cultural reproduction, language socialization research seeks to document this reproduction as well as its change and transformation through the identification and analysis of the particulars of culturally and locally organized routines, activities, and practices (e.g., Garrett and Baquedano-López, 2002). In bringing together a set of papers based on ethnographic and linguistic research conducted in a range of diverse communities, this volume aims to highlight scholarship that critically discusses and systematically examines the process of language socialization in classrooms.

An enduring tradition of research on discourse and interaction over the past few decades has uncovered a wealth of information on the structural organization and communicative practices of teaching and learning activities in classrooms (e.g., Bloome et al., 2004; Cazden, 1988; Erickson, 1982, 1996; Hicks, 1996; Margutti and Piirainen-Marsh, 2011; Markee, 2015;[1] Mehan, 1979; Mehan and Griffin, 1981; Resnick, Asterhan, and Clarke, 2015). Over a similar period, an emerging body of scholarship has documented the process of language socialization in classrooms (e.g., Baquedano-López, 1997; Burdelski, 2010; Cekaite, 2012; Cook, 1999; Duff, 1993; Fader, 2001; Friedman, 2010, 2016; García-Sánchez, 2010; He, 2000, 2015; Heath, 1982; Howard, 2009; Kanagy, 1999; Klein, 2013; Lee and Bucholtz, 2015; Lo, 2009; Moore, 2006; Ohta, 1994; Philips, 1983; Poole, 1992; Talmy, 2008; Willett, 1995; Vogel-Langer, 2008; Zuengler and Cole, 2005). As there is an immense amount of interest in classroom interaction in the fields of anthropology, applied linguistics, communication, conversation analysis, and education, this volume seeks to build upon prior research on language socialization and classroom discourse by examining ways in which communicative practices in classrooms – with their distinctive turn-taking organization, activities, participant roles, and goals – are a vehicle for socializing child, adolescent, and adult learners into language and culturally meaningful realities. Here, we consider such culturally meaningful realities to be constructed and subjective, rather than given and objective.

The volume reveals how a language socialization perspective can shed greater light on the role of classroom discourse as a medium of learners' development and growth, and at the same time show how detailed analyses of classroom discourse can illuminate the field of language socialization by highlighting teaching and learning as a robust, dynamic, and culturally organized process. The papers have implications for how to work with teachers, graduate students, and colleagues to investigate classrooms by interrogating both the more *visible/hearable* interactions (e.g., teacher-fronted lessons) and *invisible/unhearable* ones (e.g., peer interactions conducted in a quiet voice as the teacher is conducting a lesson). In these ways, the volume offers a theoretically grounded and thematically organized collection of studies on language socialization in classrooms. The individual chapters span a range of continents (Asia, Europe, and North America), languages (Danish, English, Corsican/French, Hindi/English, Japanese, Russian, and Swedish), settings (e.g., urban and rural, religious and secular), and learners (e.g., first language [L1], second language [L2], immigrant, heritage, child, and adult). The chapters all focus on classroom discourse from a common theoretical perspective – language socialization – in seeking to foster coherence and a better understanding of teaching and learning in classrooms, and the theoretical, practical, and policy implications thereof. In the remainder of this chapter, we present the theory and methodology of language socialization, and summarize the structure of the volume and chapters.

1.2   Language Socialization

Language socialization is a theoretical and methodological framework that explores the acquisition, reproduction, and transformation of knowledge and competence across the lifespan. As originally articulated in the 1980s by Elinor Ochs and Bambi Schieffelin (Ochs and Schieffelin, 1984; Schieffelin and Ochs, 1986) – and later updated by them and their former students and colleagues (e.g., Duff, 2010; Duff and May, 2017; Garrett and Baquedano-López, 2002; Howard, 2014; Kramsch, 2002; Kulick and Schieffelin, 2004; Ochs and Schieffelin, 2011, 2017; Paugh, 2016) – language socialization was proposed as a distinctive field of inquiry to bridge and build upon research on children in the fields of anthropology (where *language* was often glossed over) and language acquisition (where *culture* was often glossed over). Based on the assumption that language socialization begins from the moment a child enters the social environment, the central tenet of the theory is that the acquisition of language and culture are intertwined and mutually interdependent, principally involving "socialization *through* the use of language and socialization to *use* language" (Schieffelin and Ochs, 1986, p. 163). In other words, as children and other less experienced members participate in situated interactions with more experienced members, they develop an ability to understand and use language and discursive practices in situationally appropriate ways, while being socialized into systems of cultural meaning that include ways of speaking, feeling, and acting that are necessary for functioning in the communities they inhabit. Although the process of language socialization occurs where there are asymmetries of knowledge, competence, and experience, this process is bidirectional in that not only are novices socialized by experts but also experts are socialized by novices into new identities, stances, and actions. The roles of relative expert and novice can shift during an interaction depending on the prior experiences of participants, topic of talk, language being used or talked about, and other dimensions of the social situation (e.g., Duff, 2008; Pontecorvo, Fasulo, and Sterponi, 2001; Takei and Burdelski, 2018).

Research on language socialization examines the ways in which culturally specific linguistic, embodied, and material resources – including prosody, word choice, syntax, turn-taking, activities, code choice, genre, bodily comportment, gesture, and objects – and communicative practices and routines are the vehicles for socializing less experienced individuals into a range of cultural meaningful realities that are not *essential* (i.e., given, objective) but rather *constructed* and *subjective*. These realities include identities, stances, ideologies, morality, social acts and activities. In their early comparative study of White middle-class American (WMCA), Western Samoan, and Kaluli caregivers that launched the field of language socialization, Ochs and Schieffelin (1984) argued that "baby talk," or linguistic accommodation (e.g., grammatically simple sentences, repetition), is neither a universal practice nor a necessary condition for language acquisition to occur, as was previously assumed. Rather it is culturally variable and influenced by beliefs and ideas, or ideologies (see Section 1.2.3), about how children acquire language and their roles and statuses in relation to others in society. They showed that although WMCA caregivers verbally accommodate to children's perspectives and presumed competence by treating them as equal conversational partners through a great deal of communicative scaffolding, in the highly stratified society of Western Samoan caregivers do not make such verbal accommodations, as children are expected to accommodate *to others* of higher status. These caregivers use a "minimal grasp" strategy that requires children to repeat or reformulate their unclear utterances (i.e., child accommodates speech to others), rather than expand or guess the meaning of children's unintelligible utterances (i.e., caregiver accommodates speech to the child in WMCA society) (Ochs, 1988). Similarly, among the Kaluli of Papua New Guinea, baby talk is also not observed, but for a different cultural reason: Kaluli children are viewed to be naturally "soft" and have to be "hardened" (e.g., to use language to be assertive), and thus baby talk is not considered helpful for this goal (Schieffelin, 1990). These observations suggest that "child-directed communication" (Ochs, Solomon, and Sterponi, 2005) is influenced by cultural notions and ideologies of children's roles, rights, and responsibilities in society.

    Although early language socialization research primarily focused on domestic settings, research conducted around the same time by Heath (1982) and Philips (1983) explored schooling practices in diverse communities in the United States. Both of these studies documented ways that language socialization processes in the home, including speaking and literacy activities, converge and diverge from those in classrooms, and discussed the pedagogical and social implications of domestic language socialization practices on children's participation and success in school. Heath's (1982) study of three nearby communities in the US Piedmont Carolinas – Maintown (White middle class), Roadville (White working class) and Trackton (Black working class) – found that the process of language socialization in White working-class homes prepared children, although less well than the children in the White middleclass homes, for participation and success in school. This preparation included participating in bedtime stories, using everyday language, such as addressing adults and older children with politeness formulae, and gaining familiarity with the structuring of the classroom environment (e.g., through question–answer sequences). In comparison, in the Black working-class community, Heath observed a discontinuity between home and school socialization in relation to literacy activities and everyday language use that presented children with an unfamiliarity of classroom practices, such as responding to teacher questions that ask for what-explanations, or labeling of shapes, colors, and numbers.

Similarly, Philips' (1983) study of the Warm Springs Reservation in the US Northwest state of Oregon, examined discontinuities between home and school language socialization by aiming to provide an ethnographically grounded account of Native American children's reluctance to speak and participate in predominantly Anglo classrooms. She showed that discursive and socialization practices in domestic settings, such as long periods of Native American children's keen observation of others in tasks, group-facing discussion, and talking while engaging in physical activity, did not translate well to the Anglo-American classrooms where the children often sat in rows and were expected to demonstrate their verbal competence and academic knowledge, which was immediately subjected to public scrutiny and evaluation by the teacher and peers. From a pedagogical perspective, Philips suggested that teachers need to become more aware of the different socializing practices of children in the home and their own implicit assumptions about communication and children's participation in their classrooms. The findings of these two pioneering studies suggest that when language socialization practices in the home are radically different from those at school, children may have trouble participating in classroom discourse and achieving academic success; however, when these practices are relatively congruent, children might have an easier time participating in classroom discourse and achieving academic success.

In the early 1990s, language socialization research in classrooms expanded to examine second language (L2) classrooms both inside and outside the United States. In a study at a US university in two English as a second language (ESL) classrooms, Poole (1992) observed how the teachers' practices reflected a White middle-class communicative style in speaking with less competent members (as articulated by Ochs and Schieffelin, 1984), though the teachers had different ways of organizing the students in the classroom spaces and engaging them in activities. One teacher, who had the students sit in rows, conducted a great deal of discursive accommodation, such as by providing (1) "test questions" or known-answer questions, (2) incomplete (fill-in-the-blank type) utterances, and (3) expansions, in scaffolding students' displays of competence. The other teacher, who organized the students in a semi-circle, engaged the students in an activity beyond their level of L2 competence by providing a great deal of scaffolding, such as offering words and expressions for the students to say and repeat. Poole also observed that both teachers tended to use first person plural pronouns (*we*, *us*, and *our*) to downplay their authority and power (see Section 1.2.4) and create solidarity by inviting students to accomplish an activity together. She showed that the teachers, however, shifted to first person reference (student name or pronoun) when evaluating individual work, which conveyed independence and competence in having accomplished the task.

Around the same time, Duff (1993) conducted a first- and second-language socialization study of several classrooms in different schools in Hungary that were either English-medium (or "non-traditional") or Hungarian-medium (or "traditional") (see also Duff, 1996 for an analysis of one Hungarian-medium classroom). Importantly, her research occurred during the dissolution of the Soviet Union (end of 1991), which was a period of rapid social change in Hungary as well (as it was originally one of the Eastern Bloc countries heavily controlled by the Soviet Union). The change included gradually moving toward Western values of democracy, egalitarianism, and critical thinking. Duff was able to observe ways in which classroom practices reflected and constituted ongoing changes and tensions in the larger Hungarian society. She focused on a traditional and ritualized classroom activity known as *felelés* (oral recitation/examination), in which students were required to memorize a text or summarize the previous day's lesson and repeat it back as an assessed performance in front of the class. She observed that while some of the English-medium language classroom teachers abandoned this activity entirely, others who continued with it attempted to modify it in order to give the students more autonomy in line with the new democratic values, such as by replacing the teacher-selected presentations with student-volunteered pre-planned presentations. Her findings suggest that the tensions and problems experienced in the modified style of classroom assessment, such as difficulty with balancing student respect for the teacher and maintaining teacher author-ity and discipline in the classroom with the new Western-style practices of overt praise and fostering student independence, was a microcosm of the tensions observed in the larger society upon moving toward a more democratic ideology.

Since the late 1990s, the scope of language socialization research in class-rooms has further expanded into ethnically, linguistically, and culturally diverse settings (e.g., Garrett and Baquedano-López, 2002), such as class-rooms with immigrant and migrant children, children learning a heritage language, and adults and children learning a second or additional language. With a few exceptions (e.g., Howard, 2009; Moore, 2006), studies have mainly focused on communities in North America and to a lesser extent in Europe, as the training of graduate students and researchers in language socialization theory and methodology has largely occurred in the United States (see Duff, Chapter 12 in this volume). Language socialization research in North America and Europe has primarily investigated diversity *within* a society. Researchers who have done such fieldwork in other cultures (e.g., Howard, 2009; Moore, 2006) have been able to make what anthropologists often call the *strange familiar* by striving to make sense of the practices of a social group and (upon returning to their home country) the *familiar strange* by broadening their understanding of practices that had been previously taken for granted. This too has implications for training of graduate students and collaboration with colleagues, such as by encouraging them to reflect upon and critique their own classroom practices.

By offering this volume of 10 case studies based on ethnographic and linguistic research in schools and classrooms (and in some cases in settings beyond them) within Europe (four chapters), India (one chapter), and the United States (five chapters), we highlight ongoing and dynamic work being conducted on language socialization where multiple languages, cultures, genres, and "communicative repertoires" (Rymes, 2010) are in play. In the remainder of this chapter, we unpack language socialization theory, methodology, and prior research by detailing the following five dimensions of language socialization theory, especially as they relate to classrooms: (1) indexicality, (2) practices, (3) ideologies, (4) power, authority, and agency, and (5) participation frameworks.

1.2.1 Indexicality

Central to the process of language socialization theory is "indexicality" (e.g., Agha, 2005; Bucholtz, 2009; Inoue, 2004; Jaffe, 2016; Ochs, 1990, 1992; Silverstein, 1976, 2003), or the notion that the referential and social meanings of language resources are contextually bound. Indexicality enables language to both reflect and constitute the social "context" (Duranti and Goodwin, 1992), such as identities, stances, social acts, social activities, and other culturally meaningful realities that are co-constructed (Ochs, 1992). Ochs (1992) proposed two levels of indexicality in relation to cultural meaning: direct and indirect. She argued that linguistic forms directly index social acts and epistemic/affective stances, which in turn indirectly index or constitute particular identities (e.g., in many classrooms, the person who primarily initiates and evaluates talk is constituted as the teacher). Language socialization research in classrooms has shed light on ways teachers convey the social indexical meanings of linguistic forms. In an elementary classroom in a Northern Thai village, Howard (2009) observed how teachers instructed students to use honorific forms when addressing other teachers as an index of social hierarchy and respect, as reflective and constitutive of relationships in the larger Thai society. In a Russian heritage-language school affiliated with an Orthodox Christian church in the United States, Moore (Chapter 4 in this volume) shows how teachers made assessments of church objects to index positive affective stances in socializing children to membership in an Orthodox Christian community. In a Swedish language classroom for recently arriving immigrant children, Cekaite (Chapter 6 in this volume) finds that when defining ostensibly unknown words for children (e.g., 'to nag') teachers used language and embodied resources to index positive and playfully negative affective stances in locating the words within egalitarian parent–child relationships (e.g., parents nag children and children nag parents) that are highly valued in Swedish society. In a graduate program for teaching English to speakers of other languages (TESOL) at a US university, Friedman (Chapter 8 in this volume) observes ways in which teachers engaged students in metalinguistic practices that displayed authoritative epistemic stances, such as identifying and explaining grammatical errors and citing authoritative sources of grammar use (e.g., the APA manual), in socializing students to use language in ways that indexed an identity as competent TESOL professionals. Thus, teachers in classrooms across the globe use specific communicative resources as an index of culturally meaningful realities in ways that implicitly convey these meanings to students.

While language socialization research has often focused on the use of linguistic and other semiotic resources to index widely circulating culturally meaningful realities, the process of language socialization also involves the use of such resources to index more particularized, novel meanings in creating new and hybrid identities, performing social actions, and displaying stances (e.g., Jaffe, Chapter 5 in this volume). As pointed out by Ochs and Schieffelin (2011), a challenge for language socialization research and theory is to account for how both creativity and conformity are indexed in learners' lives. These dual aspects have been documented especially within studies of peer language socialization (e.g., Goodwin and Kryatzis, 2011; Paugh, 2012; Reynolds, 2007). This body of research is especially relevant to classrooms. In a Japanese preschool classroom, Burdelski (2013) showed how three-year-old girls used addressee honorific (*desu/-masu*) forms, which traditionally index out-group relationships and public personas (e.g., Cook, 1996), to create social distance and display affective stances in excluding an older boy from their play. In an honors Language Arts classroom at a US high school, Rymes and Leone-Pizzighella (Chapter 7 in this volume) show how students used various communicative resources to index "unofficial" classroom stances (ironic, witty, uncertain) within "side interactions" with nearby peers (such as by whispering an exchange in order to confirm an answer to the teacher's question) that positioned themselves and peers in various roles and relationships (e.g., "friend," "confidant," "less/ more expert").

In sum, the process of language socialization in classrooms and beyond entails learning to understand linguistic and other semiotic resources not only in indexing well-established culturally meaningful realities, but also in imagining, instantiating, and establishing novel and innovative ones.

1.2.2 Practices

Language socialization occurs through everyday "communicative practices" or "socializing strategies" (Ochs and Schieffelin, 2011), constructed through a rich "ecology of sign systems" (Goodwin, 2000), including linguistic, embodied, and material resources (Ochs, Solomon, and Sterponi, 2005). In classrooms, some of the key practices or strategies that have been examined include the following:

(1) questions (e.g., Heath, 1982; Poole, 1992)
(2) error correction or repair (e.g., Burdelski, Chapter 10 in this volume; Friedman, 2010; Jaffe, Chapter 5 in this volume)
(3) elicited repetition and prompting (e.g., Burdelski, 2010; Bhattacharya and Sterponi, Chapter 9 in this volume; Jaffe, Chapter 5 in this volume; Karrebæk, Chapter 11 in this volume; Moore, 2011)
(4) assessments or evaluations (e.g., Burdelski and Mitsuhashi, 2010; Lo, 2016; Moore, Chapter 4 in this volume)
(5) accounts (e.g., Karrebæk, Chapter 11 in this volume)
(6) fill-in-the-blank utterances (Jaffe, Chapter 5 in this volume; Poole, 1992)
(7) directives (e.g., He, 2000)
(8) modeling and demonstration (e.g., Burdelski, Chapter 10 in this volume; Moore, 2006)
(9) reported speech (e.g., Moore, Chapter 4 in this volume)
(10) narrative or storytelling (e.g., Baquedano-López, 1997, 2000; Ikeda, 2004)
(11) "participant examples" (Cekaite, Chapter 6 in this volume; Ikeda, 2004; Moore, Chapter 4 in this volume, Wortham, 1992).

These practices are embedded within and constitute classroom routines and activities in ways that encourage students' acquisition of academic knowledge and skills together with their formation of personhood and subjectivity. In an ethnically diverse Danish kindergarten classroom, Karrebæk (Chapter 11 in this volume) shows how teachers used accounts and requested accounts from children in relation to their not bringing rye bread in their lunchboxes, socializing them to norms and values of healthy eating practices that are valued by the school program and the mainstream society. In a classroom activity focusing on collaboratively constructing poetic texts in Corsican as a heritage language, Jaffe (Chapter 5 in this volume) shows how the bilingual Corsican-French teacher used fill-in-the blank utterances[2] followed by rising intonation that invited students to self-correct portions of their texts. The findings reveal how children were socialized to becoming competent poets and to acquiring a poetic genre valued among Corsican speakers. Other studies have shown how practices inside and outside classrooms can be interpreted by members and non-members of the culture in very different ways. In a taek-wondo lesson at a Korean heritage-language school in California, Lo (2016) observed how an instructor responded to a student's taekwondo moves and displayed attitude by producing "negative" assessments as a form of shaming (see Lo and Fung, 2011) – a social emotion, as it requires a person to be immersed among others. Although this episode was interpreted in post hoc interviews by the Korean teacher and Korean informants as indexical of caring and concern for the student's skill and social development, non-Korean observers typically viewed it as being potentially harmful to the students' emotional development and self-esteem. In addition to linguistic resources, the discursive architecture of classroom practices is constructed from material and embodied resources that socialize novices into specific ways of acting in the social world. At a Japanese heritage-language school in the United States, Burdelski (Chapter 10 in this volume) observes how teachers prepared the children for a preschool graduation ceremony by modeling and demonstrating how to receive the graduation certificate (e.g., bowing toward the principal, receiving the certificate with both hands). The teacher then engaged the children during individual rehearsal by using touch and bodily manipulation to instruct them to coordinate their verbal and embodied actions, which socialized them in how to use bodily conduct in a formal, ritual performance that is highly valued in the Japanese educational system and society.

In sum, communicative practices built from a range of multimodal resources are the vehicle through which novices are socialized to and through language. By participating in the process of language socialization in classrooms, novices gain familiarity with the practices.

1.2.3   Ideologies

Communicative practices and language resources in classrooms, and the choices of language, dialect, or register, as well as *who* teaches, are mediated by ideologies that are shaped by (and in turn shape) social, political, and economic concerns (e.g., Althusser, 1971; Blommaert, 1999; Errington, 1999; Jaffe, 1999; Kroskrity, 2004; Riley, 2011; Rumsey, 1990; Silverstein, 1979; Woolard and Schieffelin, 1994). Language ideology refers to "common-sense notions about the nature of language" (Rumsey, 1990, p. 346) and "beliefs, or feelings, about language as used in social worlds" (Kroskrity, 2004, p. 498), such as "unexamined cultural assumptions" (Riley, 2011, p. 493) about language use and episodes taken up for metalinguistic and metapragmatic commentary that can become a focus of contestation and challenge in interaction. Language ideologies play a role in sustaining languages, dialects, and communicative practices, and can also contribute to change and even "erasure" (Irvine and Gal, 2000), or the process whereby persons, activities, and language features are made invisible because they are inconsistent with a given ideological position. Most centrally, ideologies are conveyed within everyday human action (Jaffe, 1999).

Language socialization research has examined ways in which ideologies are related to identity and undergird processes of language shift and language maintenance in communities and societies (e.g., Bunte, 2009; Garrett, 2005; Jaffe, Chapter 5 in this volume; Klein, 2013; Kulick, 1992; Makihara, 2005; Paugh, 2005; Riley, 2007). In a Dominican community, Paugh (2005) observed a language policy to introduce the vernacular (Patwa) into classroom literacy activities, but found that rural villagers expressed an ambivalence that these efforts would succeed as they continued to face dominant policies and ideologies in social life that devalued and excluded Patwa from institutional discourse and the desired professions. In classrooms, language ideologies undergird educational activities, discursive practices, and socialization strategies. In a school in Spain with many immigrant children from Morocco, García-Sánchez (Chapter 2 in this volume) shows how an ideology of "tolerance" toward immigrant children was an aspirational value of the school that shaped class content and practices, but points out that this ideology was both supported and contested within the wider community. Her observations reveal subtle and overt exclusion of Moroccan children by their Spanish peers in activities as representing a microcosm of the struggles and wider tensions concerning the flow of immigrants in Spain. In some classrooms, language ideologies of "purity" (Friedman, 2010; Klein, Chapter 3 in this volume) and "correctness" (Burdelski, Chapter 10 in this volume) that are tied to identity and stance are revealed in certain practices such as error correction. In a study of a Sikh education program at a *gurdwara* in Southern California, Klein (Chapter 3 in this volume) shows how, during a class discussion in English, a student (who had been born in Punjab and lived there until the age of 12) displayed a "purist language ideological notion" by initiating a correction of another student's Anglophone pronunciation of the word *Sikhs*. Klein suggests that the student's correction indexed an authoritative stance and the positioning of himself as a gatekeeper of the language ideology that links native pronunciation of the membership category *Sikh* with authentic Punjabi identity.

In these ways, language ideologies play a role in language shift and maintenance, and impact the codes, genres, registers, and discursive practices used in classrooms. Language ideologies themselves are also conveyed by teachers and students in subtle and overt ways through metalinguistic and metapragmatic discourse surrounding what is (in)correct.

1.2.4   Power, Authority, and Agency

Human interaction and language socialization occur within asymmetrical relations of power and authority (e.g., Bourdieu, 1991; Foucault, 1980) that are manifested in everyday discursive practices (e.g., Goodwin and Cekaite, 2018; Philips, 2004; Summerson, 2010). Power and authority emerge, unfold, and are achieved in interaction in ways that *ascribe* and "position" (Davies and Harré, 1990) self and others in relation to action, knowledge, and ability (e.g., Evaldsson and Tellgren, 2009; Goodwin, 2006; Shohet, 2013). Power and authority can be not only displayed, but also concealed or modulated, and sometimes projected onto third parties. In her research on Japanese mother–child interaction, Clancy (1986) observed that by projecting power (in the form of linguistic directives) onto a non-present third party (such as a teacher, father, or doctor), mothers positioned themselves as an equal in relation to the child (e.g., Clancy, 1986). As social actors with agency (e.g., Ahearn, 2001), relative novices not only acquiesce to power/authority and thereby co-construct it, but also contest, undermine, resist, or ignore it through their own actions and silences.

In institutional settings such as classrooms, relational categories (e.g., teacher–student) are instantiated through discursive practices. The teacher–student relationship is an inherently asymmetric one, in which teachers display or downplay their power/control, authority, and knowledge in ways tied to stance and identity. At a school in a suburban New Delhi community, Bhattacharya and Sterponi (Chapter 9 in this volume) show that during the daily Morning Assembly children were required to repeat and recite a school pledge in unison after the teacher. They argue that both the content and performance of the pledge socializes Indian children to literacy and obedience to authority as an important value in Indian society based on the master–disciple relationship. Conversely, in English-speaking classrooms at a US university, Rounds (1987) showed that teachers often downplayed their power and authority through the use of first person plural pronouns (*we*, *us*, and *our*) as a non-inclusive referential (meaning *you*, students) in directing the students' actions (e.g., "Let's look at the problem *we* [=*you*] had to do for today"). She argued that this pronoun use indexed stances of alignment and group togetherness as part of an American democratic ideal. Students may resist teachers' ascription or positioning of them in relation to acts, stances, and identities (see Chapters 6, 8, and 3 in this volume, by Cekaite, Friedman, and Klein, respectively). Within peer groups, children can create their own power and authoritative structures in ways that exclude other children (e.g., Goodwin, 2006), which either fly under the radar of adults or are noticed and subject to teacher intervention. At the Spanish school mentioned above, García-Sánchez (Chapter 2 in this volume) observes that having ostensibly noticed that Spanish children were excluding a

Moroccan peer on the playground the teacher stepped in and destabilized this peer-constructed power structure of exclusion by asserting his own power and authority in encouraging the children to include the peer.

In sum, power/authority and agency are crucial to the process of language socialization in and around classrooms, as teachers display, modulate, or mask their power and authority, and novices align or contest it and form their own kinds of power and authority among peers.

1.2.5   Participation Frameworks

The process of language socialization generates various "participation frameworks" (e.g., de León, 1998; Goodwin and Goodwin, 2004; Ochs, Solomon, and Sterponi, 2005) that structure novices' development in culturally specific ways. Inspired by Goffman's (1981) original formulation, the notion of participation frameworks has come to be viewed as a dynamic configuration of actors in which linguistic, material, and embodied resources are used in ways that afford, promote, and change, as well as constrict and limit, the engagement of social actors in interaction (Ochs, Solomon, and Sterponi, 2005). Goffman's deconstruction of the categories of "speaker" (e.g., "author," "animator," "figure,") and "recipient" (e.g., "addressee," "overhearer," "observer") into various roles has invited researchers to look beyond a dyadic model of communication in examining ways novices are positioned in various roles in multiparty interaction. Among the Kaluli of Papua New Guinea, Schieffelin (1990) observed that caregivers use *elema* routines (X *elema* 'X, say') to position children as "animator" of an utterance in encouraging them to use language to be confrontational and assertive. In a Zinacantec Mayan community, de León (1998) showed how caregivers use a reported speech frame ('he/she says') to ventriloquize the wants and needs of infants and toddlers based on their proto-vocalizations and gestures. She argued that this positioned children within a complex participation framework as "embedded speakers," and was an important means through which these children "emerge" as social actors in everyday life.

Classrooms are inherently multiparty participation frameworks through which students are positioned and position themselves in various roles (e.g., addressee, observer). Philips' (1983) study of language socialization in homes and classrooms on the Warm Springs Reservation suggests that Native American children's participation in the Anglo-American classrooms was restricted in relation to their Anglo peers. She argued that this was because forms of participation in Anglo-American classrooms (such as the IRE routines and sequences discussed below) were quite different from those in Native American homes, where children engaged in a great deal of observation before being required to participate in direct ways.

A fundamental turn-taking structure observed in many classrooms is IRE routines (e.g., Mehan, 1979), canonically composed of teacher *Initiation*, followed by student *Response* and teacher *Evaluation*, where teachers have the power and authority (see Section 1.2.4) to select who speaks next and to evaluate the student's answer. While these routines are an emergent structure that is interactionally achieved (see Rymes and Leone-Pizzighella, Chapter 7 in this volume), their content and preferred organization are culturally specific (e.g., Cook, 1999). In an honors Language Arts classroom for gifted high school students in the United States, Rymes and Leone-Pizzighella argue that the predictability of the IRE routines enables students to anticipate the flow of classroom discourse whereby in the interstices of and in overlap to the routine, or what they call "unofficial" space, students accomplish various actions (e.g., confirm a candidate answer to the teacher's question), display affective and epistemic stances, and perform identity work with peers. They show how the students also performed this work in the "official" space of the classroom, or IRE routines, such as by answering the teacher's questions about the Shakespearean text in which they inserted their own linguistic markers of suburban youthfulness (e.g., "like"). In some classrooms (Cekaite and Moore, Chapters 6 and 4 in this volume), teachers use "participant examples" (Wortham, 1992) that position the students as "figures," or characters, in hypothetical scenarios, such as in explicating the meaning of unfamiliar words. Such examples may socialize children not only to the meaning of words but also into culturally specific meanings related to relationships (Cekaite, Chapter 6 in this volume) and affective stance (Moore, Chapter 4 in this volume). In a TESOL program for graduate students in the United States, Friedman (Chapter 8 in this volume) shows how, in introducing an example sentence from the textbook in which the students were asked to delete a word from a sentence in order to make it grammatical, the instructor used reported speech to "animate" what the non-native speakers of English in the classroom were likely thinking (Teacher: "the nonnative speakers are laughing like HA how would I have ever found that right?"), ascribing particular knowledge of English to them (as deficient) in relation to their native-speaking peers.

In sum, participation is an essential dimension of language socialization in classrooms through which teachers and students are positioned in relation to various kinds of social actions, stances, and identities.

1.3   Research Methodologies

The chapters in this volume take a linguistic and an ethnographic approach to the study of human development (see Garrett, 2008; Kulick and Schieffelin, 2004; Ochs and Schieffelin, 2011) through observations and recordings of focal children and teachers within specific educational activities in classrooms.

As Ochs (2000, p. 230) has observed in relation to language socialization methodology:

the gaze and camera lens of the data collecting researcher is primarily directed at the activities undertaken rather than zooming in and tracking the actions of any one participant. Activities (e.g., telling a story, playing a game, preparing and consuming food, attempting to solve a problem, having an argument) are examined for their social and linguistic organization, including the spatial positioning of more or less experienced participants, the expressed stances, ideas, and actions that participants routinely provide or elicit and, importantly, the response that such expressions receive.

In this volume, some of these activities include reciting a pledge during Morning Assembly (Bhattacharya and Sterponi, Chapter 9), throwing a ball in a group and dancing (García-Sánchez, Chapter 2), eating lunch (Karrebæk, Chapter 11), constructing verses of a poetic genre (Jaffe, Chapter 5), reviewing answers to a homework assignment on Shakespeare's *Hamlet* (Rymes and Leone-Pizzighella, Chapter 7), discussing prescriptive grammar rules (Friedman, Chapter 8), and rehearsing how to receive a graduation certificate (Burdelski, Chapter 10). Recordings were done longitudinally (from a few months to a few years) in order to capture how language, including "micro-movements of bodies, gestures, and verbal acts" (Ochs and Schieffelin, 2011, p. 12), was being used by participants in socially situated ways and how this use relates to cultural meanings that may have broader social and political implications. During the recordings, the primary researcher or a member of the research team was usually co-present in order to monitor the equipment and in some cases shadow participants who moved around the classroom or other spaces. This co-presence can subject language socialization researchers to criticism that the methodology is too invasive of people's lives or unduly influences the interactions being observed. As language socialization research-ers are highly sensitive to people's lived worlds, a great deal of care is taken in finding a balance between participating as an "outsider" of the observed community (e.g., developing a rapport with participants) and stepping back from the interactions in order to capture what is typical and ordinary. In order to elucidate the particulars of interaction and relate them to broader cultural meanings, recordings are essential. Participants usually become so engrossed in their daily activities that the video equipment and the camera person are rarely attended to. Nevertheless, the videographer does have a "participation status" (Goffman, 1981) (see Section 1.2.5), typically as an "observer" or sometimes as an "addressee" and is thus not completely immune from shaping the interactions.

Recordings of interactions were played back by researchers a number of times, in some cases while working with participants or informants, to identify, transcribe, and analyze the particulars of what people were doing in order to arrive at more generalized understandings. Some researchers employed play-back sessions of the recordings with participants, while others utilized semi-structured interviews with teachers and students (Jaffe, Chapter 5), in order to reveal various perspectives of the recorded interactions, uncover participants' ideologies that motivated their practices, and obtain other information that informed their analyses. In many cases, materials were supplemented with fieldnotes and observations of interactions that could not be recorded (e.g., due to the sensitivity of the scene).

In some of the chapters, some new methods have emerged in relation to language socialization research in classrooms, as researchers involved teachers and students in shaping the activities that were observed. Jaffe (Chapter 5) participated in a language revitalization effort of the Corsican language by working with teachers and students at two elementary schools on Corsica to introduce and carry out a poetry project in the heritage language, which was ultimately performed between the students of the two schools at another site (a museum). Rymes and Leone-Pizzighella (Chapter 7) worked closely with a classroom teacher in order to bring insights from linguistic anthropology and sociolinguistics to develop the teacher's classroom lessons. In these ways, the study of language socialization in classrooms affords researchers the oppor-tunity to collaborate with teachers and students in order to mutually inform the analysis and shape the pedagogical practices being documented.

1.4   Summary of Parts and Chapters in the Volume

The volume is divided into four parts. Following this introduction, Part I, *Socializing Values, Dispositions, and Stances*, highlights how everyday class-room routines, practices, and activities are vehicles for socializing cultural dispositions, values, and stances in ways that are crucial for becoming compe-tent members of classrooms and communities. The section consists of three chapters, focusing on children and adolescents in different languages and communities. In Chapter 2, Inmaculada M. García-Sánchez examines the classroom as a site for socializing tolerance (a socio-politically contested value in the community) in preventing exclusion of immigrant Moroccan children by their peers in a rural Spanish elementary school. García-Sánchez analyzes episodes in which children subverted the socialization of tolerance and how teachers dealt with those subversions. Specifically, she shows ways that some children attempted to exclude their Moroccan peers from participating with them in classroom activities, and ways that teachers intervened (or did not intervene) such as by avoiding labeling discrimination and prejudice overtly in negotiating the politics of inclusion and diversity among the children. In Chapter 3, Wendy Klein presents an analysis of Sunday classes held at a *gurdwara* (Sikh temple) for Sikh youth in urban Southern California by focusing on the mutual socialization of teachers and students. While bridging the domains of religious schooling and immigrant communities, Klein focuses on how teachers took on the roles of mentor in advising these youth on how to respond to their non-Sikh peers outside the classroom who categorized them in negative ways using racial, ethnic, and religious stereotypes. She examines how students with various backgrounds in the heritage culture (some were born in the United States, while others had arrived from India in early or later childhood and adolescence) socialized their peers and teachers. In Chapter 4, Ekaterina Moore takes us to an elementary school classroom in an urban community in the United States, in which children are learning Russian as a heritage language at a school affiliated with the Orthodox Christian Church. Moore investigates how children are socialized into appropriate stances, values, and feelings toward religious practices that index what it means to be an Orthodox Christian and shows how the children aligned with and resisted those stances using words and prosodic devices.

Part II, *Socializing Identities*, examines socialization into identities tied to society, roles, and knowledge, and considers their fluidity. The section is comprised of four chapters, focusing on child and adult learners. In Chapter 5, Alexandra Jaffe focuses on elementary school children's socialization to the role of "poet" and to the poetic genre of *Chjam'è rispondi* (Call and Response) in a French–Corsican bilingual school on the island of Corsica. Against the backdrop of language revitalization of Corsican in schools that she participated in and helped shape, Jaffe traces the longitudinal process of children's written production of poetic texts in the classroom to oral performances both inside and outside the classroom in shaping and transforming this traditional genre. She shows how this process socialized the children not only to existing social identities but also to new identities as poets in the heritage language. In Chapter 6, Asta Cekaite takes us to a Swedish elementary school where she focuses on teachers' vocabulary explanations to children from various immigrant backgrounds. Cekaite shows how the teachers' explanations, often in the form of narratives and participant examples, were sites for positioning children in identities embedded in traditional Swedish family and society. She also shows how the children co-constructed and at times resisted this positioning. In Chapter 7, Betsy Rymes and Andrea Leone-Pizzighella focus on an honors Language Arts class in a US high school. In identifying what they call "contrapuntal" interaction among peers that occurs in tandem to the teacher's lesson, the authors detail the ways in which the teacher encouraged such interaction, and in the process provided a space for peer socialization. In Chapter 8, Debra Friedman examines L2 socialization and identity construction in relation to a different setting and type of learners: US-raised and international students in methods courses within a graduate program on teaching English to speakers of other languages (TESOL) at a US university.

She details discourses of difference in the ways the teachers positioned US-born and international graduate students in relation to knowledge about English, and the ways the international students positioned themselves and challenged their status as relative "novices" in claiming expertise over the teacher, shedding light on the fluidity of expert–novice roles in classrooms involving adult learners.

Part III, *Language Socialization and Ideologies*, examines socialization to and through ideologies. In Chapter 9, Usree Bhattacharya and Laura Sterponi present a study of children at a village school in suburban New Delhi, India. Employing Althusser's (1971) notion of ideological state apparatus in relation to schooling, the authors explain that a central ideology in Indian society is to incorporate individuals into power structures where teachers, parents, and elders are the primary sources of knowledge. They examine the verbal, corporeal, and spatial ways in which the daily routine of the Morning Assembly in classrooms is a key site for socializing children into dispositions of authority and knowledge in relation to schooling and the broader community. In Chapter 10, Matthew Burdelski examines language ideologies surrounding "correctness" and attention to embodied form and detail in a Japanese-as-a-heritage-language (JHL) preschool classroom in the United States by focusing on socialization into the linguistic, material, and embodied moves required of children in receiving a preschool graduation certificate for an upcoming ceremony. By using verbalization, touch, and guided manipulation of children's bodies, the teachers implicitly conveyed to children the importance of the body in presenting a public self in a highly valued formal ritual in Japan. In Chapter 11, Martha Karrebæk focuses on an ethnically diverse kindergarten classroom in Denmark where ideologies about health in the school and mainstream Danish society shaped the kinds of talk about food during lunch time. She shows how teachers often requested accounts from children, especially from the children from immigrant families where food practices were often very different from the mainstream society, socializing children to an ideology surrounding healthy eating habits.

In Part IV, consisting of Chapter 12, Patricia Duff provides a commentary on the contributing chapters, details how language socialization theory informs understandings of classrooms, and identifies what the chapters contribute to language socialization theory. She also provides suggestions for future research on language socialization in and out of classrooms.

NOTES

1 This edited volume examines classroom and interaction from various perspectives, and includes a part titled "The Language Socialization Tradition" consisting of four chapters that examine language socialization in (and out) of classrooms.
2 In an examination of classroom discourse from a conversation analysis perspective, Koshik (2002) refers to these as "designedly incomplete utterances."

REFERENCES

Agha, A. (2005). Voice, footing, enregisterment. *Journal of Linguistic Anthropology*, 15(1), 43–59.

Ahearn, L. (2001). Language and agency. *Annual Review of Anthropology*, 30, 109–137.

Althusser, L. (1971). *Lenin and Philosophy and Other Essays* (translated by B. Brewster). New York, NY: Monthly Review Press.

Baquedano-López, P. (1997). Creating social identities through *doctrina* narratives. *Narrative Inquiry*, 10(2), 1–24.

Baquedano-López, P. (2000). Narrating community in *doctrina* classes. *Narrative Inquiry*, 10(2), 1–24.

Blommaert, J. (ed.) (1999). *Language Ideological Debates*. Berlin: Mouton de Gruyter.

Bloome, D., Carter S. P., Christian B. M., Otto S., and Stuart-Faris, N. (2004). *Discourse Analysis and the Study of Classroom Language and Literacy Events: A Microethnographic Perspective*. Mahwah, NJ: Lawrence Erlbaum Associates.

Bourdieu, P. (1991). *Language and Symbolic Power* (translated by G. Raymond and M. Adamson). Cambridge: Polity Press.

Bucholtz, M. (2009). From stance to style: gender, interaction, and indexicality in Mexican immigrant youth slang. In A. Jaffe (ed.), *Stance: Sociolinguistic Perspectives* (pp. 146–170). Oxford: Oxford University Press.

Bunte, P. (2009). "You keep not listening with your ears!": language ideologies, language socialization, and Paiute identity. In P. Kroskrity and M. Field (eds.), *Native American Language Ideologies* (pp. 172–189). Tucson, AZ: University of Arizona Press.

Burdelski, M. (2010). Socializing politeness routines: action, other-orientation, and embodiment in a Japanese preschool. *Journal of Pragmatics*, 42, 1606–1621.

Burdelski, M. (2013). Socializing children to honorifics in Japanese: identity and stance in interaction. *Multilingua*, 32(2), 247–273.

Burdelski, M. and Mitsuhashi, K. (2010). "She thinks you're kawaii": socializing affect, gender, and relationships in a Japanese preschool. *Language in Society*, 39(1), 65–93.

Cazden, C. (1988). *Classroom Discourse: The Language of Teaching and Learning*. Portsmouth, NH: Heinemann.

Cekaite, A. (2012). Affective stances in teacher–novice student interactions: language, embodiment, and willingness to learn. *Language in Society*, 41, 641–670.

Clancy, P. M. (1986). The acquisition of Japanese communicative style. In E. Ochs and B. B. Schieffelin (eds.), *Language Socialization across Cultures* (pp. 213–250). New York, NY: Cambridge University Press.

Cook, H. M. (1996). Japanese language socialization: indexing the modes of self. *Discourse Processes*, 22(2), 171–197.

Cook, H. M. (1999). Language socialization in Japanese elementary school: attentive listening and reaction turns. *Journal of Pragmatics*, 31, 1443–1465.

Davies, B. and Harré, R. (1990). Positioning: the discursive production of selves. *Journal for the Theory of Social Behavior*, 20(1), 43–63.

De León, L. (1998). The emergent participant: interactive patterns in the socialization of Tzotzil (Mayan) infants. *Linguistic Anthropology*, 8(2), 131–161.

Duff, P. A. (1993). "Changing times, changing minds: language socialization in Hungarian-English schools." Unpublished doctoral dissertation, University of California, Los Angeles, CA.

Duff, P. A. (1996). Different languages, different practices: socialization of discourse competence in dual language school classrooms in Hungary. In K. Bailey and D. Nunan (eds.), *Voices from the Language Classroom: Qualitative Research in Second Language Education* (pp. 407–433). New York, NY: Cambridge University Press.

Duff, P. A. (2008). Language socialization, participation and identity: ethnographic approaches. In M. Martin-Jones, A.-M. de Mejia, and N. Hornberger (eds.), *Encyclopedia of Language and Education, 2nd Ed., Vol. 3: Discourse and Education* (pp. 107–119). New York, NY: Springer.

Duff, P. A. (2010). Language socialization. In N. H. Hornberger, S. L. McKay, and S. Lee (eds.), *Sociolinguistics and Language Education: New Perspectives on Language and Education* (pp. 427–454). Bristol, UK: Multilingual Matters.

Duff, P. A. and May, S. (eds.) (2017). *Language Socialization: Encyclopedia of Language and Education, 3rd Ed.* New York, NY: Springer.

Duranti, A. and Goodwin, C. (eds.) (1992). *Rethinking Context: Language as an Interactive Phenomenon.* Cambridge: Cambridge University Press.

Erickson, F. (1982). Classroom discourse as improvisation: relationships between academic task structure and social participation structure in lessons. In L. C. Wilkinson (ed.), *Communicating in the Classroom* (pp. 153–181). New York, NY: Academic Press.

Erickson, F. (1996). Going for the zone: the social and cognitive ecology of teacher–student interaction in classroom conversations. In D. Hicks (ed.), *Discourse, Learning, and Schooling* (pp. 26–62). Cambridge: Cambridge University Press.

Errington, J. (1999). Ideology. *Journal of Linguistic Anthropology*, 9(1–2), 115–117.

Evaldsson, A.-C. and Tellgren, B. (2009). "Don't enter – it's dangerous": negotiations for power and exclusion in preschool girls' play interactions. *Educational and Child Psychology*, 26(2), 9–18.

Fader, A. (2001). Literacy, bilingualism, and gender in a Hasidic community. *Linguistics and Education*, 12(3), 261–283.

Foucault, M. (1980). *Power/Knowledge: Selected Interviews and Other Writings, 1972–1977* (edited by C. Gordon; translated by C. Gordon, L. Marshall, J. Mepham, and K. Soper). New York, NY: Pantheon Books.

Friedman, D. (2010). Speaking correctly: error correction as a language socialization practice in a Ukrainian classroom. *Applied Linguistics*, 31, 346–367.

Friedman, D. (2016). Our language: (re)imagining communities in Ukrainian language classrooms. *Journal of Language, Identity, and Education*, 15, 165–179.

García-Sánchez, I. M. (2010). The politics of Arabic language education: Moroccan immigrant children's socialization into ethnic and religious identities. *Linguistics and Education*, 21(3), 171–196.

Garrett, P. B. (2005). What a language is good for: language socialization, language shift, and the persistence of code-specific genres in St. Lucia. *Language in Society*, 34(3), 327–361.

Garrett, P. B. (2008). Researching language socialization. In K. A. King and N. H. Hornberger (eds.), *Encyclopedia of Language and Education, Vol. 10: Research Methods in Language and Education* (pp. 189–201). Boston, MA: Springer.

Garrett, P. B. and Baquedano-López, P. (2002). Language socialization: reproduction and continuity, transformation and change. *Annual Review of Anthropology*, 31, 339–361.

Goffman, E. (1981). *Forms of Talk*. Philadelphia, PA: University of Pennsylvania Press.

Goodwin, C. (2000). Action and embodiment within situated human interaction. *Journal of Pragmatics*, 32(10), 1489–1522.

Goodwin, C. and Goodwin, M. H. (2004). Participation. In A. Duranti (ed.), *A Companion to Linguistic Anthropology* (pp. 222–244). Malden, MA: Blackwell.

Goodwin, M. H. (2006). *The Hidden Life of Girls: Games of Stance, Status, and Exclusion*. Malden, MA: Wiley-Blackwell.

Goodwin, M. H. and Cekaite, A. (2018). *Embodied Family Choreography: Practices of Control, Care, and Mundane Creativity*. New York, NY: Routledge.

Goodwin, M. H. and Kyratzis, A. (2011). Peer language socialization. In A. Duranti, E. Ochs, and B. B. Schieffelin (eds.), *The Handbook of Language Socialization* (pp. 365–390). Malden, MA: Wiley-Blackwell.

He, A. W. (2000). The grammatical and interactional organization of teachers' directives: implications for socialization of Chinese American children. *Linguistics and Education*, 11(2), 119–140.

He, A. W. (2015). Literacy, creativity, and continuity: a language socialization perspective on heritage language classroom interaction. In N. Markee (ed.), *The Handbook of Classroom Discourse and Interaction* (pp. 304–318). Malden, MA: Wiley-Blackwell.

Heath, S. B. (1982). Questioning at home and at school: a comparative study. In G. D. Spindler (ed.), *Doing the Ethnography of Schooling: Educational Anthropology in Action* (pp. 102–131). New York, NY: Holt, Rinehart & Winston.

Hicks, D. (ed.) (1996). *Discourse, Learning, and Schooling*. Cambridge: Cambridge University Press.

Howard, K. (2009). "When meeting Khun teacher, each time we should pay respect": standardizing respect in a Northern Thai classroom. *Linguistics and Education*, 20 (3), 254–272.

Howard, K. (2014). Language socialization. In *Oxford Bibliographies Online*. Retrieved September 4, 2018 from www.oxfordbibliographies.com/view/document/obo-9780199766567/obo-9780199766567-0111.xml

Ikeda, E. (2004). Socializing missionary ideologies through narrative. *Texas Linguistic Forum*, 47, 81–95.

Inoue, M. (2004). What does a language remember? Indexical inversion and the naturalized history of Japanese women. *Journal of Linguistic Anthropology*, 14 (1), 39–56.

Irvine, J. T. and Gal, S. (2000). Language ideology and linguistic differentiation. In P. V. Kroskrity (ed.), *Regimes of Language: Ideologies, Polities, and Identities* (pp. 35–84). Santa Fe, NM: School of American Research Press.

Jaffe, A. M. (1999). *Ideologies in Actions: Language Politics on Corsica*. Berlin and New York, NY: Mouton de Gruyter.

Jaffe, A. M. (2016). Indexicality, stance and field in sociolinguistics. In N. Coupland (ed.), *Sociolinguistics: Theoretical Debates* (pp. 86–112). Cambridge: Cambridge University Press.

Kanagy, R. (1999). Interactional routines as a mechanism for L2 acquisition and socialization in an immersion context. *Journal of Pragmatics*, 31, 1467–1492.

Klein, W. (2013). Speaking Punjabi: heritage language socialization and language ideologies in a Sikh education program. *Heritage Language Journal*, 10(1), 36–50.

Koshik, I. (2002). Designedly incomplete utterances: a pedagogical practice for eliciting knowledge displays in error correction sequences. *Research on Language and Social Interaction*, 35(3), 277–309.

Kramsch, C. (ed.) (2002). *Language Acquisition and Language Socialization: Ecological Perspectives*. London: Continuum.

Kroskity, P. (2004). Language ideologies. In A. Duranti (ed.), *A Companion to Linguistic Anthropology* (pp. 496–517). Malden, MA: Blackwell.

Kulick, D. (1992). *Language Shift and Cultural Reproduction: Socializing, Self, and Syncretism in a Papua New Guinean Village*. Cambridge: Cambridge University Press.

Kulick, D. and Schieffelin, B.B. (2004). Language socialization. In A. Duranti (ed.), *A Companion to Linguistic Anthropology* (pp. 349–368). Malden, MA: Blackwell.

Lee, J. S. and Bucholtz, M. (2015). Language socialization across learning spaces. In N. Markee (ed.), *The Handbook of Classroom Discourse and Interaction* (pp. 319–336). Malden, MA: Wiley-Blackwell.

Lo, A. (2009). Lessons about respect and affect in a Korean-American heritage language school. *Linguistics and Education*, 20(3), 217–234.

Lo, A. (2016). "Positive and negative assessment: metalinguistic understandings of praise and criticism in Korean American interactions." Paper presented at the 115th American Anthropological Association Annual Meeting, Minneapolis (November).

Lo, A. and Fung, H. (2011). Language socialization and shaming. In A. Duranti, E. Ochs, and B. B. Schieffelin (eds.), *The Handbook of Language Socialization* (pp. 169–189). Malden, MA: Wiley-Blackwell.

Makihara, M. (2005). Rapa Nui ways of speaking Spanish: language shift and socialization on Easter Island. *Language in Society*, 34(5) 727–762.

Margutti, P. and Piirainen-Marsh, A. (2011). The interactional management of discipline and morality in the classroom: an introduction. *Linguistics and Education*, 22(4), 305–309.

Markee, N. (ed.) (2015). *The Handbook of Classroom Discourse and Interaction*. Malden, MA: Wiley Blackwell.

Mehan, H. (1979). What time is it Denise? Some observations on the organization and consequences of asking known information questions in classroom discourse. *Theory into Practice*, 18(4), 285–292.

Mehan, H. and Griffin, P. (1981). Sense and ritual in classroom discourse. In F. Coulmas (ed.), *Conversational Routine: Explorations in Standardized Communication Situations and Prepatterned Speech*. The Hague: Mouton Press.

Moore, L. C. (2006). Learning by heart in Qur'anic and public schools in northern Cameroon. *Social Analysis: The International Journal of Cultural and Social Practice*, 50(3), 109–126.

Moore, L. C. (2011). Language socialization and repetition. In A. Duranti, E. Ochs, and B.B. Schieffelin (eds.), *The Handbook of Language Socialization* (pp. 209–226). Malden, MA: Wiley-Blackwell.

Ochs, E. (1988). *Culture and Language Development: Language Socialization and Language Acquisition in a Samoan Village.* Cambridge: Cambridge University Press.

Ochs, E. (1990). Indexicality and socialization. In J. W. Stigler, R. A. Shweder, and G. Herdt (eds.), *Cultural Psychology: Essays on Comparative Human Development* (pp. 287–308). Cambridge: Cambridge University Press.

Ochs, E. (1992). Indexing gender. In A. Duranti and C. Goodwin (eds.), *Rethinking Context: Language as an Interactive Phenomenon* (pp. 335–358). Cambridge: Cambridge University Press.

Ochs, E. (2000). Socialization. *Journal of Linguistic Anthropology*, 9(1–2), 230–233.

Ochs, E., Solomon, O., and Sterponi, L. (2005). Limitations and transformations of habitus in child-directed communication. *Discourse Studies*, 7, 547–583.

Ochs, E. and Schieffelin, B.B. (1984). Language socialization: three developmental stories. In R. A. Shweder and R. A. Levine (eds.), *Culture Theory: Essays on Mind, Self, and Emotion.* Cambridge: Cambridge University Press.

Ochs, E. and Schieffelin, B.B. (2011). The theory of language socialization. In A. Duranti, E. Ochs and B.B. Schieffelin (eds.), *The Handbook of Language Socialization* (pp. 1–21). Malden, MA: Wiley Blackwell.

Ochs, E. and Schieffelin, B. B. (2017). Language socialization: an historical overview. In P.A. Duff and S. May (eds.), *Language Socialization: Encyclopedia of Language Education, 3rd Ed.* (pp. 3–15). New York, NY: Springer.

Ohta, A. S. (1994). Socializing the expression of affect: an overview of affective particle use in the Japanese as a foreign language classroom. *Issues in Applied Linguistics*, 5, 303–325.

Paugh, A. (2005). Acting adult: language socialization, shift, and ideologies in Dominica, West Indies. In J. Cohen, K. T. McAlister, K. Rolstad, and J. MacSwan (eds.), *ISB4: Proceedings of the 4th International Symposium on Bilingualism.* Somerville, MA: Cascadilla Press.

Paugh, A. (2012). *Playing with Languages: Children and Change in a Caribbean Village.* New York, NY: Berghahn Books.

Paugh, A. (2016). Language socialization. In N. Bonvillian (ed.), *The Routledge Handbook of Linguistic Anthropology* (pp. 125–139). New York, NY: Routledge.

Philips, S. U. (1983). *The Invisible Culture: Communication in Classroom and Community on the Warm Springs Indian Reservation.* New York, NY: Longman.

Philips, S. U. (2004). Language and social inequality. In A. Duranti (ed.), *A Companion to Linguistic Anthropology* (pp. 474–495). Malden, MA: Blackwell.

Pontecorvo, C., Fasulo, A., and Sterponi, L. (2001). Mutual apprentices: the making of parenthood and childhood in family dinner conversations. *Human Development*, 44, 340–361.

Poole, D. (1992). Language socialization in the second language classroom. *Language Learning*, 42(2), 593–616.

Resnick, L. B., Asterhan, C. S. C., and Clarke, S. N. (2015). *Socializing Intelligence through Academic Talk and Dialogue.* Washington, DC: American Educational Research Association.

Reynolds, J. F. (2007). "Buenos días/((military salute))": the natural history of a coined insult. *Research on Language and Social Interaction*, 40, 437–465.

Riley, K. C. (2007). To tangle or not to tangle: shifting language ideologies and the socialization of Charabia in the Marquesas, French Polynesia. In M. Makihara and B. B. Schieffelin (eds.), *Consequences of Contact* (pp. 70–95). New York, NY: Oxford University Press.

Riley, K. C. (2011). Language socialization and language ideologies. In A. Duranti, E. Ochs, and B. B. Schieffelin (eds.), *The Handbook of Language Socialization* (pp. 493–514). Malden, MA: Wiley-Blackwell.

Rounds, P. L. (1987). Multifunctional personal pronoun use in an educational setting. *English for Specific Purposes*, 6, 13–29.

Rumsey, A. (1990). Wording, meaning, and linguistic ideology. *American Anthropologist*, 92(2), 346–361.

Rymes, B. (2010). Communicative repertoires and English language learners. In M. Shatz and L. C. Wilkinson (eds.), *The Education of English Language Learners: Research to Practice* (1st ed.) (pp. 177–197). New York, NY: Guilford Press.

Schieffelin, B. B. (1990). *The Give and Take of Everyday Life: Language Socialization of Kaluli Children*. Cambridge: Cambridge University Press.

Schieffelin, B. B. and Ochs, E. (1986). Language socialization. *Annual Review of Anthropology*, 15(1), 163–246.

Shohet, M. (2013). Everyday sacrifice and language socialization in Vietnam: the power of a respect particle. *American Anthropologist*, 115(2), 203–217.

Silverstein, M. (1976). Shifters, linguistic categories, and cultural description. In K. H. Basso and H. A. Selby (eds.), *Meaning in Anthropology* (pp. 11–55). Albuquerque, NM: University of New Mexico Press.

Silverstein, M. (1979). Language structure and linguistic ideology. In P. R. Clyne, W. F. Hands, and C. L. Hofbauer (eds.), *The Elements: A Parasession on Linguistic Units and Levels* (pp. 193–248). Chicago, IL: Chicago Linguistic Society.

Silverstein, M. (2003). Indexical order and the dialectics of sociolinguistic life. *Language and Communication*, 23(3–4), 193–229.

Summerson, C. E. (2010). Enactments of expertise. *Annual Review of Anthropology*, 39, 17–32.

Takei, N. and Burdelski, M. (2018). Shifting of "expert" and "novice" roles between/ within two languages: language socialization, identity, and epistemics in family dinnertime conversations. *Multilingua: Journal of Cross-Cultural and Interlanguage Communication*, 37(1), 83–117.

Talmy, S. (2008). The cultural productions of the ESL student at Tradewinds High: contingency, multidirectionality, and identity in L2 socialization. *Applied Linguistics*, 29(4), 619–644.

Vogel-Langer, A. (2008). *Becoming One Nation: Explorations into Language Use and Identity Formation of Germany's Post- and Pre-Unification Generations*. Saarbrücken: Verlag.

Willett, J. (1995). Becoming first graders in an L2: an ethnographic study of L2 socialization. *TESOL Quarterly*, 29(3), 473–503.

Woolard, K. A. and Schieffelin, B. B. (1994). Language ideology. *Annual Review of Anthropology*, 23, 55–82.

Wortham, S. (1992). Participant examples and classroom interaction. *Linguistics and Education*, 4(2), 195–217.

Zuengler, J. and Cole, K. (2005). Language socialization and L2 learning. In E. Hinkel (ed.), *Handbook of Research in Second Language Teaching and Learning* (pp. 301–316). Mahwah, NJ: Lawrence Erlbaum Associates.

Part I

Socializing Values, Dispositions, and Stances

2 Interactional Contingencies and Contradictions in the Socialization of Tolerance in a Spanish Multicultural School

Inmaculada M. García-Sánchez

2.1 Language Socialization Perspectives on Values in the Classroom

Educational institutions have long been known as crucibles in the (re-)production of socio-culturally preferred and intelligible subjects. Rather than assuming a mimetic and predictable process like previous theories of cultural reproduction in schools (see Collins, 2009 for a thorough review of these theories), the most important contribution of language socialization research in classrooms has been to offer a detailed processual account. Such an account demonstrates how children and youth's subjectivation is fostered, discouraged, and sometimes contested and subverted through seemingly inconsequential quotidian interactions that are organized in relation to local social structures and to larger sociocultural, historical, political ideologies and expectations. One of the most productive angles, in this regard, has been the study of students' socialization into *values*. Indeed, language socialization (Ochs and Schieffelin, 2017) has a rich tradition of exploring how sociocultural values, and other preferred dispositions, are explicitly and, more crucially, implicitly socialized through classroom discourse and interaction between teachers and students.

This body of work has most often emphasized language socialization into *historically sedimented values*, or orientations that tend to be thought of as *traditional* and that are often communicated and socialized in redundant ways. While such values can certainly be contested and at times unevenly socialized, they nevertheless tend to be relatively widely shared, in part because they are often implicated in discourses that allow teachers and students to imagine themselves as belonging to a common community (e.g., Moore, Chapter 4 in this volume). In this regard, historically sedimented values tend to be at the service of forces of reproduction. These orientations have usually been examined as tied to aspects of group morality and technologies of the self, such as personal responsibility, modesty and piety (Fader, 2009), respect for authority (Bhattacharya and Sterponi, Chapter 9 in this volume; García-Sánchez, 2010; Howard 2009), obedience (Moore, 2006), and other forms of social conformity through indirectness (He, 2001). Also, although much less frequently, such values have been tied to aspects of identity politics and representation in more diverse contexts. Two important examples of this trend involve the study of the use of storytelling in the classroom to foster immigrant students' identification and pride with an indigenous-syncretic Mexican identity as constructed in mytho-historical narratives of nationhood (Baquedano-López, 2000) and to (inadvertently) advocate ideologies of belonging based on Herderian homogeneity, by promoting essentialist notions of immigrant and minority children's ethnolinguistic identities (García-Sánchez, 2016).

There has been far less analytic attention given to classroom practice and interaction during attempts to overtly socialize much more highly contested values, such as tolerance, pluralism, respect for diversity, and multiculturalism. Unlike more historically sedimented orientations, these socio-politically contested values are often reflective of wider social tensions, since they are usually invoked to cope with fundamental changes occurring in a society. Before moving on, I want to underscore that the distinction I am drawing between more historically sedimented values and those that are highly contested is a heuristic one, and that I do not consider them to be stable categories. Historically sedimented values can become highly contested at certain critical moments of socio-cultural change, and highly contested values can over time become more implicit and more widely shared. The distinction is simply meant to gesture toward the continuum that exists between values that are more or less widely shared in any given historical moment.

The educational socialization of these socio-politically contested values has become increasingly common in the school systems of a growing number of both developed and developing nations, particularly in the Western Hemisphere. This growing trend is in part due to the fact that one of the ways in which schools have tried to accommodate the increasing linguistic, racial/ethnic, and cultural heterogeneity of student bodies, as well as to prevent exclusion, bullying, and discrimination, is to implement pedagogical programs that are designed to foster inclusion and intercultural friendships through the overt socialization of highly contested values such as tolerance, justice, and respect for diversity. In this chapter, I focus on one such program of *tolerance education* in a public elementary school in Southwestern-central Spain. It is worth noting, however, that the same private philanthropic foundation that is funding these types of programs in Spain, is also active in funding very similar types of programs in another 12 countries.[1] Moreover, while the specific ethnographic context that I discuss in this chapter is Spain, one of the most comprehensive and best-known examples of these types of efforts is the "Teaching Tolerance" curricular project of the Southern Poverty Law Center in the United States.[2]

Despite this growing attention to tolerance and respect for diversity, we know very little about how these highly contested values are actually taken up by students in everyday classroom interaction. In educational research, for example, discussions about tolerance education have most often been developed through the lens of educational philosophy (e.g., Macleod, 2010). Many of the debates in this literature center upon whether the challenges presented by tolerance as an ideal are better addressed in educational contexts through the respect conception versus the coexistence conception of tolerance. All this work, however, remains largely decontextualized and not related specifically to classroom practices and interactions.

In the following sections, I explore how the values of tolerance and respect for diversity are enacted in actual classroom practice, highlighting how contingent interactions implicitly socialize the ways in which ideologies are interpreted through everyday social action in schools. Specifically, I focus on how the emergent, co-constructed nature of everyday classroom interaction can undermine pedagogical efforts to overtly socialize highly contested values. In so doing, I emphasize children's agentive role in socialization processes, who, as language socialization theory has shown (Ochs and Schieffelin, 2017), may align with or resist authority figures' attempts at socialization. I want to clarify that by focusing on interactional contingencies that lead to unintended outcomes, I am not questioning the value of these programs and curricula. In fact, I take for granted that these efforts are important and necessary. But since schools do not work in isolation from larger sociocultural ideologies or processes, I use these examples to understand where and how some of these unintended consequences may arise. I also consider how everyday classroom practice may inadvertently encourage problematic modalities of tolerance discourse. These critiques are important if tolerance education is to fulfill its justice-oriented potentialities rather than stagnate in empty public valorization of its goodness and desirability.

2.2   The Contradictions of Tolerance as a Socioculturally Contested Value

So far, I have been referring to tolerance and respect for diversity as examples of highly contested values. Part of what makes the discourse of tolerance so contradictory and problematic is the fact there is little clarity about what tolerance is and what its limits ought to be in liberal democracies. Indeed, tolerance has come to mean so many different things that Brown (2008) once suggested that its connotations had become "semiotically polyvalent, politically promiscuous, and sometimes incoherent" (p. 3).

The specific logic of tolerance that I focus on in this paper is the tolerance discourse that emerged in Europe at the end of the twentieth century as nation-states began to confront the linguistic, cultural, religious, and ethnic diversity resulting from the arrival of an increasing number of immigrants, many of whom were coming from places formally colonized by European countries. In this particular brand of tolerance discourse, tolerance is most often defined as a universal, neutral value that can function to prevent violence and to restore the civic fabric of communities beset by hate crimes and discrimination.

Tolerance education in schools has been hailed as an antidote to ethnic bullying and everyday acts of discrimination in the student body. As such, it is often used as a central strategy of antiracist pedagogy, with the double goal of achieving civic peace and promoting students' moral development. The UNESCO definition of tolerance education, for example, is a prime example of how this discursive logic has been used in schools:

Education for tolerance should aim at countering influences that lead to fear and exclusion of others, and should help young people develop capacities for independent judgment, critical thinking and ethical reasoning. The diversity of our world's many religions, languages, cultures and ethnicities is not a pretext for conflict, but is a treasure that enriches us all.[3]

Although the promotion of tolerance is often presented as an alternative to violence and discrimination, it may result in discriminatory practices as well. This is the case, for example, when the discourse of tolerance is deployed to differentiate between European students who are presumed to be capable of tolerance and Muslim immigrant students who are assumed to be intolerant, as Taha (2017) found in her analysis of debates about gender equality and gay rights in citizen education classes in a Spanish high school.

However, one of the biggest contradictions of the tolerance concept is how its usage as a universal moral virtue can mask how tolerance operates as political discourse and regime of governmentality, the purpose of which is to depoliticize the social order by substituting emotional and personal vocabularies, such as sensitivity or respect, for political ones, such as justice and equality, in formulating *solutions* to social problems (Brown, 2008, p. 16). Evidence of this depoliticization is how the discourse of tolerance has at times been embraced by both the political right and the political left, and how among all the political tropes that have come to dominate Western European discourse surrounding immigrants and immigration, *tolerance* sits uncomfortably between discourses of *cultural differences and assimilation*, more aligned with the political right, and discourses of *multiculturalism and interculturality*, more aligned with the political left.

The epitome of all these contradictions is how the political reality that tolerance is meant to address, diversity, is often rejected and constructed as problematic, even by social groups who publicly embrace the discourse of tolerance. For instance, in their study of the discourse of tolerance in Belgium, Blommaert and Verschueren (1998) showed that the discourse of tolerance is embraced in Belgium society insofar as it does not threaten ideologies of homogeneism, an ideology that casts diversity as deeply problematic and as something to be avoided. From this perspective, tolerance, in addition to being a contested value, also becomes a pragmatic strategy to manage diversity and contain opposition.

All these aspects of tolerance – as a highly contested value, a pragmatic strategy, a political discourse, and the contradictions inherent in them – reverberated in consequential ways in the local community and in the school where I worked in Spain. As I elaborate below, the school administration's public proclamation of tolerance aligned itself with the most strongly utopian aspects of tolerance as a universal value, as this definition, taken from a picture that adorned the school walls, shows: *Tolerancia es reconocer el pluralismo, respetar la diversidad, compartir las diferencias como algo positivo y enriquecedor* [Tolerance is acknowledging pluralism, respecting diversity, and sharing difference as something positive and enriching]. Yet, the school also used curricular efforts for tolerance, as a pragmatic political strategy to control and redefine community tensions arising precisely out of discomfort about, and sometimes even rejection of, diversity. This web of contradictions is significant not only in the kinds of interactional contingencies that happen in the classroom, but ultimately also in how the teachers respond to them.

2.3   Ethnographic and Methodological Notes

The analyses in this chapter center around several extended sequences of teacher–student interaction in the context of a special Performance Arts program in an elementary school in a Southwestern rural community in Spain, characterized by a high concentration of Moroccan immigrants, where I have been doing the bulk of my research since the mid-2000s.[4] While in my larger linguistic ethnographic study I have examined Moroccan immigrant children's everyday linguistic and communicative practices in the contexts of educational institutions (both secular and religious), neighborhood peer groups, participation in sports clubs, and families,[5] for the purposes of this chapter I highlight the public elementary school as a key site to probe the web of contradictions involved in the promotion of tolerance and inclusion.

As I have described at length elsewhere (García-Sánchez, 2013, 2014), because of the high concentration of children of Moroccan immigrant families in this school (almost 40 percent of the school student body at the peak of migration in this community), the school launched a major revision of its curricular programs in the early 2000s to emphasize inclusion and interculturalism, as well as to improve the overall social life of the school.

The main tenets of the new curriculum centered around promoting a spirit of tolerance and respect for the cultural and linguistic heterogeneity of the students. The school staff took steps to prevent exclusion and discrimination by institutionalizing a core set of civic values, namely respect, friendship, cooperation, justice, peace, and tolerance, that were intended to regulate the academic and social life of the school.

More specifically, all children in this school were required to participate in a special Performance Arts program that was designed to promote these values, and which was funded by a private, non-governmental philanthropic institution. This organization conceptualized the special Performance Arts program as a way to prevent violence and discrimination, as well as to promote tolerance, dialogue, and respect for diversity through the practice of artistic performance disciplines, specifically dancing, acting, and circus arts. Using classroom discourse analysis within the wider ethnographic frame of language socialization, the analysis in this chapter focuses specifically on the daily micro-interactions between teacher and students in this special Performance Arts program. However, the analysis is also informed by observations and video recordings of other school activities (math, music, social studies and language arts classes, recess, school field trips, and extra-curricular activities), and by the larger linguistic ethnographic study described above. In particular, there are two phenomena I have noted in previous work that have direct relevance for understanding the interactional contingencies and contradictions I analyze below.

One is that, as I foreshadowed above, school administrators used curricular efforts to promote the discourse of tolerance not only as an antiracist pedagogy to improve the school social climate and to promote students' moral autonomy, but also as a political pragmatic strategy to smooth out community tensions surrounding diversity in school. For example, Spanish parents often thought that the presence of Moroccan immigrant children in the school detracted from their own children's education in terms of both quality and resources (García-Sánchez, 2014). As a result, the principal spent a lot of time and energy attempting to convince Spanish parents that this program benefited *all* the children in the community, not just the Moroccan children. So, while many Spanish parents and students may have appreciated access to a performance arts curriculum that was rarely available at the elementary school level, they still felt a certain degree of ambivalence, and in some cases outright resentment, toward a program they perceived was being implemented *for the sake of the Moroccans*.

The second phenomenon of note is that in other classroom settings in this school, Moroccan immigrant children's behavior was routinely misrecognized and indirectly constructed as deviant by their Spanish peers, through a set of linguistically mediated technologies of surveillance and exclusion (García-Sánchez, 2014). A key aspect of these discriminatory practices was that they were so much a part of the covert background and fabric of everyday social interaction in the classroom that they were rarely noticed and recognized by teachers as actual forms of targeted exclusion. The interactions that I observed in the Performance Arts classes contained many of these same kinds of covert discriminatory practices found in other classroom settings, but, as I will show below, they also contained instances of Spanish children explicitly excluding and discriminating against their Moroccan peers.

2.4   Studying Highly Contested Values in the Classroom

While it is true that all values, whether more or less historically embedded, evoke a moral stance in social actors, the moral imperative that values such as tolerance bring to human relations is often deeply embedded in contemporary political struggles and practices of liberal governance. Indeed, the depoliticization of tolerance that I discussed above rests on presenting tolerance as a *virtue*, when it is actually both a moral disposition and political discourse of governmentality (Brown, 2008). Accordingly, an effective analysis of classroom interaction in relation to the socialization of highly contested values must take into account both the moral and the political dimensions of these exchanges. Even beyond the classroom, these two aspects are often so empirically intertwined that in contemporary anthropology there has been a shift to rethink the traditional scholarly separation between the ethical and the political. Fassin (2013), in particular, has argued strongly that morality and ethics focused on values oriented toward the good and the right cannot be separated from the political.

In order to bring these two aspects together in my own analysis, I draw on Pratt's (1991) classic formulation of the classroom as "contact zone," defined as "a social space where cultures meet, clash, and grapple with each other, often in contexts of highly asymmetrical relations of power" (p. 34) and on Mattingly's (2014) more recent formulation of the "moral laboratory." The latter is an analytic trope for how everyday contexts can become spaces of moral discerning, experimentation, critique, and personal transformation, when examined from the phenomenological perspective of how social actors experience and respond on the ground to quotidian moral crises or dilemmas. These two analytic tools brought together provide us with a framework for considering how difference and conflict can be addressed in the classroom, while simultaneously revealing teachers' dilemmas in relation to moral becoming, as well as their vulnerability in making moral judgments and political decisions within these situations.

2.5   Quotidian Interactional Contingencies in the Socialization of Tolerance

As I described above, one of the most conspicuous contradictions in this school is that the most aggravated forms of classroom exclusion happen precisely in classroom spaces where the overt socialization of tolerance is more important than actual disciplinary knowledge and practice. For example, in math class, where children are primarily focusing on learning math, indirect forms of exclusion of Moroccan students by their Spanish peers are almost always implicit. But in the Performance Arts program, the goal of which is to encourage tolerance and related contested values, Spanish children sometimes overtly refused to participate with their Moroccan peers in the activities of the program. Given the inconsistent ways in which discourses about tolerance were used to manage diversity, one possible explanation for this is that at least some Spanish children both simultaneously enjoy and begrudge having to participate in this program at all. The targeted discrimination occurring in these performance arts activities is so blatant that, unlike in other classroom settings, it is nearly impossible for teachers to ignore them or misunderstand them as something other than overt acts of exclusion.

In this analysis, I zero in on how teachers responded to these interactional contingencies that directly challenged the goals of the Performance Arts program (i.e., on whether and how teachers decide to intervene and how they manage these disruptions of the ongoing activities and these obstacles to their socializing objectives). In particular, I examine two representative examples capturing different levels of activity disruption: one example involving a teacher's mildly disruptive intervention and a second example involving a more protracted disruptive intervention. Thinking about these classroom spaces as contact zones and as moral laboratories, I highlight the simultaneous political and moral dimensions of these disruptions. I also use these examples as a point of departure to reflect on how teachers are able to enhance or diminish the moral experience and political subjectivation of their students by how they frame and respond to these discriminatory actions. Critical to how they respond to these actions, however, is a language ideology prevalent among teachers and administrators in this school about how to handle incidents of discrimination. Through many discussions with teachers and administrators at the school, I was able to learn that school staff tried to avoid labeling discriminatory incidents directly as such for fear that it would heighten social divisions. Teachers often recoiled at marking discrimination overtly because they thought that it would bring undue attention to the large number of immigrant children at the school. Since the latter were already often constructed as the source of tensions and problems, teachers concluded that discussing exclusion openly was unnecessarily dangerous. This belief very often translated into metalinguistic labor (Carr, 2006) – or the activation of this language ideology in their pedagogical practice – designed to avoid explicit talk about discrimination and prejudice.

Excerpt 2.1a is extracted from a lesson focusing on circus arts skills. In this excerpt, children are asked to get into a circle and to throw a juggling ball among themselves. The goal of the activity, as with most activities in the performance arts program, was twofold: on the one hand, the drill was designed to help students gain agility in handling juggling balls; on the other hand, it was aimed at building trust and strengthening interpersonal relationships among the children. Crucial to achieving both goals was supposed to be a quick and spirited throwing back and forth of a ball, leaving students no time to think or to plan who the next receiver was going to be. In order to ensure that the exchange of the ball was going to be not only spirited but also random, the teacher, David, jokingly warned that attention-seeking behaviors to get the ball would not be allowed during the activity and that students were supposed to stand still "like statues" (*como estatuas*). The teacher also tried to preempt exclusion of individual children by clearly stating that the ball could not go to the same person twice.

Excerpt 2.1a Juggling Ball

01 Teacher: *Empezamos* (.)
               ((holds up a juggling ball)) 'We start'
02 Teacher: *Vale?*
               'Ok?'
03 Teacher: (xxx) *como estatuas*
               ((inaudible)) 'like statues'
04 Teacher: *No vale decir- y no vale decir*
               'It is not allowed to say- and it is not allowed to say'
05 Teacher: *Pa'mi Pa'mi*
               'To me! To me!' ((mimics attention-getting gestures))
06 Teacher: *Yo, yo e::h pa'mi (.) vale?*
               'Me! Me! Hey, to me! (.) ok?'
07 Teacher: *Cada uno- el que esté en el medio se la va a tirar=*
               'Each one- He who's in the middle is going to throw it='
08 Teacher: *=a quien quiera él*
               'to whomever he wants'
09 Teacher: *No vale repetir (.) vale?*
               'It is not allowed to repeat (.) ok?'
10 Teacher: *No vale salir el mismo- ninguna persona dos veces*
               'It is not allowed to go the same- to anybody twice'

With these three behavioral guidelines established by the teacher during the set-up of the activity, it is interesting to see how, as the activity unfolds, the children start playing with these rules, often breaking or coming very close to breaking them. As a result, and to the frustration of the teacher, all the Spanish

Table 2.1 *Order of turns in how students pitched the ball*

Spanish children	Moroccan children
Teacher ➜ MARISOL	
1. MARISOL ➜ RAMÓN	15. (GLORIA) ➜ *MIRIAM*
2. RAMÓN ➜ ESTRELLA	16. *MIRIAM* ➜ *WAFIYA*
3. ESTRELLA ➜ ALICIA	17. *WAFIYA* ➜ *SARAH*
4. ALICIA ➜ ANTONIO	18. *SARAH* ➜ *YOUSEF*
5. ANTONIO ➜ MARTA	19. *YOUSEF* ➜ *YIMAD*
6. MARTA ➜ ROBERTO	20. *YIMAD* ➜ *KARIM*
7. ROBERTO ➜ LOLA	21. *KARIM* ➜ *MIMON*
8. LOLA ➜ *DANIELA	22. *MIMON* ➜ (*ROSA*)
9. DANIELA ➜ MANOLO	
10. MANOLO ➜ MARGARITA	(*) Asterisk indicates a student who was thrown the ball twice
11. MARGARITA ➜ JUAN	
12. JUAN ➜ SUSANA	
13. SUSANA ➜ *DANIELA ➜ ANA	
14. ANA ➜ GLORIA	
15. GLORIA ➜ *(MIRIAM)*	

children end up throwing the ball among themselves first. It is only when they think that all the Spanish students have had a turn, that they finally start throwing the ball to their Moroccan classmates. Table 2.1 shows how students actually threw the ball, with the first 15 throws going to students of Spanish origin, and the next seven going to students of Moroccan origin. The names of the Moroccan students are italicized.

What is clear almost from the very beginning of the activity is that Spanish children are subverting the intent of the activity by choosing their friends to throw the ball to. While part of what is structuring this interaction might be children's tendency to favor their friends when they have this kind of choice, the racialized nature of these friendship groups, and how children hierarchize them along ethnic lines, is also revealed in the ball-throwing pattern: non-Roma Spanish children are picked first, then Spanish children of Roma descent are picked as the number of non-Roma Spanish children available diminishes, and then finally the Moroccan children are picked, as the Spanish children think that there are no Spanish children left to throw the ball to.[6] The teacher's dilemma is then how to frame and respond to these subversions. According to the analytic framework proposed above, which emphasizes the inseparability of the moral and political aspects of highly contested values, what is most striking in the teacher's response is that there is little overt acknowledgment that there is a political and a moral crisis emerging in the activity. Instead, the increasingly frustrated teacher tries to intervene and reorient the students' actions through admonitions reminding students to keep up a quick rhythm and reminding them, in a general sense, that there are many people who have still not had a chance to participate:

Excerpt 2.1b Juggling Ball
Continuation of Excerpt 2.1a

22 Teacher: *pero tiene que ser un poquito rápido porque si no*
                'but it has to be a little fast because if not-'
[...]
28 Teacher: *Venga, tiene que llevar este ritmo*
                'Come on. It has to carry this rhythm' ((as he snaps his fingers at a quick pace))
30 Teacher: *Este ritmo (.) Tiene que llevar este ritmo*
                'This rhythm (.) It has to carry this rhythm'
[...]
38 Teacher: *Tiene que llevar este ritmo. No puede parar- No puede parar*
                'It has to carry this rhythm- It can't stop- It can't stop'
[...]
46 Teacher: *Venga-rápido-rápido-que no pierda el ritmo-que no pierda el ritmo*
                'Come on-fast-fast, so that the rhythm isn't lost-so that the rhythm isn't lost'
[...]
54 Teacher: *Vale otra persona que no haya salido, por favor (.) Hay muchas*
                'Ok, another person who has not gone, please (.) There are many'

The teacher's exhortations to adhere to activity procedures, and his invocations of a general basic sense of fairness, indicate that he seemed to sense the problem and was trying to do something to neutralize students' subversion of the goals of the activity. Mobilizing the metalinguistic labor of avoiding labeling exclusion overtly, he opted for a rule-based approach to build inclusion. While it is true that this structural approach could have had the desired effect if the rules had been adhered to, what the teacher failed to see in real time is that playing with these rules is what students are using to undermine the activity. Furthermore, this approach fails to engage students both at the political and at the moral levels: the teacher's response skirts the political dimension and greatly understates the real emergent moral crisis, which is not whether a particular student, like Daniela, got the ball twice or whether students deviate from the teacher's rhythm, but rather that an entire group of students is being excluded, or at least made to wait until those who are seen as being more legitimate members of the classroom community have had their turn. The reduction of what happened to an issue of basic fairness not only diminishes students' moral experience but also distorts, to the point of erasing it, the political signification of students' actions. Thus, the emergent potential for social and personal transformation of this fleeting moment in the classroom is lost not so much because Spanish students subvert activities that promote values that some of them (and their families) may see as not in their interest, but because the teacher shies away from engaging students in a potentially difficult conversation.

In Excerpt 2.2, extracted from a performance arts lesson focusing on dance, we find a similar pattern, even if the teacher's intervention is significantly more forceful and disruptive of the activity. The teacher, Irene, starts pairing children up to perform a dance move that requires the boy-dancer to support the girl-dancer as she jumps up in the air. Once again, as with all activities of the Performance Arts program, this activity has a double goal not only of increasing dance dexterity, strength, and flexibility, but also of promoting interethnic/racial intimacy and trust. Accordingly, Irene was very deliberate in pairing up Moroccan girls with Spanish boys and vice versa. In the following excerpt, a Spanish boy, Roberto, is paired up with Wafiya, a Moroccan student, but he refuses adamantly to participate:

Excerpt 2.2 Dance Partner

((Teacher pairs up Roberto with Wafiya))
01 Roberto: *No::::::::::::::*
          'No::::::::::::'
          ((Pointing at Wafiya))

02 Teacher: *O:::::h*
          'Awwww:::::'

03 Roberto: *No con Wafiya*
          'Not with Wafiya'
          ((Teacher mimics him))

04 Teacher: *No-*
          'Don't' ((Following Roberto
          who has left the circle))
[. . .]

Figure 2.1 Roberto refuses to be Wafiya's dance partner

((Roberto, approached by teacher, shakes his head))
((Teacher escorts Roberto back to the circle))
06 Teacher: *Aquí todo el mundo está con todo el mundo*
          'Here everybody is with everybody else'
07 Teacher: *porque de eso se trata*
          'because that is what this is about'

Unlike in the first example, here we can see a Spanish student, Roberto, more blatantly violating the rules of participation established by the teacher, as can be seen in his "response cry" (Goffman, 1978) 'No:::::::' pronounced with an extremely high pitch that affectively highlights the opposition (line 01). His opposition to dancing with Wafiya is further highlighted by a gesture, pointing to Wafiya with his finger, that accompanies the response cry and displays an affective embodied alignment (see Figure 2.1). Accordingly, the teacher intervenes more forcefully, up to the point at which the progress of the activity is disrupted. When Roberto walks away, she physically moves him back to the dance circle and explicitly acknowledges that a direct challenge has occurred by making overt reference to a breach in the ultimate purpose of the activity: 'Here everybody is with everybody else because that is what this is about' (lines 06–07).

The disruption, however, continued, as both Irene, the performance arts teacher, and Luisa, the fourth-grade regular classroom teacher, took turns talking with Roberto in private. Although I did not approach the three directly out of respect for the privacy of this conversation, I could see Roberto shaking his head defiantly. Later the embarrassed teachers told me that they had threatened Roberto with banning him from participating in the activity if he refused to dance with Wafiya. Luisa also confided how horrified she was that Roberto had boldly told them that he was not going to dance with a Moroccan girl. In a probable attempt to both defuse the situation and to minimize the pedagogical disruption, Irene turned her attention to the whole group once again and explained how the activity was to proceed, using Roberto as her example-partner. Yet, when she was done with the explanation and told students to start trying the dance with their respective partners, Roberto again refused to dance with Wafiya. This time he did not say anything. He just folded his arms and kept shaking his head "no," while maintaining his gaze fixed on the floor. At this juncture, Luisa removed Roberto from the dance group, and Wafiya was placed with another couple, consisting of Juan, a Spanish boy, and Sarah, a Moroccan girl. While the rest of the class was rehearsing the dance movements, Luisa could be seen talking to Roberto in a stern manner and took him out of the classroom. After a few minutes, both teacher and student returned, but Roberto ended up grounded in a corner of the room. At this point, over 35 minutes of class had elapsed, and Irene had not had much luck in getting the rest of the class to focus on the dance movements. Seeing that the lesson had been completely disrupted, she asked students to sit down in a big circle. Irene then spent the rest of the class period scolding the children about their behavior. The next excerpt focuses on Irene's admonishment.

Excerpt 2.3 Teacher's Admonishment

01 Teacher: *Nunca ha habido problemas en esta clase para trabajar con ningún compañero*
'Working with other classmates has never been a problem in this class'

02 Teacher: *Y bajo ningún concepto*
             'And under no circumstances'
03 Teacher: *voy a admitir que NADIE se niegue con trabajar nadie*
             'will I accept ANYBODY refusing to work with anybody else'
04 Teacher: *porque para eso es esta clase (.)VALE?*
             'because that is what *this class* is for, OKAY?'
05 Teacher: *Entonces, estamos aquí para entrenernos=*
             'So, we are here to entertain ourselves'=
06 Teacher: *=para pasarnoslo bien=*
             ='to have a good time'=
07 Teacher: *=y para todo lo que queráis*
             ='and for everything you may want'
08 Teacher: *menos para pegarnos >empujarnos< y demás (.) cosas, VALE?*
             'except for hitting one another >pushing one another< and the rest of (.)
             things, OK?'

This excerpt clearly highlights the teacher's dilemma, and her discomfort in framing and responding to students' discriminatory actions. Unlike the ball exchange example examined earlier, this teacher acknowledges directly that there is indeed an emergent crisis in the classroom. Furthermore, she makes an unequivocal reference to a breach in the purpose of the activity and to the inclusionary goals of the Performance Arts program (lines 02–04): 'And under no circumstances will I accept ANYBODY refusing to work with anybody else because that is what *this class* is for, OK?' Yet, and despite her direct acknowledgment of the crisis, much like David in the ball exchange example, Irene is also reluctant to address students' discriminatory behavior per se. Her admonition is full of ambiguity and indirectness as reflected in her linguistic choices. This ambiguity, and her eventual decision to revert to what Pollock (2005) has called "colormute talk," may itself be reflective of the teacher's struggle about naming discriminatory patterns overtly or not.

For example, she makes reference to general forms of misbehavior, like hitting and pushing, that had not been a problem in this instance but, interestingly, then glosses over the overt discrimination and exclusion that *had been* the real problem as "and the rest of (.) things" (line 08). Throughout her interventions in Excerpts 2.2 and 2.3, the nature of the moral and political crisis unfolding is discursively framed through indirect referentiality, through vague deixis (*here, this class*) in which the referent is never quite made explicit, and through indefinite pronouns (*everybody, nobody, other classmates*) that typically refer to no particular person; although, as in the ball exchange example, there was a particular group of students (Moroccan immigrant children) who were being targeted. So, while in this example there is an acknowledgment that a moral-political crisis needs to be addressed, Irene's metalinguistic labor is mobilized to avoid labeling directly what is happening. Instead, as in the ball exchange example, she diffuses the political implications of this crisis by morally retreating to a general sense of class-room fairness.

The teachers' difficulties in engaging students in disquieting conversations in both the juggling and dance lesson examples illustrate quite poignantly the intricate dilemmas that go into making everyday moral judgments with charged political implications in the classroom. To be fair to the teachers, it *is* tricky to navigate these situations in real time. As Pratt (1991) has suggested, creating a pedagogical space that is truly a "contact zone" is inherently unsafe. Such situations are also full of vulnerability and marked by radical uncertainty and unanticipated risks, as all moral laboratories are (Mattingly, 2014). As a result, teachers often avoid the political dimensions of these incidents, retreating instead, perhaps inadvertently, to an ethical comfort zone where it is safer and easier for them to try to shape students' moral development in terms of basic right and wrong. These retreats are precisely what Fassin (2013) warns against in his political anthropology of morality in contemporary societies. In addressing moral dilemmas that only acquire their full meaning in relation to political issues, Fassin (2013) has emphasized the need to reject "our Mani-chean propensity and ethical comfort" (p. 261) and to address the empirical gray zones where the ethical and the political meet. This warning is particu-larly relevant to classroom settings in which teachers are attempting to social-ize tolerance and other socio-politically contested values. In these contexts, how teachers justify the political actions they and their students are engaged in on moral grounds is of great significance for the formation of students as political subjects and for the development of their moral subjectivities.

2.6   A More Successful Enactment of Highly Contested Values in School

As a counterpoint to the previous two examples, I now discuss a third example that did not take place in the Performance Arts classroom, but rather in the playground. I include it here, however, because it also features a teacher intervening after a group of Spanish girls explicitly excludes one of their Moroccan peers from participating in one of their games. This is an episode I have described in great detail elsewhere (García-Sánchez, 2014, pp. 125–127), but which I summarize here. The episode begins as Paco, a teacher, and I were watching a group of Spanish girls play jump-rope. At some point, Mouna, a Moroccan girl, approaches the Spanish girls and asks if she can join in. The Spanish girls, through both words and actions, make very clear that Mouna will not be admitted to their game. Observing this, Paco makes a playful show of getting in line to jump rope with the other Spanish girls, bringing Mouna into the line in front of him, giving her an opportunity to enter the game. When it is Paco's turn, he jumps for a few minutes, but then, claiming to be too old and too tired to jump rope, he quits the game as Mouna continues to play with the Spanish girls. He then remained in close proximity to the girls watching over their game until the end of recess.

It is important to note that, in some ways, this example is not that dissimilar from the other two. For example, much like the other two teachers, Paco does not explicitly name the discriminatory act of exclusion, thus upholding the unwritten rule of the school to not mark ethnic tensions overtly. Nevertheless, he is more courageous in moving himself and his students out of their comfort zones. One could even argue that he exhibits considerable skill in doing this in that he transcends the dichotomy of naming overtly exclusionary patterns or not; a dichotomy that tends to dominate debates about best practices in addressing discriminatory situations. By playfully jumping into the game, Paco demonstrates his willingness to make himself vulnerable and to enter into an uncertain interactional realm with his students. From this perspective, his act of stepping into the game and inviting Mouna to join him brings attention to the political and moral crisis unfolding in the game of jump rope. He does not disrupt the game to offer explicit meta-commentary on this crisis. Yet, bringing into question the actions of the Spanish girls with his own actions, he transforms the physical and social space of the game of jump-rope into something more akin to the everyday moral laboratories described by Mattingly. It becomes a space of moral critique, and therefore, a space of hope and possibility. Also, although Paco's actions do not directly engage students in difficult conversations, as Pratt (1991) urges educators to do, his actions are political in that, by stepping into the game, he is using his own power and authority to disrupt and reframe the local power relations between the girls. By doing so, Paco, of all the teachers I observed in the school, came closest to enacting with his actions and behavior the values and ideals to which the school aspired, even though he was not himself part of the Performance Arts program.

2.7   Conclusion

In this chapter, I have examined how the overt socialization of highly con-tested values, such as tolerance, can become fraught with contradictions in actual classroom practice, particularly in contexts where diversity itself is the source of wider social tensions and constructed in negative terms, and where tolerance itself might be uncritically and apolitically promoted as a neutral, universal value. I have focused in particular on the emergent moral-political crises that arise in classroom interactions when Spanish students work inter-actionally to actively undermine the inclusionary goals of the activities of a special Performance Arts program specifically designed to reduce the incidence of violence and discrimination and promote inter-ethnic friendships. I have paid particular attention to how teachers handle these crises, by examining their metalinguistic labor in how they frame and respond to Spanish students' discriminatory actions against their Moroccan peers. In addition to not intervening too directly or labeling discriminatory behavior too overtly, a striking pattern found among the teachers facing these ethical dilemmas was a tendency to sidestep the political aspects of these crises and minimize their moral significance.

While there is some value in trying to avoid marking overtly too often or in too heavy-handed a way the discriminatory behavior of the Spanish students, interventions that avoid talking about prejudice and discrimination can also lead educators to inadvertently reproduce the very exclusion they are trying to fight, as the work of as Mica Pollock and others (2008) on antiracism has convincingly demonstrated. The growing consensus in this literature is that for any of these curricular interventions to have an effect, students need to reflect explicitly on these values.

I also wondered whether there may be aspects of teachers' and administrators' restraint that are more implicit than such an explanation may capture. For instance, teachers may find it difficult (and embarrassing) to reconcile this school's reputation as an innovative and award-winning site of educational reform for inclusion with its persisting record of everyday acts of discrimination, as well as with their own inability to confront enduring prejudices that elude and resist these reform efforts. More to the point, and addressing the school's main concern, to what extent is this fear of a community backlash and a deepening of social divisions based in reality? It is interesting to note in this regard that this belief is reminiscent of US ideologies suggesting that talking overtly about racism is divisive, ideologies that are sometimes deployed in subordinating and oppressive ways, rather than emancipatory ones. However, it is also true that, as I mentioned above, there was a group of Spanish parents who were vocal in their misperception that an over-attention to Moroccan immigrant students was diverting resources away from their own children's education. It is then certainly possible that putting these everyday classroom tensions too much in the spotlight could have been counterproductive.

The example I discussed above of the teacher intervening on the playground, however, demonstrates that teachers might have more possibilities to use educational spaces as grounds for political transformation and moral experimentation than they usually imagine, even without having to disrupt activities or to label them too overtly. If so, then perhaps the school and the teachers are only comfortable "imagining their own tolerance," in Blommaert and Verschueren's words (1998, p. 120). They might also be reluctant to challenge the ideological underpinnings of homogeneism, not only out of concern about stirring up the Spanish community's political anxieties, but also for fear of confronting their own unexamined anxieties. This fear would help explain, for example, teachers' reluctance to make themselves vulnerable in these interactions in the way Paco did. But it may be precisely this willingness to be vulnerable and enter into uncomfortable spaces of possibility with students that can make the difference in the success of the programs that attempt to socialize highly contested values.

Indeed, as the juggling ball and dance lesson examples show, everyday contradictions that subvert the inclusionary goals of these pedagogical programs are more likely to continue and become more aggravated when the basic moral and political realities of intolerance and discrimination are not directly incorporated and responded to. These interactional contingencies must then be taken seriously as political and moral interpellations of the nature of tolerance as both a political discourse and a personal and social ethics. If their political meaning is ignored and their moral significance is minimized, it will be impossible to grasp the complex contemporary moral economy of tolerance and justice in diverse classrooms and societies. Without this grasp, however, it will be difficult for schools to work as spaces of social change, despite our best efforts to teach these values. Furthermore, by not paying attention to how the political and moral realities happening inside the classroom connect to the political and moral realities happening outside of the classroom, we allow the classroom to become a zone of oppression that perpetuates inequality and discrimination, rather than a contact zone and a moral laboratory of the possible (against the probable), where familiar ways of acting and believing can actively be brought into question.

NOTES

1 Eleven other European countries (Austria, Belgium, Finland, France, Germany, Hungary, Italy, Kosovo, Lichtenstein, Portugal, and Switzerland), plus Israel.
2 For more information on this project, visit www.tolerance.org/
3 For more information, visit www.unesco.org/new/en/social-and-human-sciences/themes/fight-against-discrimination/promoting-tolerance/
4 This research has been supported by funding from a Wenner–Gren Foundation Individual Dissertation Research Grant (Grant #7296), from a Harry and Yvonne Lenart Foundation Graduate Research Travel Grant, and from a Temple University Summer Research Fellowship.
5 For more information on the methodology employed in the larger study, see García-Sánchez (2014), particularly chapter 3 (pp. 61–87).
6 As shown in Table 2.1, Rosa is inadvertently left out.

REFERENCES

Baquedano-López, P. (2000). Narrating community in doctrina classes. *Narrative Inquiry*, 10(2), 1–24.

Blommaert, J. and Verschueren, J. (1998). *Debating Diversity: Analyzing the Discourse of Tolerance*. London: Routledge.

Brown, W. (2008). *Regulating Aversion: Tolerance in the Age of Identity and Empire*. Princeton, NJ: Princeton University Press.

Carr, E. S. (2006). Secrets keep you sick: metalinguistic labor in a drug treatment program for homeless women. *Language in Society*, 35(5), 631–653.

Collins, J. (2009). Social reproduction in classrooms and school. *Annual Review of Anthropology*, 38, 33–48.

Fader, A. (2009). *Mitzvah Girls: Bringing Up the Next Generation of Hasidic Jews in Brooklyn*. Princeton, NJ: Princeton University Press.

Fassin, D. (2013). On resentment and ressentiment: the politics and ethics of moral emotions. *Current Anthropology*, 54(3), 249–267.

García-Sánchez, I. M. (2010). The politics of Arabic language education: Moroccan immigrant children's socialization into ethnic and religious identities. *Linguistics and Education*, 21(3), 171–196.

García-Sánchez, I. M. (2013). The everyday politics of "cultural citizenship" among North African immigrant school children in Spain. *Language and Communication*, 33(4), 481–499.

García-Sánchez, I. M. (2014). *Language and Muslim Immigrant Childhoods: The Politics of Belonging*. Oxford: Wiley-Blackwell.

García-Sánchez, I. M. (2016). Multiculturalism and its discontents: essentializing ethnic Moroccan and Roma identities in classroom discourse in Spain. In H. S. Alim, J. Rickford, and A. Ball (eds.) *Raciolinguistics: How Language Shapes Our Ideas about Race* (pp. 291–309). Oxford: Oxford University Press.

Goffman, E. (1978). Response cries. *Language*, 54(4), 787–815.

He, A. W. (2001). The language of ambiguity: practices in Chinese heritage language classes. *Discourse Studies*, 3(1), 75–96.

Howard, K. M. (2009). "When meeting Khun teacher we should pay respect": standardizing respect in a Northern Thai classroom. *Linguistics and Education*, 20(3), 254–272.

Mattingly, C. (2014). *Moral Laboratories: Family Peril and the Struggle for a Good Life*. Oakland, CA: University of California Press.

Macleod, C. (2010). Toleration, children and education. *Educational Philosophy and Theory*, 42(1), 9–21.

Moore, L. C. (2006). Learning by heart in Qur'anic and public schools in northern Cameroon. *Social Analysis: The International Journal of Cultural and Social Practice*, 50(3), 109–126.

Ochs, E. and Schieffelin, B. B. (2017). Language socialization: a historical overview. In P. A. Duff and S. May (eds.), *Language Socialization: Encyclopedia of Language and Education, 3rd Ed.* (pp. 3–16). New York, NY: Springer.

Ochs, E. and Schieffelin, B. B. (2011). The theory of language socialization. In A. Duranti, E. Ochs, and B. B. Schieffelin (eds.), *The Handbook of Language Socialization* (pp. 1–21). Malden, MA: Wiley-Blackwell.

Pollock, M. (2005). *Colormute: Race Talk Dilemmas in an American School.* Princeton, NJ: Princeton University Press.

Pollock, M. (ed.) (2008). *Everyday Anti-Racism: Getting Real about Race in School.* New York, NY: The New Press.

Pratt, M. L. (1991). Arts of the contact zone. *Profession*, 33–40.

Taha, M. (2017). Shadow subjects: a category of analysis for empathic stancetaking. *Journal of Linguistic Anthropology*, 27(2): 190–209.

3   Shaping Sikh Youth Subjectivities in a US *Gurdwara*

Discursive Socialization of Religious Heritage in Sikh History Classes

Wendy Klein

3.1   Introduction

This study of a Punjabi Sikh education program in Southern California employs the language socialization framework to examine the construction of religious heritage in history classes for Sikh youth. Drawing from Kulick and Schieffelin's (2004) perspective on the unique applicability of language socialization methods for examining the production of culturally intelligible subjects, this analysis will also highlight the ways that teachers and students enact and contest Sikh subjectivities of belonging in contemporary American society. Participants' discursive practices of "positioning" (Davis and Harré, 1990) and "stance-taking" (Goodwin, 2006; Jaffe, 2009; Ochs, 1996) juxtapose students' behaviors with the actions of Sikh historical figures and contemporary understandings of Sikh ideals. The close scrutiny of teacher–student and peer exchanges will chart the recurrent linguistic practices that index notions of Sikh heritage and distinguish insider and outsider alignments (Ochs, 1990, 1993). The analysis foregrounds the features of interactional sequences that constitute the collaborative, yet multivocal, practices of reimagining and relocating a religious diaspora in the United States.

The term "diaspora," which was initially used to refer to the dispersal of Jews after exile from their homeland (Cohen, 2008), has been adopted by anthropologists to describe a subjective sense of belonging tied to experiences of prejudice and loss and to a collective pride in historical heritage (Clifford, 1994). Appadurai (1996) proposes that modern subjectivities are located in "ethnoscapes" of migrants' shifting worlds. Similarly, Gupta and Ferguson (1997), building on Anderson's (1983) notion of "imagined community," theorize the notion of diaspora as a cultural imaginary constructed by a de-territorialized community. Axel (2001, p. 28) aligns with this

I would like to Matthew Burdelski, Kathryn Howard, and an anonymous reviewer for their valuable comments and suggestions on an earlier draft of this chapter. My gratitude to Matt for additional editorial feedback and clarifications. Any errors that remain are my own.

conceptualization in his description of the Sikh diaspora as an emergent "transnational social formation" linked to the socio-political configurations of Sikh life in India, the ongoing desire for a Sikh homeland, and the perspectives of Sikh migrants abroad. Few studies examine how these construals of diaspora are lived and socialized in Sikh institutional settings. Brubaker (2005) proposes that we conceive of diaspora as a stance or a practice, rather than an "ethnodemographic" entity. He states (2005, p. 12), "As a category of practice, diaspora is used to make claims, to articulate projects, to formulate expectations, to mobilize energies, to appeal to loyalties . . . It does not so much describe a world as seek to *remake* it" (italics in original). Following Brubaker's aspirational sense of the term, this study analyzes the semiotic processes that (re-)shape subjectivities of belonging for youth in Sikh history classes in the United States.

The Sikh education program discussed in this chapter has been operating since the early 1990s. The content has gradually expanded to include discussions of contemporary issues viewed as deeply impacting Sikhs in American society. Post-9/11 acts of violence and discrimination have shifted Sikh perspectives on belonging in the United States and highlighted the consequences of the mistaken belief that Sikhs are affiliates of Middle Eastern terrorist groups (Klein, 2009; Sidhu and Singh Gohil, 2009).[1] *Gurdwaras* have also been targets of attacks such as the 2012 mass shooting in Oak Creek, Wisconsin, and incidents of arson and vandalism at other *gurdwaras* around the country.

The general lack of knowledge about Sikhs in the United States has prompted many Sikh institutions to prepare youth to become active representatives in their local communities. In Sikh history classes, historical narratives trace a collective chronology that begins in the Punjab at the end of the fifteenth century and culminates in the current moment in which Sikh youth are positioned as the heirs of a spiritual tradition that has reached a critical (dis)juncture in the United States.[2] The classes include accounts of historical persecution, the ongoing struggle for a sovereign Sikh nation, and relatively recent conflicts between Sikhs and the Hindu-majority government in India. Teachers often frame the contemporary socio-political climate in the United States as the latest challenge for the stability and growth of Sikh communities.

3.2   Classroom Education and Religious Socialization in Immigrant Communities

While socialization typically starts at home, classrooms are vital contexts for investigating routine practices in which experts and novices construct knowledge, negotiate social order, and position themselves in relation to others (Duff, 2002). Social theorists have long held that schools function as incubators of social and cultural reproduction through which enduring dispositions are continually reshaped (Bourdieu and Passeron, 1990). Language socialization studies of classrooms ground this theoretical perspective in ethnographically informed analyses of interactional routines in institutional contexts. In religious education, children and youth encounter authoritative discourses on the historical and moral configurations of the spiritual traditions that delineate their belonging in a particular community as well as their differentiation from other groups (Ek, 2005; Fader, 2006). Yet as Kulick and Schieffelin (2004) note, the aim and outcome of socialization practices is not always reproduction; in some cases, the specific subjectivities produced are new and embody change or transformation.

Language socialization research in immigrant populations brings into focus the interactional processes that shape moral subjectivities and designate appropriate ways of embodying faith and enacting citizenship in transnational communities (see Lytra, Volk, and Gregory, 2016). Several studies reveal the diverse and intricate ways that religious identification and ethnic or national ties are constructed and embodied in classroom interactions. For example, Baquedano-López (1997, 2000, 2002) analyzes the socialization of religious heritage in *doctrina* and catechism classes in a Catholic parish in California. In Spanish *doctrina* classes, the story *Nuestra Senora de Guadalupe* positions Mexican immigrant students as belonging to a distinct linguistic and cultural heritage rooted in Mexico's geography, colonial history of oppression, and redemption. In contrast, catechism classes taught in English frame Mexican heritage as one of many ethnicities of Catholics in the world. In another important study of language ideologies and ethnoreligious identification, García-Sánchez (2014) examines language and belonging among Moroccan children in Spain. Her monograph includes a comparison of Arabic language classes across two settings: a Spanish public school and a local mosque. The analysis illustrates the cultivation of different diasporic layers of identification and belonging in the socialization of Arabic language varieties. While the public schoolteacher links this variety to modern, pan-Arab cultural and literary traditions, the mosque instructor views the acquisition of Classical/Standard Arabic as a religious practice that embodies Muslim faith. These indexical meanings of Classical/Standard Arabic are conveyed in instructional discourses and literacy practices across the two locations. In both settings, the "Moroccan Arabic" used by children at home is treated as a lower status code, especially by the schoolteacher, who frames his urban background as superior to that of the families of rural origin. García-Sánchez contemplates the future implications of these tensions for the ongoing development of children's subjectivities of belonging and citizenship in Spain.

Methodologically and analytically, Moore's (2006, 2008) research on Qur'anic study among the Fulbe in Cameroon offers a model for taking a language socialization approach to examining the sequential and multimodal practices that constitute religious learning. Her micro-analysis of religious lessons demonstrates the importance of investigating the multiple semiotic (nonverbal, material, bodily components along with vocalization) and provides "a processual account of how children come to be intelligible as (emergent) Muslim subjects in that setting" (2008, p. 662). Moore's (2016) research on "double schooling" examines the tensions in language ideologies and pedagogical practices between Qur'anic study in Arabic and instruction in public schools in two different populations: the Fulbe in Cameroon and the Somali diaspora in Ohio. In Cameroon, many Fulbe linked the recent changes in Qur'anic education to colonial models of schooling that secularize the nature of language study. The Fulbe lamented the exposure of their children to attitudes and behaviors in public schools that challenge their religious and cultural customs. At the same time, Fulbe perspectives associated rote memorization in Qur'anic study with better academic motivation. Moore found that the Somali diaspora in Ohio share the latter view and emphasize the crucial role of Qur'anic schools in their children's socialization into Somali Muslim cultural and religious identification in American society.

Gendered subjectivities of belonging are explored in Fader's (2009) research on Hasidic girls in Brooklyn, where teachers clearly delineate insider and outsider ways of behaving in the world. Fader's investigation includes an analysis of classroom discourse that reflects the ideological importance in this community of submitting to the authority of males, elders, and religious texts. Girls are encouraged to ask particular types of questions that respect the given hierarchy, and they are quickly sanctioned through shaming and ridicule when they challenge authority figures and religious traditions. Teachers equate students' unfavorable behaviors with the "selfish," transgressive norms of gentile society, which exists outside of the moral domain of Hasidic life; thus subjectivities of belonging are carefully circumscribed in the classroom and beyond. Similarly, Ek's (2005) analysis of socialization of Central and South American children into Christian Pentecostal Chicano identities in California reveals that teachers differentiate between two youth worlds, el camino (the path) and el mundo (the world). Students are encouraged to follow God's path by attending church and dedicating time to religious activities, rather than falling under the corrupting influences of secular youth culture. Teachers position immigrant youth as occupying a special status; they embody a shift from the previous generation's difficult lives to the promise of success in a new country, as long as they remain on el camino. In actuality, however, youth live in both worlds and must negotiate their own paths.

Ethnographic research on Sikh communities around the world has included important insights into Sikh childrearing and education abroad (e.g., Gibson 1988 and Leonard 1999 in the United States); yet most studies do not analyze linguistic and discursive practices of socialization. Hall's (2002) scholarship on Sikhs in London is an important contribution to literature that bridges this gap. Hall highlights the institutional spheres of power that affect notions of British citizenship for Sikh youth and examines youth language practices, revealing the conflicting ethnic and cultural striations that emerge in youth narratives. The analysis, however, does not extend to social interactions in religious instruction. Some recent studies have made inroads in the analysis of recurrent linguistic and embodied practices that organize learning activities of Sikh children in classrooms (Klein, 2013, 2015; Sagoo, 2016). While Klein's work examines the socialization of prayer recitation and language ideologies in Sikh religious education in the United States, Sagoo's study focuses on a Sikh-run nursery school in the United Kingdom that combines Sikh cultural and spiritual practices with English educational approaches. These studies illuminate the links between specific genres of language use and the historical and moral dispositions enacted by teachers and students in these settings.

3.3   The Ethnographic Context

The center of spiritual and social life for Sikh religious communities is the *gurdwara* (lit. doorway to the Guru), where Sikhs gather for devotional services and community events. Most *gurdwaras* in the United States also provide youth education programs that include instruction in *Gurbani* (prayer recitation), *kirtan* (singing hymns and playing traditional instruments), Sikh history, and other religious and cultural activities. The Sikh tradition began at the end of the fifteenth century in the region of Punjab, where Guru Nanak, the first of ten consecutive Sikh Gurus, developed a set of monotheistic teachings that center on daily meditative recitation, service to the community, family life, gender equality, and the rejection of caste distinction.[3] The tenth Guru proclaimed that the *Sri Guru Granth Sahib Ji* (SGGSJ), the Sikh anthology of writings, would succeed him as Guru.[4] The SGGSJ, which is regarded as the embodiment of the divine, is placed upon an elaborately draped platform in the main hall during *gurdwara* services. One of the first ritual practices to which children are introduced is paying respect to the SGGSJ. Infants as young as a few months are placed facing the altar by their parents who configure their children's bodies into a kneeling position and touch their heads to the ground. On the wall behind the altar is a vast mural of *Harmandir Sahib* (also referred to as "The Golden Temple"; see Figure 3.1), which is located in Amritsar, in the state of Punjab, India. The Golden Temple complex is a large, magnificent structure that spans several buildings and has gilded domes, minarets, and a reflecting pool in the center. This iconic depiction of Sikh spirituality and history is also displayed in photos and illustrations in families' homes and businesses.

The *gurdwara* is home to a range of semiotic representations and practices that link Sikh communities in India and abroad (Klein, 2013). Upon entering,

Figure 3.1 Mural depicting *Harmandir Sahib* in a US *gurdwara*

attendees must cover their heads and remove their shoes in deference to the divine. Females usually wear *salwar kameez* (tunics) and *chuni* (headscarves), while males wear *dastaar* (turbans) or *patka* (smaller head covering) with their everyday attire.[5] During prayer recitation classes, students learn to recite Archaic Punjabi verses (*Gurbani*) from the SGGSJ. Formulaic language often constitutes an important socialization resource for creating indexical ties between language use and social identities (Burdelski and Cook, 2012). Stories about the Sikh Gurus and other important figures in Sikh history function in a similar manner to invoke a "collective memory" (French, 2012) of shared origins. Sikh historical events are recounted in activities for children and youth and depicted in images found throughout the *gurdwara*. In the Sikh history classes analyzed in this chapter, the narratives construct a shared historical trajectory that carries implications for current Sikh youth conduct.

3.4   Data Collection, Participants, and Analytical Procedures

This study was carried out over a two-year period in a Sikh education program in Southern California (2005 to 2007) and was part of a larger ethnographic endeavor that included an additional year of data collection in families' homes in the United States and in Punjab, India, along with three months of follow-up visits in 2013 to observe a more recent cohort of students. Initially, I met Sikh community members in 2003 when volunteering for a social support organization for Indian immigrants. Sikhs were particularly active in outreach activities at that time in reaction to incidents of profiling and harassment. Although I was an outsider, I was warmly welcomed and invited to Sikh community events and religious services where I met many families over a period of several months. Most Sikhs I met who were raised in India were proficient in English, but my previous study of Hindi was helpful in acquiring basic Punjabi, which allowed me to hold simple exchanges with elder relatives and understand instructions in classes. The teachers of the Gurbani and history classes, along with a few of the youth, generously assisted me in translating when necessary. In exchange, I helped them create videos that captured children's activities. In the beginning of my research, students often asked my name and inquired about why I was there, but after the first few months, I was rarely questioned and my presence at the *gurdwara* seemed to attract little attention, probably due to the fact that I was not the only non-Punjabi woman who was around during classes. A few of the mothers who had different ethnic backgrounds (other than Punjabi/Indian) were often at the *gurdwara* while their children were in class.

Data collection was carried out during two Sundays each month, and methods included ethnographic video recording, participant observation, and open-ended interviews. The parents who participated in the study were ethnic Punjabis who were born in India.[6] In the Sunday program, students were divided into peer groups according to age, and six of the youth in the larger study fell into the eldest group (15 to 18 years old or roughly high school age). The teachers in the Sunday program functioned as mentors and role models for their students. Many were parents or older siblings of students in the program, and their curriculum integrated readings and visual media from a range of resources and websites. The history classes were taught primarily in English as all students were native or near-native English speakers, while only a few reported that they were fluent in Punjabi. Yet the majority were familiar with formulaic conversational phrases in Punjabi as well as with some of the recitation verses and religious terminology used in the history classes.

Video recordings of classes captured the visual aspects of communication that are necessary for a fine-grained analysis of participants' embodied attitudes and behavior (Goodwin, 1993). Several of the teachers and community members circulated with video cameras, sometimes recording the same classes that I was filming, which most likely contributed to students' lack of interest in the recording equipment. Classes took place in different rooms of the *gurdwara*, none of which were actual school classrooms in the conventional sense (e.g., rows of desks or tables and chairs). The spaces were sparsely furnished and often used to house visitors. Students sat on the floor with their notebooks and folders, while the teachers either sat or stood facing them. Some rooms contained white boards and television monitors for showing videos.

In classes for the younger cohort, students read stories about the Gurus, drew pictures of important historical figures and locations, and watched slide shows about the Gurus' lives. As one of the teachers noted in an interview about the children he instructed, "They have to know their Gurus, they are their ancestors. They must know them to know who they [themselves] are." The classes for the older group were organized both chronologically (e.g., successive Gurus and battles) and according to theme (e.g., "Women in Sikhism"), and probed the implications of Sikh historical narratives. The teachers who instructed the group stated that their instructional goals included "waking them [the students] up" and "giving them the support to make them knowledgeable leaders." Teachers framed the transformation of youth subjectivities as inducing an epistemological shift that will rouse students into understanding their heritage and undertaking the work of community building.

Data transcription and analysis of the corpus (82 hours) proceeded through several stages that included coding participation structures and recurring themes and topics/narratives. The analytical focus was on dominant, ubiquitous patterns of language use that constructed notions of Sikh religious heritage and socialized youth subjectivities over the two-year period. These discursive practices, which will be examined in the following sections, include: (1) marked person reference: terms of address, pronouns, and identity categories (e.g., Sikh-American, Punjabi-speaking); (2) discourses of collective self-critique and relational positioning; and (3) contemporary stances toward Sikh historical concepts. Detailed transcription and analysis were carried out on representative segments that most clearly illustrated these discursive positioning practices, which were often found within the same interactional sequence. The analysis links these interactional practices to historical, cultural, and socio-political processes of Sikh community formation. The French sociologist Hervieu-Léger (2006, p. 68) suggests that religious heritage persists through "the construction of an imaginary positioning system of individuals within a symbolic genealogy." This notion resonates deeply in the way that Sikhs construct community within the *gurdwara* setting. For example, the quotidian practice of taking attendance in *gurdwara* classes identifies students in a manner that deviates from common secondary school procedures. The teachers added the Punjabi surname, "Singh" to all male students' names when taking roll (except for those students whose last name was Singh). To the female students' names, the teachers attached the last name "Kaur."[7] The adoption of these surnames in Sikh communal contexts is linked to the Sikh egalitarian ideal; Indian surnames typically identify caste, thus adopting the same surnames is a way to avoid caste designations. The use of shared surnames also socializes egalitarianism and kinship among students with different historical circumstances of immigration and a range of socio-economic backgrounds (in contrast, see Howard (2007) for the socialization of hierarchy through the use of kinship terms in Thailand). The custom of using familial terms to designate fictive kin relationships among Sikhs is socialized early in Sikh education (Sagoo, 2016), but the discursive practices employed in the history classes reflect more specifically situated notions of heritage and belonging.

3.5　Socialization into Religious Heritage in Sikh History Classes

3.5.1　Discourses of Self-Critique

Sikh history classes were organized around accounts of the lives of the Gurus, the development of Sikh teachings, and important historical events. Classes covered the past persecution of Sikhs, which emphasized themes of hardship, sacrifice, and loss, and socialized students into chronicling their shared spiritual and ancestral history. As Baquedano-López (2000) demonstrated, historical narratives are important discursive vehicles for socialization in religious instruction. In the following interaction, which was recorded during the fourth month of observation, there were two instructors (T1 and T2) team-teaching the class. Both were recent college graduates (one male, one female) who served as mentors to the students.

Excerpt 3.1 Brutal History

(Harjot = female student; Ss = multiple students)

```
01   ((T1 writes three dates on the board: 1746, 1762, 1984.))
02   T1:     We discussed seventeen forty-six last time. Vaddā Ghallūghārā was our
03           second holocaust, and more people died in this one in a day.
04   Harjot: How many people did they kill in one day?
05   T1:     Back then they didn't have a census so best estimate is (0.8) probably
06           thirty thousand [(at least).
07   Ss:                     [What::t? (Naa)
08           ((many students express surprise and disbelief))
09   T2:     We had a very brutal history.
```

The history teachers frequently used the term "holocaust" (line 03) when discussing three specific events in Sikh history. The term was used interchangeably with "genocide" and "massacre" when referring to these historical events, and its usage frames these incidents as highly calamitous in terms of the number of Sikhs killed.[8] The vast majority of the students had studied the Jewish Holocaust in school; employing the term here interprets Sikh suffering through the lens of Jewish experience and indexically links Sikh and Jewish histories with imperatives for collective remembering. This connection was made explicit toward the end of the first year of data collection during a discussion about potential field-trip locations.

Excerpt 3.2 Jewish Holocaust

(S1, S2 = unidentified students)

```
01  T2:  Have you been to the Museum of Tolerance?
02       ((many students raise their hands))
03  T2:  What is that place about and why does it matter?
04  S1:  (°Holocaust of the [Jews°)
05  S2:                    [What happened in World War Two.
06  T2:  Why does the Jewish holocaust matter to us and not our own?
07       (1.2)
08  T2:  Nineteen eighty-four was not that long ago.
09       ((topic changes when another location is suggested))
```

When discussing historical content, teachers often embedded discourses of collective self-critique that called into question current youth behaviors and ways of speaking. When Teacher 2 asks, "Why does the Jewish holocaust matter to us and not our own?" (line 06), she invokes a sense of collective shame in the apparent collective neglect of tragic Sikh historical episodes. The teacher treats her recipients as accountable for caring about and displaying interest in Sikh historical events by employing "collective self-reference terms" ("us" and "our") (Lerner and Kitzinger, 2007, p. 526). These forms invoke shared subjectivities and are referred to by Silverstein (2000, p. 118) as "we-voicing" in his analysis of Benedict Anderson's notion of imagined communities. There are over 100 tokens of collective self-reference as subjects ("we"), objects ("us"), and possessives ("our") in teachers' and students' assessments of youth behaviors. While these pronominal forms index the group, they are often *not* inclusive of the speaker, as in the teacher's question above, which positions diasporic Sikhs as indifferent to the traumas experienced by past generations. The teacher's we-voicing here is an example of the "instructional we," which strategically emphasizes solidarity and avoids the more confrontational, accusative, "you" that might distance her from the students.

It was not only teachers who made critical comments about student behavior in class discussions. Students were also negatively evaluated by their peers.

Excerpt 3.3a Jag's Question

(Jag, Gurjeet = male students)

```
01  Jag:      Didn't the Moghul army pay money to kill Sikhs or something,
02  Gurjeet:  Seeks?
03  Ss:       Huh? (xxx)
04  Gurjeet:  Sikhs not See::ks. I hate it when people do that.
05  T2:       Okay, okay, fair point. Why should we say Seek? Hispanic people, when
06            they pronounce names in their language, like R(rr)oberto.
07            They don't say Robert-o,=
```

08 Ss: *((laughter))*
09 T2:   = or Robert.

After Jag asks a question about persecution against Sikhs in the eighteenth century, Gurjeet targets Jag's pronunciation of "Sikhs." In his other-initiated repair (line 02) and his correction (line 04), Gurjeet contrasts the Punjabi phonetic pronunciation of "Sikh," in which the vowel is pronounced as a short i [ɪ], with the Anglophone pronunciation, "seek" ([i]).[9] Gurjeet's subsequent remark, "I hate it when people do that," attributes this error to generic "people," thus linking Jag to non-Sikhs. As Friedman (2009, p. 360) points out in her study of "corrective feedback" in a Ukrainian language classroom, when students repair one another's speech in the classroom, they display their linguistic expertise as well as their knowledge of the social implications of such errors. It is important to note that Gurjeet was born in Punjab and did not move to the United States until his family immigrated when he was 12 years old. Gurjeet's Punjabi pronunciation and authoritative stance mark him as aligning with the purist language ideological notion of an authentic Punjabi untainted by native speakers of English (Woolard and Schieffelin, 1994). Kattan (2010) describes a similar phenomenon among Israeli youth who mock non-Israeli (i.e., American Jewish) pronunciations of Hebrew as inauthentic.

Gurjeet's expert status was, in part, often cultivated by some of the teachers who often aligned with his comments. Here, however, his correction is reformulated by the teacher as a collective critique in her question, "Why should we say Seek?" (line 05). In this instance, the use of the instructional "we" mitigates the indignity of Jag's mispronunciation by framing it as an error that other students have made. There were three other occasions when students were criticized by both teachers and their peers for making this error associated with non-Sikh mispronunciations. While the teachers did not always comment on students' pronunciations of Punjabi words and phrases, they often lamented that many students neglected their linguistic heritage, and this refrain became one of the recurrent discourses of collective recrimination, which was often followed by moral imperatives to gain or maintain Punjabi language skills in order to communicate with elders and teach future generations.

In their discursive practices of collective self-scrutiny, teachers also employed what Bucholtz and Hall (2005, p. 598) refer to as "the relationality principle." Teachers often pointed to *non*-Sikh minority groups as effective models for self-representation. By aligning Sikh youth with speakers of other heritage languages, the teachers positioned them relationally, as social actors who are responsible for authentic, legitimate displays of identification. In the above extract, when the teacher links pronunciation to community representation, she offers the following example: "Hispanic people, when they

pronounce names in their language, like R(rr)oberto. They don't say Robert-o"
(lines 05–07). Here the teacher praises "Hispanic people" in the United States
who pronounce the Spanish trilled /r/ phoneme and employ Spanish inton-
ational patterns when uttering Spanish names, even when speaking in English.
Phonological loyalty to one's heritage language is viewed as a marker of group
authenticity and an appropriate way of linguistically navigating belonging in
American society. Teachers' comparative, aspirational discourses that com-
mend the community advocacy activities undertaken by non-Sikhs are an
interesting departure from other immigrant and minority groups that condemn
youth who enact the behaviors of outsiders (Ek, 2005; Fader, 2006).

3.5.2   Contemporary Stances toward Sikh Ideals

One discursive thread observed over the two years of classes was the call for
young Sikhs to embody the *Sant-Sipahi* ideal, the spiritual-soldier model,
which is tied to the notion *Miri-Piri*, or temporal and spiritual power.[10] This
latter concept is emblemized in the image of the two swords worn by Guru
Hargobind, the sixth Sikh Guru, and represents the mandate of Sikhs to be
spiritually knowledgeable as well as protect the weak and vulnerable from
powerful oppressors. This ideal was intrinsic to another recurrent comparative
discourse genre in which teachers juxtaposed contemporary Sikhs in the
diaspora with the lives of Sikh historical figures. Excerpt 3.3b continues from
the segment above as the other teacher (T1) redirects the class's attention to the
historical discussion.

Excerpt 3.3b Jag's Question

Continuation of Excerpt 3.3a
(Sunita = female student)

10	T1:	But let's hear Jag's question. *((points to Jag))*
11	Jag:	My father said that people were paid to kill Sikhs.
12	T1:	Yes. When the Mogul emperors were trying to convert all Sikhs into
13		Muslims, there was a price on every Sikh's head, so if you gave a Sikh's
14		head to them, they will give you. (.) let's say fifty rupees.
15		And so Sikhs could not live in villages – they had to live in forests.
16		They acted as protectors and sometimes when they were in danger,
17		they attacked outta no:where, (0.8) but not for revenge, for justice.
18		So that's why we were feared. And Sikhs were rarely caught.
19		Hard to believe stuff like that – in today's world,
20		none of us have the courage – to even get up in the morning
21		(.) for (0.6) Japji [Sahib.
22	Ss:	[(It's hard).
23	T1:	Why is that?

24 Sunita: We're lazy.
25 Gurjeet: I'[m not.
26 T2:   [Now is not a time to be lazy.
27 (S):   (xxx) *Seva* and serve our community?
28 T1:   Yes, we must come back to *Sikhi*.

Jag's query (line 11) is formulated as a statement and is an instance of reported speech (e.g., Goodwin, 2007) that cites his father as the source of knowledge about the historical persecution of Sikhs. He takes up a stance of 'epistemic authority' (Heritage and Raymond, 2005), which counters his previous positioning by Gurjeet as an unknowledgeable outsider. The teacher immediately confirms (line 12: 'Yes') and goes on to recount the bravery of Sikhs in the past. He then comments, "in today's world, none of us have the courage – to even get up in the morning (.) for (0.6) *Japji Sahib*" (lines 19–21), referring to the ritual of waking up early for prayer recitation. After a few students express resistance (line 22), the teacher questions them. Sunita then characterizes the Sikh youth today as "lazy" (line 24), invoking the collective ("we") in her assessment. Yet Gurjeet refuses to engage in this self-condemnation practice. Through his oppositional stance (line 25: "I'm not"), Gurjeet positions himself as more virtuous than most of his peers who were raised in the United States. His contributions point to the heterogeneity of subjectivities within this classroom community and reflect diasporic divisions that have been described in earlier ethnographic work (e.g., Leonard, 1999).

The current generation of Sikh youth is repeatedly positioned as inhabiting a critical juncture in which the future of Sikh communities in the United States may be at risk. The teacher declares, "Now is not a time to be lazy" (line 26), a statement that marks the deictic "now" as temporally requiring youth engagement and action. One student raises the topic of *seva*, which refers to embodying a selfless attitude while performing actions that contribute to community wellbeing (line 27). The teacher agrees and concludes, "we must come back to *Sikhi*" (line 28), a moral stance that implies that youth have collectively strayed from Sikh ideals.[11] This statement emphasizes the moral (rather than geographic) distance of today's youth and demands a return to Sikh teachings.

Appraisals of contemporary youth were frequently embedded in teachers' discussions of the lives of Sikh historical figures. During the sixth months of class observations, one of the teachers recounted the battles between Guru Gobind Singh and the Mogul Empire in the early eighteenth century. He pointed out that even when the Guru's two young sons, six and nine years old, were imprisoned, tired, and underfed, they still managed to recite their evening prayers. The teacher then paused to ask the students, "Why are we getting weak? We must follow the teachings of our Guru. We forget to do our meditation. When we stay away from Guru, that's it. Guru is the one who gives us the courage to stand for our rights, for everybody's rights." The teachers' frequent comparisons of Sikh youth in the United States to important historical figures was followed by a series of moral imperatives ("We must follow the teachings of our Guru") and admonishments to engage in religious practices and social justice, the principles of *Miri-Piri* (temporal and spiritual power).

During the second year of research, some students in the history class discussed problems they encountered traveling with their families over the summer. In one case, a youth's father was asked by airport TSA (Transportation Security Administration) agents to remove his turban in a private room while his family waited outside, and they ultimately missed their flight.[12] For the family, more disturbing than the inconvenience was the experience of being targeted as potential terrorist suspects. One of the students then referenced a teacher's previous comment about Sikh persecution.

Excerpt 3.4 Miri-Piri

(Sam = male student, Mandi = female student)

```
01 Sam:    Remember you said that if you are a Sikh, you would be a target, (.) that
02         back in the day they received twenty bucks (xxx) for a Sikh head.
03 T1:     Yes. (.) So if we can survive tha:t, we can definitely get through today.
04         (1.0) ((Mandi raises her hand and T2 points to her))
05 Mandi:  And we've got to defend ourselves. Be strong, you know, do not let people
06         take us down with names.
07 Jay:    I'll mess them up.
08 T2:     NO. What is miri piri symbolic of? Civic and religious power. So it's
09         asserting your freedom and independence.
10 Harjot:  Like Guru Hargobind ji.
11 T2:     Uh huh. Like Martin Luther King. >Like what's going on in today's world
12         in the name of national security< (.) a lot of civil rights have been
13         violated. (.) Violence won't help. Speaking up will.
14         Sikhi is not just a Sunday ritual.
```

When referencing the *Miri-Piri* model, teachers and students often debated the nature of effective social activism in the United States. Historically, several of the Gurus engaged in battle, and physical attacks were an acceptable method of self-defense. Yet teachers frequently condemned violence and redefined appropriate forms of social justice that aligned with the nonviolent aspects of the American Civil Rights Movement. One student's declaration (line 07: "I'll mess them up") is immediately condemned by the teacher, who equates *Miri-Piri* with "asserting your freedom and independence" (line 09) and "speaking up" (line 13). While the teacher agrees with one student who mentions a Sikh Guru as a model (line 11: "Uh huh"), she goes on to equate the Sikh fight against civil rights violations with Martin Luther King's struggle (line 11). This is another instance in which teachers' relational discourses ultimately transform and relocate the Sikh historical model of moral personhood on a contemporary American socio-political landscape. The teacher's assertion that "*Sikhi* is not just a Sunday ritual" (line 14) emphasizes that Sikh teachings require more than weekly collective enactments of faith. Following *Sikhi* is a moral calling to represent and advocate for Sikhs in a society that often questions their citizenship and rights of inclusion. In subsequent classes, students developed projects (e.g., school presentations, writing poems, stories, volunteering) with the purpose of increasing Sikh visibility and civic participation.

3.6 Discursive Positioning in Sikh Instructional Practices

In Sikh instructional activities, particular instantiations of "collective memory" (French, 2012) are discursively constructed through linking historical accounts of important Sikh figures and pivotal events to contemporary narratives of belonging in American society. French (2012, p. 340) defines the term collective memory as "a social construction constituted through a multiplicity of circulating sign forms, with interpretations shared by some social actors and institutions and contested by others in response to heterogeneous positions in a hierarchical social field in which representations of the past are mediated through concerns of the present." This process aptly captures the semiotic dimensions of Sikh youth subjectivities in *gurdwara* instruction: the teachers' assessments of youth behaviors in relation to Sikh figures from the past; the historical framing of the current predicament of Sikhs in US society; and the divergent subjectivities embodied by Sikh youth in relation to their peers.

Tables 3.1 and 3.2 identify the types of positioning enacted in the excerpts analyzed in this chapter. Table 3.1 highlights the operation of relational discourses in the positioning of Sikh youth in comparison to previous Sikhs and to specific religious and ethnic groups in the United States. These utterances are tied to underlying thematic issues that were constructed relationally through the indexing of specific actors and practices that were held up as models for Sikh youth to emulate. At the same time, the actions of these youth were targeted and critiqued as insufficient in comparison.

The utterances in Table 3.2 indexically positioned students as linked to their predecessors and placed them at a critical juncture on the Sikh historical timeline. Deictic terms such as pronouns and temporal expressions situated Sikh youth at a temporal precipice; their collective history mandates them to embody Sikh historical ideals while advocating for the present community and their future survival in contemporary US society.

Table 3.1 *Relational positioning: comparative models and collective discourses of self-critique*

Issue	In relation to	Discursive links	Excerpt: utterances
Persecution	Jews	Holocaust	3.1: Vaddā Ghallūghārā was our second holocaust. 3.2: Why does the Jewish holocaust matter to us and not our own?
Heritage language	Hispanics	S[ɪ]kh Roberto vs. S[i]kh Robert	3.3a: Sikhs not See::ks. I hate it when people do that. 3.3a: Why should we say Seek? Hispanic people, when they pronounce names in their language, like R(rr)oberto.
Temporal shift in adherence to *Sikhi*	Historical Sikhs	Eluding conversion to Islam	3.3b: in today's world, none of us have the courage – to even get up in the morning (.) for (0.6) Japji Sahib. 3.3b: We're lazy.
Social activism	African Americans	American Civil Rights Movement MLK	3.4: So it's asserting your freedom and independence. Like Martin Luther King. >Like what's going on in today's world in the name of national security< (.) a lot of civil rights have been violated.

Table 3.2 *Indexical positioning of diasporic subjectivities*

Temporal frames	Linguistic/ discursive forms	Excerpt: utterances
Historical	Collective self-reference	3.1: We had a very brutal history.
Contemporary: deictic	Time marker; deictics	3.2: Nineteen eighty-four was not that long ago. 3.3b: Now is not a time to be lazy.
Contemporary: agentive/epistemic stances	Collective self-reference and epistemic modals	3.3b: we must come back to *Sikhi*. 3.4: So if we can survive tha:t, we can definitely get through today. 3.4: And we've got to defend ourselves. Be strong, you know, do not let people take us down with names. 3.4: Violence won't help. Speaking up will.

Along with deixis, agentive and epistemic stances constructed a pathway for Sikh youth to embark upon; embedded in these recurrent discursive practices was the positioning of Sikh youth as accountable agents in their own socialization.

3.7   Conclusion

Sikh history classes are a critical site for constructing youth perspectives on religious heritage and belonging in American society. In their discussions, teachers and students located youth as temporarily occupying a precarious subject position that requires them to reconstitute Sikh historical models of community and social justice. The attitudes and behaviors of Sikh youth were often deemed a problem in the collective self-critiques that youth engaged in with their teachers and peers. These discursive practices positioned youth as the descendants of the Gurus, but also as indifferent progeny who were not necessarily living up to the Sikh model of moral personhood (*Sant-Sipathi*). Teachers re-envisioned this model for a contemporary, diasporic community context and ultimately positioned Sikh youth as accountable agents in their own socialization. In addition to a historical axis that contrasted them with Sikhs of the past, youth were evaluated along a contemporary axis in comparison to minority groups who work to educate the public about their historical circumstances, inflect their speech with heritage language pronunciations, and fight for civil rights. The frequent references to the past predicaments, current activism and community building efforts of other minority groups invoked models for diasporic Sikhs in their pursuit of recognition and social justice.

Research on classroom discourse in history classes, citizenship classes, and second language learning classrooms has highlighted the role educational instruction plays in the construction of political and social identities (see Friedman, 2010; Vogel-Langer, 2008). History instruction, as scholarship in the philosophy of history has noted, is not simply a context for students to acquire discrete units of information such as names and dates; youth encounter ideological perspectives that either confront or sidestep the thorny problems of constructing neutral accounts of events and framing agency and causation (Lee, 1983). The teaching of history in religious education, however, tends to be less "meta-historical" and more focused on cultivating group sensibilities and contextualizing religious concepts. In Sikh history classes, participants' discursive positioning practices mobilized Sikh students from diverse backgrounds into a unified collective with a moral obligation to participate in community endeavors. Although most students took up the prescribed stances, others expressed varying levels of commitment and resistance, revealing the multivocality of youth subjectivities.

Language socialization studies illuminate the interactional practices through which classrooms and other educational settings become the locus of cultural and socio-political activity. From a language socialization perspective, the questioning and probing of Sikh historical narratives constitutes a diasporic framework for the mutual socialization of teachers and students into moral, affective, and epistemological stances that impact participant understandings of their religious heritage and belonging in American society.

NOTES

1 These circumstances are linked to anti-immigrant sentiments as well as to the mis-recognition of the Sikh turban as an Islamic article of faith. Although some Sikhs have reacted by distancing themselves from Muslims, others emphasize solidarity in view of their shared status as non-white, non-Christian "double minorities" (Singh, 2013: 116).

2 'The Punjab' is an historical area that spans parts of contemporary Northern India and Eastern Pakistan.

3 Although the principle of equality is a Sikh ideal that transcends caste or gender, divisions and discrimination still remain in differing degrees, depending on the context or location.

4 The title, *Sri Guru Granth Sahib Ji*, includes three linguistic markers of respect: *Sri* is an honorific title, *Sahib* is another polite form of address used for individuals and holy places, and *Ji* is an honorific suffix. *Guru Granth* refers to the book of holy teachings of the Guru.

5 Other important semiotic practices include the "Five K's," which refers to the five kakars, or symbols of Sikh faith: *kes* (uncut hair), *kang* (comb), *kirpan* (sword), *kara* (iron bracelet), and *kachcha* (undergarments). The Sikh turban is now representative of Sikh faith, egalitarian status of all Sikhs, and a commitment to Sikh moral codes; however, it is primarily worn by men. Some Sikh women do wear turbans and are viewed by some as making a statement of gender equality (Kalra, 2005).

6 Most Sikhs trace their ancestry back to the state of Punjab in India, either directly or through migration from another diasporic community (e.g., Singapore, East Africa), but a few parents had converted when they married Sikhs. Another group that adheres to Sikh teachings are the mostly Caucasian American congregations that emerged in the 1970s and are referred to as "*Gora* (white) Sikhs" (Dusenbery, 2008).

7 The literal meanings of "Singh" and "Kaur" are 'lion' and 'princess,' respectively. These names appear to index gendered notions of personhood; however, some scholars point out that the name "Kaur" is not inherently female (i.e., the literal meaning is 'prince') and that this practice was intended to put an end to families defining their heritage and ancestry based on male surnames, and instead emphasize gender equality within the Sikh community (Kaur Singh, 2005).

8 Although typically associated with the systematic killing of Jews and other groups by the Nazis during World War II, the term "holocaust" is also used by Sikh scholars to refer to the persecution of Sikhs (Shani [2002] ties its usage to Sikh diasporic nationalist discourses).

9 This English pronunciation is often referred to the "anglicized" pronunciation. Yet it is not due to phonological transfer from English. It has been hypothesized that the English pronunciation emerged for lexical reasons.

10 *Miri-Piri* is also translated as secular/socio-political/material (*miri*) and religious power (*piri*) (Kalra, 2014).

11 *Sikhi* is the Punjabi term for Sikh teachings and faith (Sikhism). The literal meaning of the word "Sikh" is 'disciple'.

12 After several years of Sikh organizations lobbying for changes, the TSA adopted new screening procedures in 2007.

REFERENCES

Anderson, B. (1983). *Imagined Communities: Reflections on the Origin and Spread of Nationalism.* London: Verso.

Appadurai, A. (1996). *Modernity at Large: Cultural Dimensions of Globalization.* Minneapolis, MN: University of Minnesota Press.

Axel, B. K. (2001). *The Nation's Tortured Body: Violence, Representation, and the Formation of a Sikh "Diaspora".* Durham, NC: Duke University Press.

Baquedano-López, P. (1997). Creating social identities through doctrina narratives. *Issues in Applied Linguistics*, 8(1), 27–45.

Baquedano-López, P. (2000). Narrating the community in doctrina classes. *Narrative Inquiry*, 10(2), 1–24.

Baquedano-López, P. (2002). Language socialization in children's religious education. In J. H. Leather and J. van Dam (eds.), *Ecology of Language Acquisition* (pp. 107–121). Norwell, MA: Kluwer Academic Publishers.

Bourdieu, P. and Passeron, J. C. (1990). *Reproduction in Education, Society and Culture.* London: SAGE.

Brubaker, R. (2005). The "diaspora" diaspora. *Ethnic and Racial Studies*, 28(1), 1–19.

Bucholtz, M. and Hall, K. (2005). Identity and interaction: a sociocultural linguistic approach. *Discourse Studies*, 7(4–5), 584–614.

Burdelski, M. and Cook, H. M. (2012). Formulaic language in language socialization. *Annual Review of Applied Linguistics*, 32, 173–188.

Clifford, J. (1994). Diasporas. *Cultural Anthropology*, 9, 302–338.

Cohen, R. (2008). *Global Diasporas: An Introduction, 2nd Ed.* New York, NY: Routledge.

Davies, B. and Harré, R. (1990). Positioning: the discursive production of selves. *Journal for the Theory of Social Behaviour*, 20, 43–63.

Duff, P. A. (2002). The discursive co-construction of knowledge, identity, and difference: an ethnography of communication in the high school mainstream. *Applied Linguistics*, 23, 289–322.

Dusenbery, V. A. (2008). *Sikhs at Large: Religion, Culture, and Politics in Global Perspective.* New Delhi: Oxford University Press.

Ek, L. D. (2005). Staying on God's path: socializing Latino immigrant youth to a Christian Pentecostal identity in Southern California. In A. C. Zentella (ed.), *Building on Strength: Language and Literacy in Latino Families and Communities* (pp. 77–92). New York, NY: Teachers College.

Fader, A. (2006). Learning faith: language socialization in a community of Hasidic Jews. *Language in Society*, 35, 205–229.

Fader, A. (2009). *Mitzvah Girls: Bringing Up the Next Generation of Hasidic Jews.* Princeton, NJ: Princeton University Press.

French, B. (2012). The semiotics of collective memory. *Annual Review of Anthropology*, 41, 337–353.

Friedman, D. (2009). Speaking correctly: error correction as a language socialization practice in a Ukrainian classroom. *Applied Linguistics*, 31(3), 346–367.

Friedman, D. (2010). Becoming national: classroom language socialization and political identities in the age of globalization. *Annual Review of Applied Linguistics*, 30, 193–210.

García-Sánchez, I. M. (2014). *Language and Muslim Immigrant Childhoods: The Politics of Belonging*. Malden, MA: Wiley-Blackwell.

Gibson, M. (1988). *Accommodation without Assimilation: Sikh Immigrants in an American School*. Ithaca, NY: Cornell University Press.

Goodwin, C. (1993). Recording human interaction in natural settings. *Pragmatics*, 3(2), 181–209.

Goodwin, C. (2007). Interactive footing. In E. Holt and R. Clift (eds.), *Reporting Talk: Reported Speech in Interaction* (pp. 16–46). Cambridge: Cambridge University Press.

Goodwin, M. H. (2006). *The Hidden Life of Girls: Games of Stance, Status, and Exclusion*. Malden, MA: Blackwell.

Gupta, A. and Ferguson, J. (1997). Beyond "culture": space, identity, and the politics of difference. In A. Gupta and J. Ferguson (eds.) *Culture, Power, Place: Explorations in Critical Anthropology* (pp. 33–51). Durham, NC: Duke University Press.

Hall, K. (2002). *Lives in Translation: Sikh Youth as British Citizens*. Philadelphia, PA: University of Pennsylvania Press.

Heritage, J. and Raymond, G. (2005). The terms of agreement: indexing epistemic authority and subordination in talk-in-interaction. *Social Psychology Quarterly*, 68 (1), 15–38.

Hervieu-Léger, D. (2006). In search of certainties: the paradoxes of religiosity in societies of high modernity. *The Hedgehog Review*, 8(1–2), 59–68.

Holland, D. and Leander, K. (2004). Ethnographic studies of positioning and subjectivity: an introduction. *Ethos*, 32(2), 127–139.

Howard, K. M. (2007). Kinterm usage and hierarchy in Thai children's peer groups. *Journal of Linguistic Anthropology*, 17(2), 204–230.

Jaffe, A. (2009). Introduction: the sociolinguistics of stance. In A. Jaffe (ed.) *Stance: Sociolinguistic Perspectives* (pp. 3–28). Oxford: Oxford University Press.

Kalra, V. S. (2005). Locating the Sikh Pagh. *Sikh Formations*, 1(1), 75–92.

Kalra, V. S. (2014). Secular and religious (Miri/Piri) domains in Sikhism: frames for Sikh politics. In P. Singh and L. E. Fenech (eds.) *The Oxford Handbook of Sikh Studies* (pp. 262–270). Oxford: Oxford University Press.

Kattan, S. (2010). "Language socialization and linguistic ideologies among Israeli emissaries in the United States." Unpublished doctoral dissertation, University of California, Berkeley.

Kaur Singh, N.-G. (2005). *The Birth of the Khalsa: A Feminist Re-Memory of Sikh Identity*. Albany, NY: SUNY Press.

Klein, W. (2009). Turban narratives: discourses of identity and difference among Punjabi Sikh families in Los Angeles. In A. Reyes and A. Lo (eds.) *Beyond Yellow English: Toward a Linguistic Anthropology of Asian Pacific America* (pp. 111–130). Oxford: Oxford University Press.

Klein, W. (2013). Heritage language socialization and language ideologies in a Sikh education program. *Heritage Language Journal*, 10(1), 36–50.

Klein, W. (2015). Responding to bullying: language socialization and religious identification in classes for Sikh youth. *Journal of Language, Identity and Education*, 14(1),19–35.

Kulick, D. and Schieffelin, B. B. (2004). Language socialization. In A. Duranti (ed.), *A Companion to Linguistic Anthropology* (pp. 349–368). Malden, MA: Blackwell.

Lee, P. J. (1983). History teaching and philosophy of history. *History and Theory*, 22 (4), 19–49.

Leonard, K. I. (1999). Second generation Sikhs in the US: consensus and differences. In P. Singh and N. G. Barrier (eds.) *Sikh identity: Continuity and Change* (pp. 275–298). New Delhi: Manohar.

Lerner, G. H. and Kitzinger, C. (2007). Extraction and aggregation in the repair of individual and self-reference, *Discourse Studies*, 9(4), 526–557.

Lytra, V., Volk, D., and Gregory, E. (2016). Introduction. In V. Lytra, D. Volk, and E. Gregory (eds.), *Navigating Languages, Literacies and Identities: Religion in Young Lives* (pp. 1–17). New York, NY: Routledge.

Moore, L. C. (2006). Learning by heart in Qur'anic and public schools in northern Cameroon. *Social Analysis: The International Journal of Cultural and Social Practice*, 50(3), 109–126.

Moore, L. C. (2008). Body, text, and talk in Maroua Fulbe Qur'anic schooling. *Text and Talk*, 28(5), 643–665.

Moore, L. C. (2016). Moving across languages, literacies, and schooling traditions. In V. Lytra, D. Volk, and E. Gregory (eds.), *Navigating Languages, Literacies and Identities: Religion in Young Lives* (pp. 126–140). Oxford: Routledge.

Ochs, E. (1990). Indexicality and socialization. In J. W. Stigler, R. A. Shweder, and G. Herdt (eds.), *Cultural Psychology: Essays on Comparative Human Development* (pp. 287–308). New York, NY: Cambridge University Press.

Ochs, E. (1993). Constructing social identity: a language socialization perspective. *Research on Language and Social Interaction*, 26(3), 287–306.

Ochs, E. (1996). Linguistic resources for socializing humanity. In J. Gumperz and S. Levinson (eds.), *Rethinking Linguistic Relativity* (pp. 407–437). Cambridge: Cambridge University Press.

Sagoo, G. K. (2016). Engendering 'dispositions' through communicative and semiotic practices: insights from the Nishkam nursery project. In V. Lytra, D. Volk, and E. Gregory (eds.), *Navigating Languages, Literacies and Identities: Religion in Young Lives* (pp. 193–212). New York, NY: Routledge.

Shani, G. (2002). The territorialization of identity: Sikh nationalism in the diaspora. *Studies in Ethnicity and Nationalism*, 2(1), 11–19.

Sidhu, D. S. and Singh Gohil, N. (2009). *Civil Rights in Wartime: The Post-9/11 Sikh Experience*. Surrey: Ashgate.

Silverstein, M. (2000). Whorfianism and the linguistic imagination of nationality. In P. V. Kroskrity (ed.), *Regimes of Language* (pp. 85–138). Santa Fe, NM: School of American Research Press.

Singh, J. (2013). A new American apartheid: racialized, religious minorities in the post-9/11 era. *Sikh Formations*, 9(2), 115–144.

Vogel-Langer, A. (2008). *Becoming One Nation: Explorations in Language Use and Identity Formation of German's Post- and Pre-Unification Generations.* Saarbrücken: VDM Verlag Dr. Mueller.

Woolard, K. A. and Schieffelin, B. B. (1994). Language ideology. *Annual Review of Anthropology,* 23, 55–82.

4   Affective Stance and Socialization to Orthodox Christian Values in a Russian Heritage Language Classroom

Ekaterina Moore

4.1   Introduction

Becoming a competent member of a community involves acquiring a set of affective demeanors and the socio-cultural acts and identities associated with them. Expressing affective stance, or "mood, attitude, feeling and disposition, as well as degrees of emotional intensity vis-à-vis some focus of concern" (Ochs, 1996, p. 410) in socio-culturally appropriate ways is learned from early childhood through a process of language socialization (e.g., Ochs, 1988), in which caregivers attempt to create the desire within children to adhere to a certain discourse (Fader, 2011). In any society, adults attempt to raise children to become competent members of their community, as individuals who possess, express, and engage in appropriate feelings, dispositions, and behaviors. Affective stances are shaped in everyday interactions between children and their caregivers and siblings, and such stances are central in indexing social acts, social identities, and culturally specific values (Ochs, 1996).

Socialization of affective stances is not limited to early childhood and family settings, but also occurs through formal educational experiences across the lifespan. As the social and academic dimensions of classrooms are not separable entities (Erikson, 1982), and as teaching is "first and foremost an ethical enterprise" (Larrivee, 2008, p. 344), classroom interactions are a central site in which children learn and develop not only important skills, facts, and abilities, but also appropriate ways of being, acting, and feeling in the social world. Research on language socialization of affective stance in classrooms demonstrates that this socialization is a dialogic "value-suffused process" (Cekaite, 2012, p. 668), where the role of teachers is central as they are in a position to evaluate children's stances based on classroom and societal norms while simultaneously exposing children to these norms (Cekaite, 2013). This socialization is not a unidirectional process, but involves novices' "willing engagement with, and appreciation of, the values and ideologies . . . of educational activity" (Cekaite, 2012, p. 643). In classrooms, affective stance is closely connected with identity, such as displaying gender (Burdelski and Mitsuhashi, 2010), being a problematic student (Cekaite, 2012), or a "knowingly hurtful child" (Lo, 2009, p. 231). Considerations of identity in the socialization of affective stance are especially important for second and heritage language classrooms, as learning additional languages involves "appropriate identities, stances ... and other behaviors associated with the target group and its normative practices" (Duff, 2007, p. 310).

The present chapter discusses the socialization of affective stance and values in an Orthodox Christian Russian heritage language Saturday school in California. I demonstrate how, through the use of "assessments," or practices of "evaluating in some fashion persons and events ... described in ... talk" (Goodwin and Goodwin, 1992, p. 15), within *hypothetical stories* implemented during instructional activities, teachers socialize children into positive feelings and attitudes toward church practices, which is considered a necessary quality of being a "normal" Orthodox Christian. This socialization involves not only displays of positive stances toward religious practices by the teachers, but also stance negotiation and rejection of the children's use of negative characterizations or negatively-laden language in relation to church practices. The chapter demonstrates that learning subject matter, such as vocabulary items (see Cekaite, Chapter 6 in this volume) for talking about church-related practices, is inseparable from learning the appropriate stances associated with these practices. It also shows how these stances are socialized through a variety of semiotic resources, including lexicon, syntactic structures, facial expressions, and prosody.

4.2   Setting and Methodology

The present study was conducted at a Russian heritage language school in Southern California. This heritage language school is based on an Orthodox Christian parish built by the first wave of Russian immigrants[1] who arrived in the United States shortly after the October Revolution of 1917. These were mostly members of the Russian elite who opposed the new communist regime in the country. They established the parish as a conscious effort "to unite them all in their nostalgic feeling for the lost homeland ... creating a cultural center as the custodian of the spiritual values of the lost homeland" (book dedicated to the twenty-fifth anniversary of the Parish, 1953).[2] Shortly after opening the parish, a Saturday school was established with the goal of providing organized aid to Russian children abroad.

Throughout the years, the school has seen various levels of enrollment, with about 50 children aged five to 17 attending the school today. The students are grouped according to age; each group consists of five to 15 children with a lead teacher, who is usually an expert in Russian language and literature and only teaches that particular group in a given academic year. The school employs nine teachers (seven women and two men). Most of the teachers are native

Russian speakers, 30 to 60 years old, who emigrated from the former Soviet Union, where they received a minimum of a Bachelor's degree. The two male teachers, a graduate of a seminary and one of the two parishes' priests, are usually assigned to lead God's law classes.[3]

The school operates on Saturdays between 8:00 am and 3:00 pm. A typical day consists of five 45-minute lessons: Russian language, Russian literature, music, God's law, and Russian history classes, all taught in Russian with translation into English provided upon the teacher's discretion. In addition, every school day starts with a special short church service for the children, teachers, and parents, followed by the five lessons with short breaks and a 30-minute lunch period in between. A few Saturdays a year, during the Great and Christmas Lents,[4] the students and their families attend longer church services, conducted especially for the school children before the beginning of classes. Modifications to the regular schedule are made to accommodate cultural and religious celebrations, festivals, and concerts that are seen as an integral part of the school's life and as promoting cultural and religious affiliation.

Learning the Russian language, culture, history, and foundations of Orthodoxy are some of the explicitly stated goals of the school. Other goals include "providing assistance to the parents in moral upbringing of the children and bringing up the next generation of Orthodox Christians" (from the school's website). Reflected in these objectives, learning about, affiliating with, and appreciating the Russian culture and the Russian Orthodox Christianity are considered of primary importance in the school. Further, the teachers consider Russian cultural and Orthodox Christian practices to be closely connected with, and even inseparable from, the Russian language. It is believed that a deep emotional connection among the Russian language, culture, and Orthodox Christian practices, such as prayer, exists for Russian Orthodox Christians. Teachers and parents believe that being a proper Russian Orthodox Christian involves not only knowing about church and religious practices but also experiencing a special feeling when these practices are performed in Russian.

To examine language socialization practices at the school, I conducted a longitudinal study using combined methods of discourse analysis and ethnography. I spent a year and a half observing and audio-visually recording classroom interactions of two groups of elementary-age students in their classes with four different teachers. I also conducted semi-structured interviews, participated in unstructured conversations, and observed children and teachers in their interactions with each other, parents, and clergy before, after, and between classes, and at lunchtime and organized school events. I also socialized with some of the teachers and the students' families outside the school by visiting their homes.

Informed by these ethnographic insights, my analysis in this chapter focuses on teacher-fronted lessons (one group of students with one teacher; but see note 3) that were transcribed using the conventions proposed by Sacks, Schegloff, and Jefferson (1974), and linguistic transliteration conventions (see Appendix). In addition, frame grabs, including facial expressions, and pitch tracks (generated with PRAAT) that were relevant for action produced by interlocutors were added to the transcripts, as both hearable and "seeable structure in the environment can ... contribute crucial semiotic resources for the organization of current action" (Goodwin, 2000, p. 157).

Combining long-term ethnography with detailed analysis of talk allowed me to identify central themes of cultural affiliation and evaluate how beliefs are practiced, constructed, and reinforced in everyday classroom interactions. Specifically, one central theme concerning the necessity of having proper feelings toward religious practices by Orthodox Christians became apparent during my informal conversations with teachers and parents. Conducting discourse analysis of classroom interactions allowed me to examine how this belief is expressed and transmitted to the children. Although the analysis of classroom talk provided great insight on how positive affective stance toward the church is socialized in this school, it did not explain why the socialization practices are employed. At the same time, interviews and ethnographic observations alone did not provide a clear understanding of the mechanics of the socialization process. The methods described above allowed me to uncover the intricate ways in which interlocutors utilized multiple semiotic resources in interaction and how these resources are informed by beliefs and norms of community members.

4.3   Teachers' Use of Hypothetical Stories for Socializing Affective Stances

Although school teachers and parents explicitly discussed having proper feelings toward Orthodox Christianity as a necessary component of being a "normal" Orthodox Christian, such conversations were not observed in communication with the children. Rather, in classrooms, the appropriate affective stances toward religious practices were socialized in the midst of instructional practices, such as teaching vocabulary items associated with these practices, fusing the intellectual and the socio-cultural. Frequently, these instructional practices incorporated "participant examples," or interactions that portray a "hypothetical (narrated) event which includes at least one person who is also participating in the narrating [class] event" (Wortham, 1994, p. 21; see also Cekaite, Chapter 6 in this volume).

As narratives of primarily past experience have been considered to be important vehicles of language socialization into affect and identity (Baquedano-López, 1998; Capps and Ochs, 1995; Ochs, 2007, Ochs and Capps, 2001), in this Russian as a heritage language classroom stories of "hypothetical events" (e.g., Haight, 2002, p. 96) played a central role in this socialization. In hypothetical stories and scenarios, present and absent parties become characters in future and imagined scenes (Goodwin, 1990; Murphy, 2011, Ochs and Capps, 2001). This allows the party telling the story to create scenarios not "hindered by nagging questions about reflections of truth" (Murphy, 2011, p. 246). In addition, it allows for the creation of a "desired truth" that reflects the teller's own views of reality. Incorporating hypothetical stories in the instructional practices, teachers in this heritage language classroom present to the children a reality where engaging in church practices becomes not only normal, but also desirable. Through these stories, instructors teach language associated with the church practices as they encourage children's appreciation and positive affect toward the practices, while children contribute to storytelling in various ways (Ochs and Capps, 2001).

The examples presented here are excerpts from a God's law class where eight- to ten-year-old children are learning vocabulary to refer to items used during church services, such as words for individuals participating in the services, pieces of priest's clothing, candles, icons, and incense. The discussion of these items was part of a larger project of creating a "My Church" poster. Over the course of several weeks, children colored and cut out pictures of church items and glued them on a poster board that was later displayed in the school hallway. As the students colored the pictures, the teacher, a male Seminary graduate in his early thirties, engaged them in discussions of the words associated with the items in the pictures and their functions.

Excerpt 4.1 (divided into Excerpts 4.1a and 4.1b) is a participant example where the teacher initiates a hypothetical story and positions the children as characters who take an imaginary friend to church. In Excerpt 4.1a, the teacher first introduces the story by presenting the children as novices who attend a church service for the first time (lines 01 and 02). After a pause, however, the teacher redoes the beginning of the story positioning the children as knowledgeable parties who will take a newcomer friend to church (beginning in line 03).

Excerpt 4.1a Bringing a Friend to Church
(Teacher = male teacher, Ženja = female student, Maša = female student)

01	Teacher:	*Vot vy (.) naprimer vy prišli v cerkov.*
		'Here you all for example you came to church,'
02		*Pervyj raz v žizni naprimer.* (1.0)
		'For the first time in your life for example.'
03		*Ili vot (.) prišël k vam drug i govorit,*
		'Or here a friend came to you and says,'
04		*Nadja ili Adrej ili Maša ili eh-=*
		'Nadja or Adrej or Maša or,'
05	Ženja:	*=ili Ženja*
		'Or Ženja,'

06 Teacher: *Ili Ženja ili* ⌈ *Sofija*
            'Or Ženja or │ Sofia'
07 Maša: │ *ili Sofi*
                        ⌊ 'Or Sofy'
08 Teacher: *A skaži mne (1.5) a č::to >takoe cerkov'.<*
            'Tell me what is a church?'
09   *Ja xoču pojti s toboj v cerkov'. (1.0)*
            'I want to go to church with you.'

In the present interaction, the teacher produces hypothetical direct reported speech of the friend, using several of the children's names (line 04), allowing them to maintain "a role within the example, as well as their ongoing role as … student[s] in the classroom" (Wortham, 1994, p. 1). Teachers' use of hypothetical reported speech is a commonly occurring language socialization practice in this school (Moore, 2014) and a central vehicle for the socialization of affect in relation to church practices. The quotes are usually structured in a way that makes them relevant for all the children present. In Excerpt 4.1a, the teacher utilizes second person pronoun *vy* 'you' (as meaning 'you all') (in lines 01 and 03) to frame the quote. Furthermore, the quote is made relevant for individual children through the use of children's names (lines 04 and 06) and singular familiar 'you' (line 09). Children demonstrate that they understand this story and the reported speech as something that is relevant to them and co-participate in the production of the reported speech through the insertion of their own (line 05) and classmates' names (line 07) in the story, demonstrating their alignment to the proposed hypothetical scenario. In this scenario, attending church services is presented as a normal occurrence for the children and a desirable one for their friend who is presented by the teacher as not only wanting the children to take them to church (line 09) but also asking them a question about church (line 08).

By producing a story in which children become characters for whom it is normal and desirable to attend church services, the teacher emphasizes a practice that is valued among Orthodox Christians: regularly attending church. Furthermore, this practice is introduced as something that others also strive to do, indexing a shared affective stance through the desiderative form *xoču* 'want' (line 09). In producing the friend's hypothetical reported speech, the teacher does not ask the children a question as to whether they will be going to church but uses a declarative sentence in which the children are told that the friend wants to go to church together with them, which puts the children in an experiential position. In addition, the teacher locates affect within the children's identity, positioning them as individuals who regularly attend church services, and links this affect to their peer relationships. In these ways, the teacher socializes the children not only to the practice of going to church regularly, but also to feeling good about it as an event that is desirable for their friend.

4.4 Teachers' Use of Assessments in Socializing Affective Stances

Within hypothetical stories, teachers in the Russian heritage language class-room frequently indexed positive affective stance toward religious practices through the use of assessments. Assessments are interlocutors' evaluations of people, objects, and events discussed in talk. Evaluation is a distinct element in stories that may occur throughout a narrative (Labov, 1972) as segmental or non-segmental phenomena (Goodwin and Goodwin, 1992), such as in the form of "affect specifiers" (i.e., features that specify "particular affective orientations of utterances") and "affect intensifiers" (i.e., features that modulate "the affective intensity of utterances") (Ochs and Schieffelin, 1989, p. 14). Assessments are crucial in the socialization of affective stance as expressions of affect are pervasive in assessments and central for their organization (Good-win and Goodwin, 1992). In addition, because of their public nature, assessments allow for judging novices' competence to "properly evaluate the events they encounter" (Goodwin and Goodwin, 1992, p. 155).

The teacher highlights the positive affective stance associated with church services as his story unfolds. In Excerpt 4.1b (an immediate continuation of Excerpt 4.1a), he presents vocabulary items associated with church services, specifically the words 'priest' and 'deacon'. As the teacher presents these words, he evaluates them through the use of assessments "to display [his] experience of the event, including [the] affective involvement in the referent being assessed" (Goodwin and Goodwin, 1987, p. 9). In addition, by using these assessments as part of hypothetical reported speech, the teacher presents the evaluations as those of the children's friend.

Excerpt 4.1b Bringing a Friend to Church
Continuation of Excerpt 4.1a
(Teacher = male teacher, Andrej = male student, Ženja = female student)

10	Teacher:	*I vot predstavljaete i vy voz'mëte ego za:: ruku,*
		'So imagine you take his hand,'
11		*Vašego druga ili podrugu (.) i privedëte v cerkov'. (1.5)*
		'Your friend, and bring him or her to church.'
12		*Predstavljaete čto (.) on budet spraši̇vat' vas (.)*
		'Imagine what he will ask you.'
13		*°A čto sejčas delajut° (.) a čto sejčas delajut.* ((whispers)) *(.)*
		'And what are they doing now? And what are they doing now?'
14		*A čto vot èto. A čto vot èto. (.)*
		'And what is this? And what is this?'

(lines 15–21 skipped)
22 Teacher: *A vot- i potom vyxodit vot takoj čelove::::k.*
               'And this- and then this person comes out,'
23   *Vot takoj vot.* ((shows a picture of a priest))
               'Like this.'
24   *Takoj kak zdes'.* ((points to the picture of a priest))
               'Just like here'
25   *I u vas vaš drug sprosit,*
               'And your friend will ask you,'
26   *.hha? A kto èto tak krasivo ode::::tyj. (1.5)*
               'hha? and who is this dressed so beautifully?'
27   *A vy emu skažete čto,*
               'And you will tell him what?'
28   (2.0)
29 Andrej: *Èto (.) èm- svajaščennik?=*
               'This is a hmmmm priest?'
30 Teacher: *=èto svjaščennik, da::::.*
               'This is a priest yes.'
31   *A on spro::::sit a kto èto vtoroj takoj tože- (0.2)*
               'Also who is this second one also,'
32   *Tože očen' krasivo odetyj.*
               'Also dressed very beautifully?'
33   *Vtoroj (on) nemnozko po – drugomu u nego netu* ⎡ *kresta* ::: .(1.5)
               'The second one is a little different, he doesn't have a ⎢ cross.'
34 Andrej: ⎢ *a*
35 Teacher: *U nego netu kresta u svjaščennika krest est'.*   ⎣
               'He doesn't have a cross while the priest does.'
36   *A vot u è:::togo (.) čeloveka netu kresta.*
               'But this person doesn't have a cross.'
37   *I on spro- a kto vot èto takoj kotoryj pomogaet svjaščenniku.*
               'And he'll ask, who is this one who is helping the priest?'
38   (3.0)
39 Teacher: *Vy emu skažete,*
               'You will tell him,'
40   (1.0)
41 Teacher: *Čto vy emu skažete,*
               'What will you tell him?'
42   *Èto(.) d'ja::::*
               'This is de-'
43 Andrej: *D'javol?=*
               'Devil'?
44 Teacher: ⎡ *= Ne :: t*   *vy čt(h)o(h) ::: kak(h)o(h)j d'(h)ja(h)vo(h)l.*
              ⎢ 'No   wha :: t are you saying (h)what devil(h)!'
45 Ženja: ⎣ (h)a ⎦

46 Ženja: *D'javol (.)*   ⌈ *èto* ⌉   *TOL'KO V ADE.* =
              'Devil' | is | only in hell'
47 Teacher: | haha |
48   = *Èto užas.* ⌊ *Net.* ⌋   *Èto d'jakon.*
         'This is horrible. No. This is a deacon.'

((Lesson continues for about seven minutes as the teacher explains to the children the roles of different clergy, including the discussion of the deacon.))

49 Teacher: *I vot (.) vaš drug naprimer kotorogo vy v pervyj raz priveli v cerkov',*
          'So your friend for example whom you brought to church for the first time,'

50   *I on sprašivaet,*
          'And he asks'

51   *.hhh da::: èto svjaščennik. A kto pomogaet vot èto svjaščenniku.*
          'Yes this is a priest? And who is this helping the priest?'

52   ⌈ *On,*
        | 'He'
53 Andrej: | *D'jakon.*
        ⌊ 'Deacon.'

In Excerpt 4.1b, the teacher presents to the children the vocabulary items 'priest' and 'deacon' using "Initiation–Response–Evaluation (IRE) sequences" (Mehan, 1979) (lines 27–30 and 41–48) that are prefaced by and embedded within the teacher's story that employs hypothetical reported speech. In this story, the children are positioned as knowledgeable church-goers who bring their friend to a church service. Throughout the story, the teacher produces a layering of voices (Bakhtin, 1981) by giving voice to an unknowing friend who asks questions about what is happening at the church (line 13) where there is a 'beautifully' dressed person (priest) (line 26), and another 'beautifully' dressed person (deacon) (line 32) who helps the priest (line 51). In addition to asking questions in the voice of a friend, the teacher adds his own assessments, or evaluations of "persons and events being described in [his] talk" (Goodwin and Goodwin, 1992, p. 154). Specifically, he uses affect specifiers and intensifiers to index a positive affective stance toward the church items (lines 26 and 32), and a negative stance toward a child's incorrect answer (lines 44 and 48). The teacher's use of the lexical item 'beautifully' dressed (lines 26 and 32) indexes positive affective stance toward the clothes worn by the church clergy, whereas the use of the word *užas* 'horror' (line 48) – in response to the child's answer 'Devil' (line 43) – indexes a negative stance toward the child's wrong answer that evokes negative associations. In addition to the use of lexical items, the teacher indexes positive affective stance regarding the clothes worn by the clergy through affect intensifiers, such as a whispering voice (line 13), in-awe-like inhaling (line 26), and vowel lengthening (lines 26 and 51). Simultaneously, the teacher treats the child's incorrect answer of 'devil' as laughable through the insertion of a laughing voice in his evaluation of this answer (line 44). He emphasizes that the answer is wrong by stretching the vowels in *ne::t* 'no' and *čto::* 'what' (line 44). Similar to previous research (DuBois and Kärkkäinen, 2012; Goodwin and Goodwin, 2000; Moore, 2014), prosody is a central resource in this classroom for indexing affective stance.

The use of assessments that are produced at various points in the hypothetical stories, utilizing affect specifiers and intensifiers becomes a means of not only socializing the children *to use* language but also socializing them *through* the use of language into how to feel toward the church. The instructional practice of teaching the children vocabulary associated with church practices that uses an array of positive assessments is a vehicle that encourages the children to develop an appreciation and positive feelings associated with the vocabulary. Assessments indexing positive affective stance toward church practices are prevalent in the teacher's talk that is produced both in his own voice and in hypothetical reported speech. Assessments, both positive and negative, are also common in student talk, as discussed in the next section.

4.5   Children's Reactions to Socialization Attempts

In this school, children usually align with teachers' positive assessments of religious practices. In Excerpt 4.2, a girl (Ženja) demonstrates such an alignment by co-producing the teacher's utterance. The teacher describes clothes worn by a priest on his arms, expressing a positive affective stance; Ženja completes the teacher's utterance producing a congruent assessment through the use of positive vocabulary, prosody, and facial expression.

Excerpt 4.2 Armlets
(Teacher = male teacher, Ženja = female student)

01 Teacher: *A na rukax u nix u vsex vidite kakie krasivye (.)*
              'And on their arms they all you see have these beautiful'
02   ⌈ *Vešči s krestom.*
              ⌊ 'things with a cross.'
03 Ženja: ⌈ *Uzo :: ry*   ⌈ *Uzory* ((smiles slightly))
              ⌊ 'Patterns'   ⌊ 'Patterns'
04 Teacher: ⌈ *Uzory. Oni nazyvajutsja poručni.*
                                      ⌊ 'Patterns. They are called armlets.'

In this interaction, the teacher starts the description of a new word (line 01), which will eventually become the word *poručni* 'armlets,' but then hesitates (as indicated by the micropause in line 01). Ženja takes this pause as an opportunity for a turn and completes the teacher's utterance with the word 'patterns' (line 03), which is produced simultaneously with the teacher's 'things with a cross' (line 02). Ženja then repeats the word 'patterns' (line 03), which is in turn used by the teacher who then introduces the word *poručni* (line 04). By recycling the vocabulary item produced by Ženja, the teacher utilizes Ženja's prior displayed knowledge before introducing the new vocabulary item while at the same time engaging in a collaborative dialogue, where "language use and language learning can co-occur" (Swain, 2000, p. 97).

While we see that the teacher's introduction of the new word is done in a collaborative manner, we also observe that in the midst of the co-construction of meaning, both the student and the teacher engage in the expression of affective stance. The display of positive affect toward the priest's armlets starts with the teacher's use of the word 'beautiful' (line 01). Aligning with this positive stance, Ženja not only completes the teacher's utterance with an appropriate part of speech ('patterns,' a plural noun), but also with a congruent positive stance using this highly positive word. In addition, Ženja smiles slightly as she produces a vowel stretch (line 03: *uzo::ry* 'patterns'). In response, the teacher aligns with Ženja's stance through his repetition of this word (line 04).

Along with opportunities to learn language (e.g., new vocabulary items), opportunities for stance displays and socialization are created and utilized through the use of language as the teacher and the students "co-participate in the experience offered by the assessment through an exchange of affective displays" (Goodwin and Goodwin, 1992, p. 159). Although Excerpt 4.2 demonstrated a highly collaborative interaction with aligning stance displays, this type of alignment does not always take place immediately. In the following interaction, it takes the teacher a few turns of producing positive assessments for the students to align. In Excerpt 4.3, the teacher describes incense used during church services. Prior to the description, he asks the children whether they know what incense is, to which the children answer 'no.'

Excerpt 4.3 Incense
(Teacher = male teacher, Ženja = female student, Nadja = female student)

01 Teacher: *Èto takoe-*
              'It is a-'
02   *Očen' dušistye takie kamuški   kotorye sdelany iz   smaly dereva.*
              very fragrant these stones-DIM which   made   from sap   tree
              'Very fragrant these stones which are made out of tree sap.'

03   (0.6)

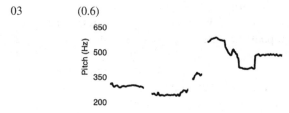

Figure 4.1 Pitch track for "sap"

04 Ženja: *S m a **L Y**:::::: .*   = ((high pitch; see Figures 4.1 and 4.2))

            'Sap?'

Figure 4.2 Facial expression for "sap"

05 Teacher: =*Iz smaly dereva i   smala očen' dušistaja.*
            'From tree sap and the sap is very fragrant.'
06   *I   kogda smalu derevjannuju (0.8) i   dušistuju ložiš' na ugol',(0.3)*
            and when   sap tree   and fragrant put-2PS on coal
            'And when you put the fragrant tree sap on the coal,'
07   °*Načinaetsja takoj očen očen duši:::styj (.) dym*°
            Start   this very very fragrant   smoke
            'This very very fragrant smoke starts to form.'

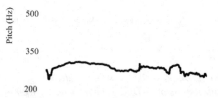

Figure 4.3 Pitch track for "Yes I love it"

08 Ženja: *Da* :::: *ja ljubljùeto.* ⎡((See Figure 4.3))
                 'Ye ::: s I love it.' ⎢
09 Teacher: ⎢*Èto tak zdorovo*
                                   ⎣'It is so nice'

10 Nadja: *Možno v tualet scxodit'.*
            'May I go to the bathroom?'
11 Teacher: *Da xorošo idi tol'ko ne dolgo.=*
            'Yes ok go but don't take long.'

Figure 4.4 Pitch track for "So good it smells"

12 Ženja: = *Tak* ⎡*xorošo* ::: *paxnet* ((see Figure 4.4))
             'So ⎢good it smells'
13 Teacher: ⎢*Èto očen' èti èto očen'zdorovo paxnet.*
                     ⎣'It's very, it smells very nice.'

The teacher describes incense as 'very fragrant these stones which are made out of tree sap' (line 02), projecting a positive affective stance toward the object. He uses affect specifiers such as the positively connoted adjective *dušistye* 'fragrant' combined with an affect intensifier *očen* 'very' and a diminutive suffix *ušk* in the word *kamuški* 'stones' (line 02). A 0.6 second pause follows this description (line 03). In response, Ženja repeats the word 'sap' that the teacher used in his talk. Its production (her facial expression [see Figure 4.2] and vocalization), however, does not align with the positive stance projected by the teacher. Ženja produces a high-pitched utterance with a very distinguished rise–fall intonation and stretching of the final sound /y/. The pitch range of the utterance is about 168 Hz, with a minimum pitch being 245 Hz and a maximum 413 Hz (line 04; see Figure 4.1).

Such production demonstrates Ženja's negative stance, possibly disagreeing with or challenging the teacher's stance. Similar to many disagreeing stance displays, the girl's utterance is "delayed" (Pomerantz, 1984), coming after a 0.6 second pause. Ženja's production of the utterance is also consistent with the intonation pattern usually associated with expressing disagreeing questioning in Russian (Bryzgunova, 1977). In addition, sound lengthening in Russian is also "known to be one of the most frequent means of expressing emotive evaluation" (Yokoyama, 1994, p. 685). In response to this evaluation, the teacher produces a further description of the incense. He frames his description as a hypothetical scenario that puts the recipients of the description, the children, including Ženja, in an experiential position.

In this scenario, a generic protagonist puts the incense on the coals, after which it starts to produce a fragrant smoke. The teacher's use of a present tense second person singular verb 'put' and omission of the subject[4] makes "anyone who engages in the posited activity" experience it (Ochs and Capps, 2001, p. 167).[5] The teacher's description is filled with positive assessments. In lines 05, 06, and 07, he describes both the incense and the smell that it creates as 'fragrant' (a highly positive adjective) adding an intensifier *očen očen* 'very very'. In his description, the teacher reverses the canonical word order, placing a verb *načinaetsja* 'starts' before a subject *dym* 'smoke' (line 07) and the adjective *dušistuju* 'fragrant' after the noun *smalu* 'sap' (line 06). The reversal of the subject–verb order allows the teacher to present the phrase 'fragrant smoke' as an existential. Simultaneously, an assertion rather than a presupposition (Robblee, 1994; Thompson, 1977), achieved through the reversal of the adjective–noun word order (line 08), emphasizes the noun descriptors. The syntactic structure of the teacher's description allows for emphasis of the qualities of the smoke and the positive adjective 'fragrant'.

In addition to syntax and vocabulary, the teacher utilizes prosody to further highlight positive affective stance. Following Ženja's negative stance display (line 04), the teacher latches his description to her utterance (line 05), not allowing any more evaluations from the students. He produces "format tying" (Goodwin, 1990) of Ženja's utterance 'sap' changing both its intonation and pitch in *smaly dereva* 'tree sap' (line 05). The teacher uses a very even intonation pattern (pitch range 20 Hz) maintaining a relatively low pitch (about 113 Hz). By recycling Ženja's utterance this way, the teacher adds a different, positive and intimate "coloring" to the utterance, intensified by the use of a lower volume and pronouncing the word 'fragrant' after a 0.8 second pause (line 06), and stretching the accented vowel (line 07). Such production contributes to the creation of the feeling of intimacy associated with the practice of using the incense.

Following the teacher's expression of affective stance, Ženja corrects her previous negative stance display and communicates a stance similar to that of the teacher through production of an upgraded positive assessment (lines 08 and 12). She uses a positive affect specifier 'good' to describe the smell of the incense (line 12) and explicitly states that she loves it (line 08). In addition, she intensifies the positive assessment (lines 08 and 12) through the use of prosody. The even intonation pattern (similar to that of the teacher) with a low pitch range (53 Hz and 25 Hz, see Figures 4.3 and 4.4) combined with vowel stretching allows for an expression of a positive stance the teacher expresses and seeks.

4.6   Conclusions

Learning one's heritage language cannot be separated from learning the "complex contextual dimensions in continuingly evolving, culturally sensible ways" (He, 2014, p. 589). The language socialization approach utilized in the present research allowed for an investigation into how such complex contextual dimensions are made relevant for heritage learners of Russian in an Orthodox Christian Saturday school in California. The research shows that displaying appropriate affective stances during classroom interactions becomes a key part in the process of socializing children into cultural values and identity associated with being a Russian Orthodox Christian.

The language socialization methodology utilized in the present research provided tools for examining both this central theme of cultural affiliation and the ways this cultural knowledge of values is transmitted to a new generation of Russian Orthodox Christians during routine classroom interactions. Combining discourse analysis and ethnographic methodologies allowed for the uncovering of ways in which interactional resources are informed by community members' beliefs and norms. Ethnographic fieldwork conducted in the school demonstrated that becoming a competent member of a Russian Orthodox Christian Diaspora and a member of the new generation of Orthodox Christians, involves the ability not only to speak Russian and understand the meaning of cultural and church practices, but also to *express* appropriate affective stances toward these practices. The ethnographic insights unveiled *why* affect is made relevant in discussion of church practices. The discourse analytic component of the language socialization approach enabled us to understand *how* positive stances toward church are socialized in the midst of instructional activities designed to teach the meaning of these practices.

As they are learning vocabulary associated with church-related practices, children are simultaneously socialized into gaining appreciation of and positive feelings for these practices and the values linked to them. The teachers in this Russian heritage language school represented religious practices in ways that express their positive stance toward these practices while simultaneously evaluating and responding to children's stance displays. They (1) provided positive evaluations of the church-related objects (e.g., priests' clothing), including when challenging children's negative characterizations; (2) positioned the children as individuals actively involved in church practices (e.g., attending services); and (3) aligned with the children's positive evaluations of church-related objects (e.g., repeating positive vocabulary used by a child). These three components of stance display (DuBois, 2007) become especially powerful as the teachers implement them in hypothetical stories and participant examples known to be useful for allowing the students to "experience certain ... emotions" (Wortham, 1994, p. 171), and, I would argue, for socialization of affective stances and values.

This chapter contributes to our understanding of stories as a powerful socialization strategy in classrooms. Stories engage the students in various ways and become a site for socializing children to affective stance, values, and identity in relation to religion. In addition, the chapter contributes to the recognition of the centrality of hypothetical stories and scenarios in the socialization of affective stance. One does not need to actually experience an event to learn from it, as to my knowledge no children were ever asked to take someone to church or engaged in the lighting of church incense (see note 6). The teacher's instructional strategy that included hypothetical stories allowed the teachers to present to the children the preferred affective stances associated with religious practices and evaluate children's stance displays. In the hypothetical stories and scenarios, children were presented as complex characters who experience and express certain emotions. Through exposure to such "hypotheticals," a child attending the school does not simply learn how to be a speaker of Russian; she learns how to be an individual who has proper feelings toward culturally embedded religious practices. The children are not told that they are to feel a certain way when they perform a prayer in Russian or smell the smoke produced by incense. Rather, through the use of hypothetical scenarios, children are put in a position of experiencing feelings, and they learn the meaning of being a member of a Russian Orthodox Christian diaspora through concrete experiences, real or imagined, and the interpretations of these experiences by teachers.

Appendix: Cyrillic Alphabet Transliteration Conventions

A a	K k	X x
Б b	Л l	Ц c
В v	M m	Ч č
Г g	H n	Ш š
Д d	O o	Щ šč
E e	П p	Ь '
Ё ё	P r	Ъ "
Ж ž	C s	Э è
З z	T t	Ю ju
И i	У u	Я ja
Й j	Ф f	

Interlinear Gloss Abbreviations
2P second person plural
DIM diminutive marker

NOTES

1 Three waves of immigration to the United States from Russia are discussed in the literature (Andrews, 1999; Zemskaja, 2001).

2 The title of the book and the school's website are not disclosed because of confidentiality concerns.

3 One female teacher also taught "God's law" during my fieldwork in the school. My discussion in this paper is based on the interactions of one male teacher (Seminary graduate) with one group of students during "God's law" classes. It is noteworthy, however, that the classroom practices analyzed in the paper are not unique to this teacher; I observed similar practices (e.g., hypothetical stories) in other classes in the school (Moore, 2014) and during "God's law" classes taught by the female teacher.

4 Great and Christmas Lents are fasting periods before Easter and Christmas. During these periods, Orthodox Christians observe abstinence from certain foods and practice intensified prayer, self-examination, confession, etc.

5 Russian is a null-subject language.

6 Only designated males, usually older children (servants) are responsible for lighting of the incense during Orthodox Christian services.

REFERENCES

Andrews, D. R. (1999). *Sociocultural Perspectives on Language Change in Diaspora.* Amsterdam: John Benjamins.

Bakhtin, M. (1981). Discourse in the novel. In M. Holquist (ed.), *The Dialogic Imagination: Four Essays by M. M. Bakhtin* (pp. 259–422). Austin, TX: University of Texas Press.

Baquedano-López, P. (1998). "Language socialization of Mexican children in a Los Angeles Catholic parish." Unpublished doctoral dissertation, University of California, Los Angeles.

Burdelski, M. and Mitsuhashi, K. (2010). "She thinks you're kawaii": socializing affect, gender, and relationships in a Japanese preschool. *Language in Society*, 39(1), 65–93.

Bryzgunova, O. E. (1977). *Zvuki i intonatsiia russkoĭ rechi* [Sounds and intonation of Russian speech]. *Moskva:* Russkiĭ iazyk

Capps, L. and Ochs, E. (1995). *Constructing Panic: The Discourse of Agoraphobia.* Cambridge, MA: Harvard University Press.

Cekaite, A. (2012). Affective stances in teacher–novice student interactions: language, embodiment, and willingness to learn in a Swedish primary classroom. *Language in Society*, 41, 641–670.

Cekaite, A. (2013). Socializing emotionally and morally appropriate peer group conduct through classroom discourse. *Linguistics and Education*, 24, 511–522.

Duff, P. A. (2007). Second language socialization as sociocultural theory: insights and issues. *Language Teaching*, 40, 309–319.

Du Bois, J. W. (2007). The stance triangle. In R. Englebretson (ed.), *Stance in Discourse: Subjectivity in Interaction* (pp. 139–182). Amsterdam: John Benjamins.

DuBois, J. W. and Kärkkäinen, E. (2012). Taking a stance on emotion: affect, sequence and intersubjectivity in dialogic interaction. *Text & Talk*, 32(4), 433–451.

Erikson, F. (1982). Taught cognitive learning in its immediate environment: a neglected topic in the anthropology of education. *Anthropology and Education Quarterly*, 13, 149–180.

Fader, A. (2011). Language socialization and morality. In A. Duranti, E. Ochs and B. B. Schieffelin (eds.). *The Handbook of Language Socialization* (pp. 322–340). Malden, MA: Wiley-Blackwell.

Goodwin, C. (2000). Practices of seeing: visual analysis: an ethnomethodological approach. In T. van Leeuwen and C. Jewitt (eds.), *Handbook of Visual Analysis* (pp. 157–182). London: SAGE.

Goodwin, C. and Goodwin, M. H. (1987). Concurrent operations on talk: notes on the interactive organization of assessments. *IPrA Papers in Pragmatics*, 1(1), 1–52.

Goodwin, C. and Goodwin, M. H. (1992). Assessments and the construction of context. In A. Duranti and C. Goodwin (eds.), *Rethinking Context*, (pp. 147–190). Cambridge: Cambridge University Press.

Goodwin, C. and Goodwin, M. H. (2000). Emotion within situated activity. In N. Budwig, I. Uzgiris, and J. Wertsch (eds.) *Communication: An Arena of Development* (pp. 33–53). Stamford, CT: Ablex.

Goodwin, M. H. (1990). *He-Said-She-Said: Talk as Social Organization among Black Children.* Bloomington, IN: Indiana University Press.

Haight, W. L. (2002). *African-American Children at Church: A Sociocultural Perspective.* Cambridge: Cambridge University Press.

He, A. W. (2014). Heritage language socialization. In A. Duranti, E. Ochs, and B. B. Schieffelin (eds.) *The Handbook of Language Socialization* (pp. 587–609). Malden, MA: Wiley Blackwell.

Labov, W. (1972). The transformation of experience in narrative syntax. In W. Labov (ed.), *Language in the Inner City: Studies in the Black English Vernacular* (pp. 354–396). Philadelphia, PA: University of Pennsylvania Press.

Larrivee, B. (2008). Development of a tool to assess teachers' level of reflective practice. *Reflective Practice*, 9(3), 341–360.

Lo, A. (2009). Lessons about respect and affect in a Korean heritage language school. *Linguistics and Education*, 20, 217–234.

Mehan, H. (1979). *Learning Lessons: Social Organization in the Classroom.* Cambridge, MA: Harvard University Press.

Moore, E. (2014). "You are children but you can always say …": hypothetical direct reported speech and child–parent relationships in a Heritage Language classroom. *Text & Talk*, 34 (5), 591–621.

Murphy, K. M. (2011). Building stories: the embodied narration of what might come to pass. In J. Streeck, C. Goodwin, and C. LeBaron (eds.), *Embodied Interaction: Language and Body in the Material World*, (pp. 243–253). Cambridge: Cambridge University Press.

Ochs, E. (1988). *Culture and Language Development: Language Socialization and Language Acquisition in a Samoan Village.* Cambridge: Cambridge University Press.

Ochs, E. (1996). Linguistic resources for socializing humanity. In J. J. Gumperz and S. C. Levinson (eds.), *Rethinking Linguistic Relativity* (pp. 407–437). Cambridge: Cambridge University Press.

Ochs, E. (2007). Narrative lessons. In A. Duranti (ed.), *A Companion to Linguistic Anthropology* (pp. 269–289). Malden, MA: Blackwell.

Ochs, E. and Capps, L. (2001). *Living Narrative: Creating Lives in Everyday Storytelling.* Cambridge, MA: Harvard University Press.

Ochs, E. and Schieffelin, B. B. (1989). Language has a heart. *Text*, 9(1), 7–25.

Pomerantz, A. (1984). Agreeing and disagreeing with assessments: some features of preferred/dispreferred turn shapes. In J. M. Atkinson and J. Heritage (eds.), *Structures of Social Action* (pp. 57–101). Cambridge: Cambridge University Press.

Robblee, K. (1994). Russian word order and the lexicon. *Journal of Slavic Linguistics*, 2(2), 238–267.

Sacks, H., Schegloff, E. A., and Jefferson, G. (1974). A simplest systematics for the organization of turn-taking for conversation. *Language*, 50, 696–735.

Swain, M. (2000). The output hypothesis and beyond: mediating acquisition through collaborative dialogue. In J. Lantolf (ed.), *Sociocultural Theory and Second Language Learning* (pp. 97–114). Oxford: Oxford University Press.

Thompson, I. (1977). Russian word order: a comparative study. *The Slavic and East European Journal*, 21(1), 88–103.

Wortham, S. E. F. (1994). *Acting Out Participant Examples in the Classroom.* Amsterdam: John Benjamins.

Yokoyama, O. (1994). Speaker imposition and short interlocutor distance in colloquial Russian. *Revue des Etudes Slaves*, 66(3), 681–697.

Zemskaja, E. A. (2001). *Jazyk Russkogo Zarubezja: Obscie Processy I recevye portrety* [The Language of the Russian Diaspora: Common Processes and Language Portraits]. Moska: Jazyki Slavjanskoj Kul'tury.

Part II

Socializing Identities

5   Learning to Be a Poet

Chjam'è Rispondi in a Corsican School

Alexandra Jaffe

5.1   Introduction

This chapter examines language socialization practices in two Corsican bilingual schools surrounding apprenticeship to the poetic genre of the *Chjam'è rispondi* 'Call and Response'. Traditionally practiced by expert, male poets, the *chjam'è rispondi* involves one poet improvising a six-line poem and his opponent responding immediately with another six-line verse. The analysis focuses on the sociolinguistic and cultural implications of shifts in the *site* of socialization to this practice as well as shifts in the social identities and linguistic competencies of those being socialized.

In Corsica, bilingual (French and Corsican) schools are a language revitalization strategy serving primarily French-dominant children. Their goals are (1) to replace the intergenerational transmission of Corsican that is no longer happening in the home; (2) to redress French language hierarchy by incorporating Corsican into a high-status institutional context; and (3) to create a privileged cultural and affective role for Corsican in the children's lives. These objectives engage multiple and sometimes conflicting criteria of linguistic authenticity and legitimacy. On the one hand there is the legitimacy and authority of the school as a site of practice; on the other, there is the ideology of the "native speaker" that links speaking Corsican with traditional, non-academic speech forms and genres. Secondly, as a site of socialization, the school is connected with authoritarian regimes of language, which conflicts with affective/identity goals that seek to positively differentiate children's relationships with Corsican vs. French and motivate children to become speakers in a society where speaking the minority language is no longer a default choice. One consequence of these tensions is that speaking/writing "school Corsican" is often not recognized as culturally authentic by the society at large.

Against this backdrop, teaching *chjam'è rispondi* emerges as a strategy that mediates these tensions by apprenticing children to a form of socially

Editorial note. Just before this volume went for clearance review, we learned of the untimely death of Alexandra "Misty" Jaffe, an amazing scholar and colleague, who contributed a great deal to our understanding of stance, identity, and ideology over a lifetime of work. The editors have made only minor adjustments to the chapter in order to adhere to publishing guidelines.

recognized and valued linguistic expertise with a high affective and collective, cultural content.

At the same time, this socialization is an agent of sociolinguistic change because it involves the transformation of the practice itself to accommodate children's novice levels of competence in Corsican. The teaching of the *chjam'è rispondi* thus offers an opportunity to explore and expand the focus, in school-based language socialization research, on "the discursive positioning of self and other (e.g., as knower, insider, outsider, legitimate, or ethnic minority) and its consequences" (Duff, 2008, p. 111). In short, I look at language socialization as a nexus of both sociolinguistic and cultural continuity and change. Language socialization practices, on this account, do not just socialize children/novices to existing social and linguistic identities but also play an active role in the imagination and instantiation of new social and linguistic identities in a context where the link between linguistic practice/competence and legitimacy has been disrupted by language shift and revitalization. A parallel point can be made about the forms of apprenticeship documented in the schools involved in this project. It not only incorporated children into progressively more central forms of participation in an existing community of practice (Corsican poets) but also played a role in the reshaping of that community of practice to include written and online composition practices as well as novice participants.

Below, I provide an account of a collaborative project that I took part in with two Corsican bilingual primary school classes in 2011–12, tracing the process of text production and circulation between schools over a school semester that culminated in a joint field trip/encounter at a museum and the two classes' participation in poetry festivals. Drawing on ethnographic and interview data and illustrated with an extract of interactional data, I show that children are simultaneously socialized to linguistic practice and to valued social and inter-actional identities and stances that include the role of "poet" and the ability to engage in a style of joking exchange (glossed by the Corsican term *a macagna*). Finally, I argue that the practices both presuppose traditional and create new forms of community around the use of Corsican and new under-standings of what being a "speaker" of Corsican means. Through its attention to the temporal dimension of socialization in educational contexts, the analysis thus also contributes to the literature on the structuring and attribution of participant roles to students over time (Jaffe, 2009; Wortham, 2006).

5.2   Sociolinguistic History

Language shift on Corsica – from Corsican to French – began in the early 1900s and accelerated after World War I as Corsicans got access to opportunities for social advancement through schooling in French and jobs off the island. By the late 1960s, many young Corsicans no longer spoke the language, and in the context of social (and ethnolinguistic) movements in France and elsewhere, the language became the object of a revitalization movement. A 2012 survey commissioned by the Corsican Territorial Collectivity estimated the number of speakers of Corsican at 100,000; among those surveyed, 58 percent self-evaluated their competence as "good" or "quite good," with stronger competencies reported among men and older speakers. Only 3 percent of respondents reported contemporary family language transmission of the language.

Today, Corsican educational policy requires all schools to provide three hours a week of Corsican language teaching and has established bilingual schools in which approximately 25 percent of primary school age children are enrolled. In these schools, up to 50 percent of the curriculum is delivered in Corsican by bilingual teachers who model bilingual practice and identity. Overall, Corsican bilingual education is an effort to repair the sociolinguistic rupture created by language shift – to restore or create the kind of seamless, integrated experience of competence, authority, and authenticity enjoyed by speakers of dominant languages.

As suggested above, the sociolinguistic context poses a number of challenges to this goal. First, because the overwhelming majority of adults outside the schools (even Corsican-speaking ones) use French with children, children have little opportunity to acquire everyday conversational competence in Corsican. Secondly, children who do learn Corsican are not necessarily acknowledged as legitimate conversational partners by Corsican-speaking parents and grandparents, who did not themselves learn Corsican in school and do not necessarily view school registers as "authentic." Third, one of the unintended consequences of successful educational use of Corsican is that some students view it as just another obligatory school subject, not to be used outside the classroom. Bilingual Corsican schoolteachers are thus concerned with creating the kinds of affective and cultural ties with the language that will provide lifelong motivation to children to continue to learn and use Corsican, since they know that without this, elementary school teaching will not "reverse" language shift.

5.2.1   *The* Chjam'è Rispondi*: From Traditional to Pedagogical Practice*

The *chjam'è rispondi* is a traditional Corsican improvisational poetic duel. The basic poetic unit is a three-couplet verse with eight syllables per line, which is sung rather than spoken. The three most common rhyme schemes are ABCBDB, ABABAB, and ABCBCC. In the "call," one poet composes a verse and a second poet responds almost immediately with another six-line verse. The first line of the response either repeats the first poet's last line verbatim or takes up its theme. The themes are light and teasing, often casting aspersions on the opposing poet's skill, place of origin, etc. The Corsican word for this key is *a macagna*. Audiences evaluate these poetic duels with reference to esthetic criteria that include fidelity to form (syllables and rhyme schemes), quality of vocabulary, cleverness and humor, and the use of "more difficult" rhymes.

The teaching of the *chjam'è rispondi* in schools is part of a larger phenomenon of the genre being expanded into new social contexts since the early 2000s. In the past, apprenticeship to the practice was exclusively male, and was learned through repeated exposure in traditional sites of sociability (cafés, agricultural fairs, village festivals, etc.). It fell victim to both social and linguistic change in the post-war years and was the object of a deliberate revival in the 1980s. By the early 2000s, however, there were few poets under the age of 60.

The Internet, however, has played a decisive role in creating new contexts for learning and practice of the genre that is illustrated by the case of Christophe Limongi, the teacher in one of the schools described below. In his early 20s, he began to participate in a Corsican-language online forum that included both novices like himself and proficient speakers/writers, some of whom were singers and well-known poets. Around 2008, he and a number of other young men began to exchange verses in writing on the forum, starting with asynchronous messages and then imposing faster and faster response times on themselves in an effort to approximate the improvisational demands of the traditional face-to-face practice.

After becoming a regular participant on the forum, Christophe attended a live event where many of the poets on the internet forum were performing. He recounted that at one point in the performance, one of them called out to him, saying something like, "you've been doing pretty well online, let's see if you've got the stuff to do it in person." Despite considerable stage fright, he managed an oral performance that was the beginning of a "live" apprenticeship, which, by the time I met him in 2011, had earned him a regular presence on the poetry performance circuit.

Ultimately, Christophe's own simultaneous apprenticeship to language and to poetic practice served as a model for his own pedagogy when he became a bilingual school teacher, where he implemented the blend of written and oral composition that had been part of his own apprenticeship. By 2011, he had been integrating the genre into the curriculum in his multi-age classroom (ages 7 to 11) of 12 students for about three years.

5.3   The School Exchange Project: A Multi-Sited, Collaborative Methodology

Christophe's teaching of the *chjam'è rispondi* in the village school of Pedicroce had caught the attention of another bilingual primary school teacher,

Sonia Foti, whose partner was another young poet on the *chjam'è rispondi* performance circuit. She was eager to add the genre to her existing classroom focus on Corsican poetry. In 2011–12, my interest in the pedagogy led the three of us to set up a project in which the children from Christophe's class exchanged verses with the children in her class at the Bonafedi school in the city of Ajaccio. Thus, the research methods in this project reflected both the teachers' and my own interests in actively intervening in the process of socialization to the poetic genre. All three of us were oriented toward the notion of exchange and community as central elements of the genre, and as central forms of motivation for the learning of minority languages by children who seldom have other child interlocutors outside the classroom with whom they use Corsican. Between January and June of 2012, I observed both classes. I recorded both their composition and rehearsal sessions and a "final" audio or video product. I then physically took that product to the other school site, where the children read, viewed, and listened to their partner class's work. Our thinking was that my role as a messenger made the other classroom more "real" to the children than a simple file exchange on the Internet. The exchange culminated in a field trip by both of the classes to the Corsican Ethnographic Museum, where they met for the first time. There, they sang their whole poetry cycle, listened to archives of poets performing the *chjam'è rispondi*, took part in poetry workshops, and were the audience to an improvisational performance by several contemporary poets. After that event, I conducted small-group and individual interviews with most of the children from both classes, asking them to reflect on and assess their experiences.

The ethnographic research methodology thus focused on the interactional process through which the poems were composed and, as I will argue below, through which students were socialized to occupy legitimate positions as speakers of Corsican and as poets. In addition to looking at language socialization in specific moments, the research project explored the temporal and spatial distribution of these practices in multiple sites; interviews allowed students to recount their histories of apprenticeship to the genre. This focus on trajectories of texts and oral practices is aligned with work at the intersection of language socialization and narrative that points to the way identities and stances are attributed to and/or accrue over time and in institutional context (Jaffe, 2009; Wortham, 2006).

All in all, the two classes produced a sung poetry cycle of six poems with four- to six-line stanzas (as opposed to the single six-line stanzas usually exchanged in live jousts). Table 5.1 shows an abridged version of the first two cycles exchanged.

The first "call" came from Sonia's class at the Bonafedi school. Due to the relatively younger age of her 30 third-graders (age eight) and their limited Corsican proficiency, Sonia did extensive scaffolding in a process of collective

Table 5.1 *First two poetic verses exchanged between the schools*

1. Prima Chjama, Scola di Bonafedi	**1. First Call, Bonafedi School**
Noi semu à u mare	We are by the seaside
Voi site à a muntagna	You are in the mountains
Noi manghjemu i zini	We eat sea urchins
E voi qualchì castagna	And you, a couple of chestnuts
Noi sottu à un bellu sole	Under our sunny skies we
V'appruntemu una macagna	Prepare a "macagna" [joke] for you
Voi site cum'è i rimiti	You are like hermits
A ghjurnata in lu bughjone	In the dark all day
No à i ragi di sole	Under the rays of the sun
Cantemu duie canzone	We sing a couple of songs
Pinsendu à i paisani	Thinking of the village folk
Dì nasu in u nivaghjone	Up to their noses in snow
Quandu si face una chjama	When a call is sent
Una risposta si deve	A response is due
Sperendu ch'ella sarà	Hoping that it will be
Prestu in la vostra pieve	Quick in your region
Sè dumane i cantunieri	If tomorrow the road crew
Vi caccianu questa neve…	Removes the snow for you
2. Risposta di a scola di Pedicroce	**2. Response from the Pedicroce School**
Noi, ind'a nostra muntagna	We, in our mountain
Liberi cum'è l'acelli	Free as birds
Accumpagnati di sole	Accompanied by the sun
Cantemu i riturnelli	Are singing a jingle
E cun a neve d'inguernu	And with the winter snow
Ghjucanu tutti i zitelli.	All the children are playing.
Noi simu paisani	We are villagers
E di quessa simu fieri	And proud of that fact
Noi ghjuchemu in paese	We play in the village
Quandu ùn ci n'hè più duveri	When we don't have any homework
Spassighjemu in muntagna	We take walks in the mountains
Simu boni cavaglieri.	We are good horsemen.
Avete u vostru risposta	Now you have your response
Noi ne vulemu un'altra	We want one in return
Emu finitu u scrittu	We have finished writing
D'a nostra muntagna alta	From the heights of our mountain
Tocca à voi di risponde	It's up to you to respond
Sè a vostra rima ùn salta.	If you can manage to rhyme.

composition. It began with a brainstorming session by the whole class on the theme, possible topics, and vocabulary. Then, Sonia wrote up a draft poem, sometimes leaving blanks at the ends of the lines for the students to fill in with words that rhymed. The following day, the students reviewed, read out loud, commented on, and modified that draft. Once they completed a full text, there was both individual and group oral rehearsal before the class performed a final version to be recorded and sent to the other school.

In the Pedicroce school, Christophe engaged in much less scaffolding since the children had both higher Corsican-language competence and greater experience with the genre. When the first and subsequent verses were received from Bonafedi, the class would listen and discuss the content and then move immediately to oral brainstorming of single lines or couplets for the poetic response. Each stanza was the outcome of a process of collective composition and evaluation in which individual children proposed a one- or two-line text. These oral proposals were written on the board by Christophe, where their form and content were evaluated and often modified by him and by the other children. As in Sonia's class, when a poem was completed, the children practiced their pronunciation and delivery before a final recording was made.

In the next section, I discuss some of the general implications of these pedagogical practices and the participation framework of the project for the children's Corsican language socialization and socialization through Corsican before turning to a more detailed look at the interactional process of composition itself.

5.4   Language Socialization and Socialization through Language: Project Overview

The process of linguistic and poetic apprenticeship in the collective composition sessions described above socialized children *to* language, including both generic linguistic skills (acquiring/reinforcing Corsican grammar, vocabulary, pronunciation, and literacy) as well as more specific, valued linguistic competencies associated with poetry as a genre (rhyme and meter). This socialization to language was intertwined with socialization *through* language to (relatively) expert stances toward that language and thereby, to legitimate identities as poets. Teacher scaffolding in each class conferred linguistic and poetic *agency* – defined as the ability to produce and be recognized as producers of written and oral texts – on the students by creating the conditions in which they were able to participate in the creative process at the maximum level their proficiency allowed. That agency was not purely individual but enacted by a group. The process of group composition therefore, created and distributed *ownership* of the poems to all of the students in the class, even those who played a smaller role in their production, responding to the challenge of legitimacy posed by learners who do not master the linguistic code associated with authentic cultural membership (see Jaffe, 2009, 2014). Literacy practices also played a role in this process: after each composition session, each child copied the text into her poetry notebook, the official institutional record of individual learning. Through oral repetition and rehearsal of the poems (see Moore, 2006), all the children had access to an experience of fluency and fluid oral practice that was inaccessible to many of them in activities involving spontaneous linguistic production of Corsican.

Their ownership of the texts was further reinforced by the final field trip and exchange at the museum. First, the texts were given a new, "official" materiality by being printed by Christophe in pamphlet form and distributed as "books" to all the children. Then, the children performed the entire exchange, with each class physically arrayed facing each other and singing "their" verses to the other class in front of an audience composed of teachers, adult poets, museum personnel, and accompanying parents. The poems also became part of the classes' repertoires in other public performance contexts the following month, when both schools took part in (different) poetry festivals where they performed their poems on stage. I also documented them spontaneously singing fragments of their poems in a variety of contexts on these field trips: when they were greeted by the festival patrons in a small café, while traveling in the buses that took them to the venues, and during workshop activities with other children. In this respect, even though most of the children were not able to "improvise" in tightly time-constrained poetic turns like expert adult practitioners of the *chjam'è rispondi*, they were able to deploy the poems in their repertoire in creative ("improvisational") ways in response to new social circumstances (see Howard, 2009, p. 340) to enjoy or affirm valued identities as Corsican users.

These identities as "users" of Corsican were, at least for some of the children, not linked solely to having full linguistic or poetic expertise, but to the dedicated process of acquiring it, a stance modeled to them by their teachers. Previous research in language socialization has seldom questioned, as Duff (2008) points out, the credentials of "native" speakers or adult "experts" (but see Friedman, Chapter 8 in this volume); more generally, as she also suggests, such research has been founded on stable models of language and identity: the target social and linguistic competencies of the socialization process. In the case of Corsican bilingual education, and the *chjam'è rispondi* project documented here, we see a socialization process that both reflects sociolinguistic change and orients to shifting conditions for the acquisition and use of Corsican. Neither of the two teachers viewed or portrayed themselves as "native speakers" of Corsican, but both portrayed the process of apprenticeship and creative practice as valued and valid forms of identity and participation through the Corsican language.

Another important form of socialization through language illustrated in the data presented above is the key of the genre (*a macagna*) that is made explicit in the "call" of the Bonafedi class that initiated the exchange. The teasing is focalized around competing claims of superiority related to contrasts in both material and cultural geography and climate between the two schools. At the time of its composition, the mountainous interior of the island where the Pedicroce school was located was experiencing heavy snowfall that briefly closed roads (and schools); the city of Ajaccio remained relatively sunny and mild. The city/village contrast was also made culturally salient in the exchange, which evokes differences in food preferences and activities of daily life that implicitly index the authenticity of the rural center (references to eating chestnuts, riding horses, and telling stories around a fire) vs. the cosmopolitanism of coastal life. The final line of the Pedicroce response also casts aspersions on the other class's poetic prowess, a common target among expert practitioners of the genre.

In an interview, one of the older girls (Julia) in the Pedicroce class explained, in response to my question about what distinguished a good from a not-so-good *chjam'è rispondi*, that *il faut qu'il y ait un bon sens, rigolo, et pas méchant* ('it has to make sense, be funny and not mean'). Below, we will explore both of these criteria in a transcript of a composition session in which she played a central role.

5.5 Scaffolding Expertise and Practicing the Key of *A Macagna* in Interaction

In this section, we turn to a transcript from a *chjam'è rispondi* composition session at the Pedicroce school that took place before the project with the other school was underway. It illustrates the outcome of years of socialization to both the language and the poetic genre among the oldest and most proficient students in the class as well as the way that this expertise was conferred and confirmed interactionally. The context for this exchange in the Pedicroce school was that the English teacher, who came once a week, had complained to Christophe privately that the children had not done their English homework. After she left, Christophe reported to them what she said and then improvised the following verse (Text 5.1):

Text 5.1 Christophe's Call about the Homework

01 *Di ciò ch'ete fattu oghje*
   'For what you did today'
02 *Un ci vole à esse fieri*
   'You shouldn't be proud'

03 *Perchè vi site scurdati*
    'Because you forgot'
04 *Di fà i vostri duveri*
    'To do your homework'
05 *E aghju da ghjunghje à crede*
    'And I am led to believe'
06 *Chì voi site sumeri*
    'That you are all donkeys'

He challenged the children to come up with a response. Text 5.2 shows their first responding verse, composed through the collective process described above. We can note the repetition with variation (negation) of his last line.

Text 5.2 The Pedicroce Class's First Responding Stanza

01 *Noi ùn simu sumeri*
    'We aren't donkeys'
02 *Perchè simu intelligenti*
    'Because we are intelligent'
03 *Avemu da travaglià*
    'We are going to work'
04 *Seranu bellu mumenti*
    'And times will be good'
05 *Averemu belle note*
    'We will get good grades'
06 *D'un ùn ci sera cuntenti*
    'We won't be satisfied with just one'

The session continued, with Christophe improvising responses to this, and several more of the children's collectively composed stanzas. Below, Text 5.3 was one of their preferred compositions.

Text 5.3 Our Brains Will Explode

01 *Site voi u prufessore*
    'You are the teacher'
02 *Eppo noi i zitelli*
    'And we are the students'
03 *Sè ci sò troppu duveri*
    'If there is too much homework'
04 *Spluseranu i cerbelli*
    'Our brains will explode'
05 *E scambiaremu di scola*
    'And we will change schools'
06 *Faleremu in Fulelli*
    'We'll go down to Fulelli'

In Excerpt 5.1, below, we trace the interactional process through which Text 5.3 was composed by the children. The transcript begins after the successful composition of lines 01 and 02 in Text 5.3, which were written on the board. In lines 01 and 02 of Excerpt 5.1, Julia, mentioned in the interview above, proposes two lines of verse. This prompts a series of reformulations, corrections, and alternative proposals by other children and the teacher, leading to the final selection of Lucia's line (line 07) about the brains exploding from too much homework.[1]

Excerpt 5.1 Composition in Action

01 Julia: *S'ellu hè troppu duveri, chjoderemu i purtelli*
'If it is too much homework assignments we will close the windows'

02 Alain: *Innò, voi chjoder...*
'no, you will'

03 Teacher: *Sè (.) ci (.) sò (.) troppu (.) duveri, chjuderemu i purtelli?*
'If (.) there (.) are (.) too (.) many (.) assignments, we will close the windows?'

04 Julia: **Je voulais dire (...)**
'I meant to say (...)'

05 Rosa: *Chjuderemu ste cerbelli*
'We will close our brains'

06 Teacher: *Ah, i cerbelli allora*
'Ah, so it's brains'

07 Lucia: *Splusemu i nostri cerbelli*
'We explode our brains'

08 Teacher: *Ah! Allora, què, sè (.)ci (.)sò (.)trop(.)pu duveri*
'Ah! so that, if (.)there (.)is (.)too (.)much (.)homework'

09 Julia: *Maestru, s'ellu ci sò troppu duveri, ùn culleremu (...)*
'Teacher, if there is too much homework, we won't go up to (...)'

10 **Ça veut dire qu'on n'y montera pas**
'That means we won't go up'

11 Teacher: **Oui**, *ma, hà dettu qualcosa chì face ride, è chì hà un sensu, Lucia (...)*
'Yes, but Lucia said something that was funny, and made sense (...)'

12 Children: *Splusanu i cerbelli*
'The brains explode'

13 Teacher: *Sè ci sò troppu duveri, ma, s'elli splosanu ùn hè micca avà, ghjè ind'u futuru, dunque, splu::*

14 'If there is too much homework, but if they explode, it isn't now, it's in the future, so they::'

15 Children: *seremu*
'[we] will explode'

16 Teacher: *splu::?*
'splu::?'

17 Children: *Spluseranu*
'They will explode'

18 Teacher: *Spluseranu i cerbelli*
'The brains will explode'

19 *E i dui ultimi?*
'And the last two?'

20   *listessu: stranieri, belli, cultelli, fratelli,*
              'the same: strangers, beautiful, knives, brothers'
21 Child: *meli*
              'apple trees'
22 Teacher: *meli. ma meli ...*
              'apple trees, but apple trees ...'
23 Child: *Fulelli*
              'Fulelli' [place name of nearby town]
24 Child: *cullà è*
              'to go up and'
25 Teacher: *fallà in Fulelli*
              'to go down to Fulelli (...)'
26 Julia: *Maestru, ne aghju una*
              'Teacher, I have one [line]'
27 Teacher: *Ah, ma ci vole duie*
              'Ah, but you need two [lines]'
28 Julia: *Maestru, "scambieremu di scole, faleremu in Fulelli"*
              'Teacher, "we will change schools, we'll go down to Fulelli"'
29 Teacher: *Allora, "scam (.) bie (.) re (.) mu di scola, allora, manc'una, chì pudemu mette?*
              'So, "[we] (.) will (.) change (.) schools," so there's one [syllable] missing, what can we put?'
30 Child: *Noi scambieremu*
              'We will change' [adds in dropped pronoun]
31 Teacher: *No, noi,*
              'No, we'
32   *"e, scam (.) bi (.) er (.) e (.) mu di sco (.) la, fa (.) le (.) re (.) mu [in Fulelli"*
33   '"and, we (.) will (.) change (.) schools, we (.) will (.) go (.) down [to Fulelli"'
34 Children: *[in Fulelli"*
              ['to Fulelli'
35 Julia: *Maestru, u possu leghje?*
              'Teacher, can I read it?'
36 Teacher: *Iè, allora ti stemu à sente*
              'Yes, go ahead, we're listening'

Teacher scaffolding and intervention in this excerpt focus on both linguistic/poetic and social competencies (see also Jaffe, 2013). The linguistic socialization includes a grammatical reformulation of Julia's use of 'if it is' (line 01) to 'if there are' (line 03) to introduce the plural word for homework (*duveri*) and a focus on verb endings (lines 16 to 18), where Christophe prompts the children to use the future tense of the verb 'to explode' and to switch their first person plural to the third person plural. He does this first with a common instructional discourse: an incomplete utterance whose rising intonation is understood as an invitation to fill in the blank, followed by an explicit reference to time sequence (line 16). Both the children and Christophe also employ an "embodied practice" (e.g., Bhattacharya and Sterponi, Chapter 9 in this volume; Burdelski, Chapter 10 in this volume) that he had socialized them to use earlier: counting out each syllable on the fingers as it was pronounced. Christophe models this practice (lines 03, 08, 29, and 32) while simultaneously exaggerating pauses and syllable stress in his oral delivery as he repeats back the children's proposals. Both Lucia and Julia count on their fingers each time they voice a proposed verse and in line 34 all the children do the same as they chime in, overlapping Christophe on the final word of his slightly exaggerated, staccato delivery of the syllables that ratifies the final, "approved" line of the verse. In one sense, then, counting syllables on the fingers marks the children as novices; no expert poet does this. However, in the institutional context, counting back is also a form of teacher ratification, and thus the children's participation in this practice aligns them with the expert stance of Christophe *as a teacher*.

Christophe attributes an expert stance to the children in several other places in the transcript. A child proposes a word that rhymes (line 21), but does not make sense (*meli* 'apple trees'). Christophe withholds ratification by saying 'apple trees, but apple trees ...' (line 22). The pause here follows falling intonation; thus, rather than being an *invitation* to fill in the blank, it represents the children as *being able* to fill in the blank: as already knowing that there is something less-than-satisfactory about 'apple trees.' Here, then, he construes them as knowledgeable by presupposing their ability to recognize and evaluate poetic choices that marry form, esthetics, and meaning. Further on, we see another example of socialization *to* practice that indexes a child's ownership of a valued poetic stance and identity, where Julia says that she thinks she has 'a line' (line 26). Christophe withholds the floor from her by saying 'but you need two' (line 27). Here, he alludes to a recent shift in his guidelines that held them responsible for a higher level of linguistic production: he had told them that they needed to think and invent in couplets, not single lines. In doing so, he established an indexical link between this way of composing and an expert identity ("poet") and positioned the children as being on a trajectory toward that identity. It is noteworthy that he imposed this "rule" in particular on Julia and Lucia, who were the oldest and most linguistically and poetically proficient students in the class. That is, alongside socialization practices that addressed the children as a collectivity, Christophe calibrated his expectations to individual linguistic profiles.

Finally, Christophe ratifies Lucia's proposal as both 'making sense' and 'being funny' (line 11). This brings us back to the key of the *a macagna*. Learning how to tease and be teased is a recurrent theme in language socialization research. Going back to Labov (1972), the role of teasing routines/ genres, including poetic ones, has been understood as a form of conflict management; a linguistic/interactional skill for managing tensions and competition (for example, Miller, 1986; Morgan, 2009). The *chjam'è rispondi* about the homework exemplified socialization to this social function because Christophe's improvised call was not simply an academic exercise, but it reflected genuine displeasure that the students had not taken the English homework seriously. The poetic exchange mitigated the scolding but did not undermine its basis.

As is the case with other similar genres, being successful at *a macagna* is a subtle expressive and social skill, a subject that was developed at some length in interviews with Julia, Lucia, and Alain. There were the ground rules – "being polite," "not being mean" – and then there was the social knowledge that allowed participants to avoid saying things that might be taken "badly" or the "wrong way" by one's opponent. Lucia said, "*Il faut savoir qui il est*" ('you have to know who [the other poet] is'); Julia agreed: "*Il faut pas le faire à n'importe qui parce qu'il est capable de le prendre très mal on va dire*" ('You can't do it to just anyone, because they might take it badly, we'll say'). With respect to the exchange with the Bonafedi class, Alain commented that had they met the other children before initiating the exchange, they could have perhaps "pushed it further." He thus construed the verses they composed in the school exchange to be conservatively polite, calibrated to their (lack of) prior social interaction. This reflects socialization to a set of social norms as well as how they are indexed by specific communicative practices: in this case, the connection between degrees of restraint in teasing and degrees of intimacy vs. social distance.

The "rules" for *a macagna* formed the basis for evaluations that were simultaneously linguistic, poetic, and moral. Julia and Lucia provided several examples that they had witnessed of "good" and "bad" practice.

Julia said,

Mais même, je vois dans les foires, j'y vais, je vois les gens, je les connais des fois. Et il me fait "Tu vois, lui, je vais lui faire un chjam'è rispondi tout à l'heure, je vais lui dire tout ce que je pense de lui." Mais des fois c'est gentil, mais des fois c'est méchant.

But even so, I see in festivals, I go, I see people, sometimes that I know. And they tell me, "you see that guy over there? I'm going to do a *chjam'è rispondi* on him in a moment, I'm going to tell him what I think of him." Sometimes it's nice, sometimes it's mean.

Examples of good practice included their observation of older poets at a festival teasing Christophe about his youthful appearance, saying he couldn't possibly be a teacher, or one of the poets at the museum field trip who began an improvisation directed at Christophe with a bit of praise ("You responded well with your poets," presumably referring to the children). They were critical, however, of gratuitous insults and deliberate attempts to "go after" someone, as implied above. They also criticized some of the children in the other school for "not being polite," though they conceded that their age explained some of their behavior. In short, their socialization to the *chjam'è rispondi* was part of a wider framework of social and moral evaluation; learning to use the genre thus positioned the children as having social expertise/capital.

5.6   *Chjam'è Rispondi* as Collaborative Practice

As we have seen, the ethos of the *a macagna* in the practice of the *chjam'è rispondi* implies community in a number of ways. First, it presupposes shared knowledge of criteria of production and evaluation of the linguistic and social content of poetic turns. Socialization to *a macagna* is thus socialization to an esthetic community that recalls the qualities of the audience to performance evoked by Bauman (1977) and Labov's (1972) early definition of speech community on the basis of shared recognition of sociolinguistic indexicalities. Second, in the enactment of *a macagna*, choices of greater or lesser "risk" in levels and types of teasing index levels of social solidarity. Finally, as Pagliai (2010) points out in her study of the *contrasto*, an Italian version of the *chjam'è rispondi* practiced primarily in Tuscany, the performance of conflict (and the exchanging of insults in performance) can be a form of collaboration that creates and sustains face and can align participants in their embrace or critique of the wider cultural and political context.

Below, I explore some of the implications of the necessarily dialogical (and in that sense collaborative) dimension of the genre and of the process, evoked above, of collective composition used in the bilingual classroom.

First, and most obviously, the *chjam'è rispondi* requires a minimum of two participants; it cannot be done alone. Its value and meaning thus lie squarely in exchange. If we look at the processes of minority language shift and school-based revitalization, it is clear that it is difficult to create conditions of non-academic exchange between linguistic novices and linguistic experts (other than teachers). Thus, few Corsican learners are able to experience their school-based linguistic capital in an interactional context, through the dynamic of social exchange. Socialization to the *chjam'è rispondi* provided the children with a communicative resource that, even without being fully mastered, had meaning founded on the principle of exchange/interaction. This was experienced by the children in Pedicroce in dialogue with their teacher and enhanced by the exchange with the Bonafedi school. So, in this sense, learning the *chjam'è rispondi* was more than a form of legitimation/validation of Corsican language competence through the acquisition of a "traditional" genre: it was a non-traditional use of the genre that, in new sociolinguistic circumstances, reproduced some of the features of the traditional form.

Secondly, the process of collective composition in itself constituted a form of collaboration in and through the Corsican language. In Excerpt 5.2, an extract from an interview with Julia and Lucia, the girls describe the habitual, democratic process through which they fielded and selected themes and specific lines for the verses (lines 01 to 13).

Excerpt 5.2 Collective Composition: "One Father and Two Mothers"
(AJ = researcher)

01 Julia: *Chacun donne son idée, et puis après, on la prend.*
          'Each person gives their idea, and then afterwards, we take it.'
02 Lucia: *La mieux qui est placée, enfin on vote, par exemple, je donne une*
          'The best one that's given, so we vote, for example, I give a'
03   *macagna, et Julia donne une macagna, et Marie choisit*
          'macagna, and Julia gives a macagna, and Marie chooses'
04   *"Ah moi, je donne mon avis. Il vaudrait mieux mettre celle-là ou*
          '"Me, I'm going to give my opinion. It would be better to use that one or'
05   *celle-là." Et après les autres disent, "Ah oui oui oui !" Et un dit par*
          that one." And then the others say, "Oh, yes yes yes!" and one might say'
06   *exemple, "Non non non" parce qu'il donne un avis ou quoi,*
          'for example, "No no no," because he gives an opinion or something,'
07   *il dit pourquoi et on choisit l'autre. Voilà, comme ça.*
          'He says why and we choose the other one. There, it works like that.'
08 AJ: *Donc ça là, c'est un peu, on fait quelque chose ensemble.*
          'So there, it's a bit like, you do something together.'
09 Julia: *Voilà, c'est comme un petit jeu en famille, on va dire comme ça.*
          'Right, it's like a little game in the family, we'll put it that way.'
10 Lucia: *Oui, c'est vrai.*
          'Yes, it's true.'
11 AJ: *Une grande famille.*
          'A big family.'
12 Lucia: *Voilà, une famille très nombreuse.*
          'Right, a very big family.'
13 Julia: *Un père, deux mamans.*
          'One father and two mothers.'

In response to my prompt (line 08) about doing something together, the girls invoke a metaphor of family to describe both affect and intimacy and the guiding role played by relatively expert "parents": Christophe, the teacher, and themselves as the "two mothers." The girls' discourse is thus indirect evidence of the way that the collaborative composition process socialized children to a model of collective, or "distributed," competence rather than to a model of purely individual linguistic performance.

5.7   Conclusion

The deliberate choice to socialize children to the *chjam'è rispondi* in these two schools and in the specific project responded in several key ways to the challenge, for Corsican language educators, of teaching linguistic skills, forging affective and cultural ties between the children and the Corsican language, and creating conditions in which novices can experience linguistic ownership and expertise and be recognized as legitimate interlocutors. The examples show how the children, through interaction and collaboration with both their teachers and the other class, were able to exercise agency in the process of creating and performing the poems. This agency translated into *ownership* of a set of texts with compelling social and interactional meanings beyond their role as a school, or even as a linguistic activity. Ownership – and through it, identity – was not just linguistic but sociocultural, as emphasized in the analysis of the children's socialization to Corsican cultural values and dispositions indexed by *a macagna* as both practitioners and as audiences/ evaluators. As the notion of "distributed competence" emphasizes, this ownership was gained through and intimately associated with collective membership and collaborative practice.

Children's poetic agency was mediated by teacher scaffolding, which allowed them to progressively align with expert identities of various kinds and levels. While this is a banal finding in the context of socialization more widely, it is uniquely inflected in the context of minority language education because of the tensions of legitimacy and authenticity I have evoked above. In a sense, being socialized to an expert genre – one that is beyond the reach or practice of many a competent Corsican speaker – served to recast and revalorize the children's identities as "novice" speakers whose competencies might fall short measured against expectations about spontaneous, everyday conversational skills. In other words, along a continuum of levels and types of expertise (see Table 5.2), the children's guided participation in the genre of the *chjam'è rispondi* situated them somewhere in a middle ground (shaded in gray) between "school" competencies and the kinds of expertise displayed by expert improvisational poets.

This "middle ground," I would argue, is a space of sociolinguistic change and development, where practices like schoolchildren becoming apprentice poets are playing a role in the potential redefinition of what speaking and writing Corsican means in the twenty-first century. Language socialization has often been framed with sole reference to established norms, identities, and linguistic practices. The analysis of deliberate language socialization practices in minority-language schools provides a window on the potential for language socialization to be simultaneously retrospective and prospective. In the case of the *chjam'è rispondi,* this involves a critical take on the definition of the "authentic" minority language speaker. These practices can thus be seen as a launching point for sociolinguistic trajectories whose endpoints are not fixed but are in the process of being defined for both the individual and the society at large.

Table 5.2 *Continua of types of expertise*

"School" Corsican	"Social" Corsican	School *Chjam'è Rispondi*	Improvisational *Chjam'è Rispondi*
		• Academic	
• Academic	• Non-academic	• Poetic	• Poetic
• Non-spontaneous	• Social	• Social	• Improvisational
	• Spontaneous	• Semi-improvisational	• Expert linguistic skill
• Low/novice linguistic skill	• High linguistic skill	• Community of novice/ expert production	• Expert poetic skill
• Written	• Oral	• Written and oral	• Oral (in performance) and written (online)

NOTE

1 Regular text = Corsican; bold = French. Double quotation marks indicate text that is read aloud. Exaggerated pauses between syllables are indicated by (.).

REFERENCES

Bauman, R. (1977). *Verbal Art as Performance*. Prospect Heights, IL: Waveland Press.
Duff, P. A. (2008). Language socialization, participation and identity: ethnographic approaches. In M. Martin-Jones, M. de Mejia, and N. Hornberger (eds.), *Encyclopedia of Language and Education, 2nd Ed., Vol. 3: Discourse and Education* (pp. 107–119). New York, NY: Springer.
Howard, K. (2009). Breaking in and spinning out. *Language in Society*, 38, 339–363.
Jaffe, A. (2009). Stance in a Corsican school: institutional and ideological orders. In A. Jaffe (ed.), *Stance: Sociolinguistic Perspectives* (pp. 119–145). Oxford: Oxford University Press.
Jaffe, A. (2013). Anthropological analysis. In J. Holmes and K. Hazen (eds.), *Research Methods in Sociolinguistics* (pp. 213–228). Boston, MA: Wiley-Blackwell.
Jaffe, A. (2014). Minority language learning and communicative competence: models of identity and participation in Corsican adult language courses. *Language and Communication*, 33(4): 450–462.
Labov, W. (1972). *Language in the Inner City: Studies in the Black English Vernacular*. Philadelphia, PA: University of Pennsylvania Press.
Miller, P. (1986). Teasing as language socialization and verbal play in a white working-class community. In B. B. Schieffelin and E. Ochs (eds.), *Language Socialization across Cultures* (pp. 199–212). Cambridge: Cambridge University Press.
Morgan, M. (2009). *The Real Hiphop: Battling for Knowledge, Power, and Respect in the LA Underground*. Durham, NC: Duke University Press.

Moore, L. C. (2006). Learning by heart in Qur'anic and public schools in northern Cameroon. *Social Analysis*, 50(3), 109–126.

Pagliai, V. (2010). Conflict, cooperation, and facework in *contrasto* verbal duels. *Language in Society*, 20(1), 87–100.

Wortham, S. (2006). *Learning Identity: The Joint Emergence of Social Identification and Academic Learning*. New York, NY: Cambridge University Press.

6 Teaching Words, Socializing Affect, and Social Identities

Negotiating a Common Ground in a Swedish as a Second Language Classroom

Asta Cekaite

6.1 Introduction

Becoming a speaker of a second language (L2) is intimately linked with socialization to use language and the development of interactional competence, including the ability to recognize culturally appropriate affective stances and social identities, and to master communicative norms of language (Cekaite, 2007; Duff, 2011). This socialization involves developing an intricate understanding of cultural practices and ways of acting in a particular community. In many societies, an important setting of children's L2 language socialization is classrooms (e.g., Cekaite and Aronsson, 2004; Poole, 1992; Willet, 1995). This chapter examines L2 socialization practices aimed at teaching vocabulary in Swedish at the primary school level. By examining vocabulary teaching practices in the form of vocabulary explanations, it will show how these practices serve as a crucial site for learning words together with their cultural meanings in the majority language, Swedish. The teaching of vocabulary is discussed here as a prime example of socialization *to use* language (as social action) and socialization *through* the use of language (Ochs and Schieffelin, 2011).

6.2 Affect, Social Identities, and Common Ground in a Sociocultural Context

A central premise of language socialization is that social actors index their affective and epistemic stances that are linked to and typify specific social identities (Ochs, 1996, p. 424). Affective stance is "defined broadly as emotion, feelings, moods, dispositions and attitudes, associated with persons and/or situations" (Ochs and Schieffelin, 1989, p. 7; see also Moore, Chapter 4 in this volume). In social interaction, participants display how they align themselves toward other participants as well as to their actions (Goffman, 1981; Goodwin, Cekaite and Goodwin, 2012). Social actors produce stance displays – public acts – by means of which they simultaneously evaluate objects, position subjects (self and others), and align "with other subjects, with respect to any salient dimension of the sociocultural field" (Du Bois, 2007, p. 163). Affective stances conveyed through "recurring linguistic routines" also indicate culturally shaped preferences and "desires" through which members are socialized to "recognize and respond to socially sanctioned ways of behaving, thinking, evaluating and acting" (Kulick and Schieffelin, 2004, p. 354). Such implicitly or explicitly shared values, routine practices, and ways of conceiving particular phenomena in the community are conceptualized as "common ground" (Clark, 1996). Language serves as an important socialization device in that it "is a typifying medium par excellence" (Hanks, 1996, p. 131). According to the sociologist Alfred Schutz (1970, pp. 74–80), "typification" is a fundamental process that forms our relations to the world. Indexicality and typification are "routine processes that make habitual life possible" (Keane, 2016, p. 155) in that they "underwrite people's everyday experience of one another" and connect lexical items with stances and values that are amplified "by their recurrence from one context to another" (Keane, 2016, p. 156). Typifications are used as a way of understanding objects or phenomena as belonging to certain categories, acts, stances, identities, and normative expectations (see also Goodwin et al., 2012; Ochs, 2002). When social actors communicate, at whatever level of effectiveness, what they share in directing and interpreting their words is "the ability to orient themselves . . . to each other and their social worlds" (i.e., their common ground) (Hanks, 1996, p. 229). For L2 learners and their teachers, the establishment of a common ground (i.e., shared world knowledge or appropriation of normative views) constitutes one of the crucial conditions for achieving mutual understanding. This chapter argues that in definitional practices of L2 vocabulary, we can witness how participants' stances display judgments that are typified and objectified as characterological features of social identities.

6.3   Research on L2 Teaching and Socialization

There has been little work done to date on how lexical items are taught and learned in L2 classrooms (but see, for instance, Watanabe, 2016). It has been suggested that vocabulary explanations usually include a metastatement/generic definition, which is followed by an explanation and an optional recycling of a definition (Lazaraton, 2004). Prior research on vocabulary teaching and learning has primarily taken a cognitive perspective in which word definitions are usually viewed as decontextualized, abstracted references to a linguistic system. A few studies from a sociocognitive perspective have suggested that learning L2 vocabulary is also a culturally embedded process (Churchill, 2008; Nguyen and Kellogg, 2010). The language socialization perspective is a useful framework for examining vocabulary teaching and learning, as it has foregrounded the bidirectional character of socialization, stressing novices' active role and negotiated participation (Ochs and Schieffelin, 2011; see also Persson, Thunqvist, and Axelsson, 2012). One tenet of language socialization is that, rather than simply internalizing experts' norms and values, novices are involved in a reciprocal process, one in which they actively co-construct their socialization. Socialization processes do not necessarily run smoothly and predictably, however, as they may be colored by the novices' and/or the majority community's ambivalence, resistance, and contestation (Duff, 2011; García-Sánchez, Chapter 2 in this volume; Rymes and Pash, 2001; Talmy, 2015). Language socialization is not limited to comprehension and appropriation of language resources, but also involves novices' normatively expected engagement with, appreciation of, or contestation of the values and ideologies that go along with the discursive structures of the community (Cekaite, 2012, 2017). The cultural anchoredness of language classrooms is also demonstrated in studies on heritage language (e.g., He, 2011) and language revitalization (e.g., Friedman, 2010). For instance, in several studies of heritage language classrooms in the United States, research shows ways in which Confucian values saturate directives in Chinese (He, 2011); notions of personhood are enacted through teachers' embodied classroom instructions and children's embodied performance in Japanese (Burdelski, Chapter 10 in this volume); and moral values are mediated through discursive structures, grammatical, and lexical resources in Russian (Moore, 2014). In a study of US citizenship classes for immigrants, Griswold (2010) shows that the teachers used personal narratives and "participant examples" (i.e., stories and other examples that included classroom participants) (Wortham, 1992; see also Moore, Chapter 4 in this volume) in positioning learners and highlighting the desirable personal and social identities.

The present study extends the research on L2 classroom language socialization by examining language socialization practices in a Swedish as an L2 class for middle-school immigrant children. Moreover, it furthers the general understanding of the sociocultural (rather than primarily cognitive) anchoredness of L2 teaching and learning. It shows that as teachers instruct children in vocabulary, they not only teach them the referential meaning and definitions of words, but also socialize them to cultural norms and ways of thinking, acting, and feeling that are deemed important in the majority Swedish society.

6.4   Method and Setting

The data include a video-ethnography involving one-and-a half years of fieldwork (utilizing observations, video recordings, and interviews) in a primary school located in a socio-economically disadvantaged and highly segregated immigrant area in a middle-sized Swedish town. In this school, 98 percent of students were first-generation or 1.5-generation immigrants (see Cekaite 2012, 2017). The study focuses on one class of instruction in Swedish as an L2 for recently arrived immigrant children, aged 10 to 13 years old. Swedish language introductory classes are intended to provide students with basic Swedish language knowledge and to prepare them for education in regular school classes (usually located at the same school, where all teaching is conducted in Swedish). Each student usually spends a period of one year in the language introduction class. Two Swedish teachers worked in the observed classroom, which was attended by 12 children who had all recently moved to Sweden from a range of Asian, Middle Eastern, and African countries (Somalia, Iraq, Syria, Lebanon, Kurdistan, and Thailand). Their life experiences in their home countries and in Sweden were characterized by a number of differences, such as weather, seasons, basic life conditions, child–adult/student–teacher roles, intergenerational relations, food, pets, and religion (Sweden being one of the most secular countries). In interviews, the teachers acknowledged that their teaching tasks were multifaceted. They involved both teaching Swedish and providing a cultural introduction into the Swedish schooling system and society. The students were immersed in a sociocultural context where the dominant society (through the educational institution) advocated strong child-centeredness, and where the child's individual wishes, resistant agency, and negotiation skills, rather than adult authority (e.g., Aronsson and Cekaite, 2011; Kusserow, 2004), were celebrated as prerequisites for egalitarian childhood.

The students joined classes at various times during the academic year and their low and heterogeneous proficiency levels resulted in teachers organizing language teaching and accommodating children's understanding by employing significant linguistic and discursive adjustments. The teachers picked out words from the text or interactions to highlight, repeat, and query the meaning based on their anticipation of what might give the students problems. In addition to teacher-organized vocabulary teaching, vocabulary explanations evolved spontaneously during everyday educational practices as the teachers responded to the children's questions and difficulties in understanding Swedish words during reading activities.

6.5   Vocabulary Explanations: A Site of Language Socialization

The teachers' vocabulary explanations were not neutral semantically oriented activities that mediated the abstract meanings of linguistic forms. Rather, through vocabulary explanations the teachers socialized the children into culturally appropriate understandings and values, and ways of thinking and behaving in Sweden, their new community. These recurrent practices provided affordances for the shaping of the lifeworlds and identities of the L2 learners and the teachers. Several discursive grammatical features and affective stances characterizing vocabulary explanations contributed to these socializing potentials. These included the teachers' (1) active solicitation of the students to participate; (2) use of concrete, participant examples (e.g., Griswold, 2010; Moore, Chapter 4 in this volume; Wortham, 1992) including "hypothetical stories" (e.g., Moore, Chapter 4) that positioned one or more children as social actors and protagonists (who think, feel, and/or act) in ways that comprise and highlight normatively appropriate affective stances and identities; and (3) use of generalizations of word meanings as a way of establishing a common ground. Through vocabulary explanations, the teachers socialized the students into affect (i.e., positive or negative stances) and social identities, associated with "culturally intelligible subjectivities" (Kulick and Schieffelin, 2004) of the dominant society, mediating how they and the students were to feel and think. Vocabulary explanations recurrently implied conventionalized notions of Swedish children's everyday lives, likes and dislikes, and habits (such as food, weather, and other features), which were interpreted and explained within the context of the students' earlier and current language and cultural experiences.

Vocabulary explanations were interactive events characterized by active teacher–student participation where the participants explained, appropriated, or contested social categories, typifications, and stances. Word meanings were introduced through "local" (i.e., participant-level) discursive resources such as embodied demonstrations, short narratives including autobiographical and participant examples, synonyms, and physical objects in the proximity. To promote the students' understanding of the linguistic forms, the teachers appealed to their life experiences and shared interactional history. Care was taken to imbue language knowledge with extralinguistic knowledge of the world, informing about the local, Swedish, cultural context, and orienting to it as a common ground. By locating the participants (students and teachers) in narrative events, the teachers cast them in socioculturally relevant social typifications (Keane, 2016; Schutz, 1970) that the words in question evoked in a wider context of Swedish society. In this way, vocabulary practices served as a meaning-making and socialization site where a system of beliefs, perspectives, and ways of conceiving things in a community (i.e., common ground, as in Clark, 1996) between the teachers and language novices was invoked, negotiated, and adjusted.

6.5.1   Interactional–Dialogic Organization of Vocabulary Explanations

Vocabulary explanations were initiated when the students displayed a problem in understanding, or when the teachers had ostensibly anticipated that certain Swedish words might cause difficulties for children, such as when the class was engaged in a reading comprehension activity. The teachers initiated vocabulary explanations by asking students to explain the meaning of a lexical item. In general, the students were actively responsive to the teachers: they asked questions, made comments, and offered their own interpretations and examples. The teachers paid close attention to the students' verbal and non-verbal uptake, and usually treated the students' responses as needing additional explanations or corrections. This extended interactional organization afforded the students with significant attention to words, which was advantageous for low-proficiency users of Swedish. The dialogic structure of vocabulary explanations provided the language beginners with additional opportunities to understand and discuss the referential and cultural meanings of the Swedish words (e.g., Griswold, 2010).

In Excerpt 6.1a, the students are reading a story aloud one-by-one about a girl Anna, when the teacher asks whether the students know what the verb *att längta* 'to long for' from the story means (line 01).

Excerpt 6.1a To Long For

(Participants: Swedish language teacher; girls: Nura and Fatma [Iraq]; boys: Doy [Thai], Abdi [Somali], Mohamed [Lebanon])

01	Teacher:	*vad är längta:r?*
		'What is lo:ngs for?'
02		(2.0)
03	Nura:	°*längtar*°?
		'°Longs for°?'
04	Teacher:	*mh. Anna längta:r. vad gör hon då?*
		'Mh. Anna lo:ngs for. What does she do then?'
05	Fatma:	*så a:h.*
		'Like this a:h.' ((acts surprised, afraid))
06	Nura:	*hon (.) kanske förvånat.*
		'She (.) maybe surprised.'*
07	Fatma:	*hon här (.) förvånad.*
		'She here (.) surprised.' ((points at book))
08	Doy:	*göra så. ah ah!*
		'Do like this. Ah ah!' ((surprised face, then "falls" on the desk))
09	Students:	hahahhaha
10	Teacher:	*va? vad var det?*
		'What? What's that?' ((mock surprise))
11	Students:	hahaha

* Translation to English reflects the ungrammatical Swedish of the students.

When no definition is forthcoming (line 02), the teacher revises her question by recycling the sentence from the text (line 04: 'Anna lo:ngs for. What does she do then?' [Implies: 'What actions does 'to long for' imply?']). Several students suggest that the word means 'surprised' and use embodied demonstrations (lines 05–08), but the teacher does not confirm their guesses.

As shown in Excerpt 6.1b (a continuation of Excerpt 6.1a), the teacher asks another vocabulary-related question (line 12: 'Let's say that I̲: lo:ng for summer. What do I want then?').

Excerpt 6.1b To Long For

Continuation of Excerpt 6.1a

12 Teacher: *om jag lä:ngta- om vi säger att ja̲:g lä:ngtar till sommaren.*
13   *vad vill jag då?*
            'If I lo:ng- Let's say that I̲: lo:ng for summer. What do I want then?'
14 Doy: *jag vet.*
            'I know.'
15 Fatma: *a. jag tycker om (.) sommaren.*
            'Yeah. I like (.) summer.'
16 Teacher: *jag v̲i̲l̲l̲ att sommaren ska komma.*
            'I w̲a̲n̲t̲ summer to come.' ((points at herself))
17 Fatma: mh.
18 Teacher: *jag längtar till nåt. jag vill att-*
            'I'm longing for something ((points at herself)). I want-'
19 Students: *a.*
            'Yeah.'
20 Teacher: *det är nåt som jag vill h̲a̲.*
            'It's something I w̲a̲n̲t̲.'
21 Abdi: *samma jag.*
            'I same.'
22 Teacher: ((turns to Abdi))
23 Fatma: hahaha
24 Teacher: *längtar du också till sommaren?*
            'Are you longing for summer as well?'
25 Abdi: *a::.*
            'Yea::h.' ((with relish))

The teacher's question moves the interpretive ground from the denotational text the students are reading to real-life experiences, as the teacher presents a hypothetical situation where she is a social actor who has desires (lines 12–13: 'What do I want then?'). The hypothetical scene centers on an experience-based association that invokes socioculturally salient affect and desire: in Sweden, the summer season is highly appreciated, especially after a long and dark winter (this particular lesson took place at the end of winter), and is celebrated in Swedish songs and festivities, such as midsummer celebration. While Fatma offers an aligning response (line 15: 'Yeah. I like summer'), which displays a positive affective stance, the teacher embellishes her partici-pant example (line 16: 'I w̲a̲n̲t̲ summer to come') and then moves from a local to a more general characterization (line 18: 'I'm longing for something'; line 20: 'It's something I w̲a̲n̲t̲').

Hence, in order to help them make sense of the new vocabulary item, the students are called upon to invoke their world knowledge of the feelings and desires of the majority society by interpreting the feelings of the teacher (as a member of the society) in a local context. Importantly, the teacher's explanation is audience-designed. She monitors the students for their verbal and nonverbal signs of comprehension, and their aligning perspectives on phenomena in the world. Abdi, a Somali boy, responds to the teacher's example by displaying an affectively congruent perspective and positive affective stance (line 21: 'I same'). When the teacher attempts to confirm his preference (line 24: 'Are you longing for summer as well?'), Adbi provides an emphatic response (line 25: 'Yeah' [with relish]). The teacher ostensibly interprets that Abdi's alignment is a confirmation that he has understood the referential and cultural meaning of the word, and ends the word explanation sequence.

Here, a vocabulary explanation worked as a multifunctional educational activity that was organized dialogically to provide affordances for the students to use Swedish to display and adjust their lexical and sociocultural knowledge, including affect toward objects and phenomena.

6.5.2   Socializing Appropriate Understanding, Affective Stances, and Identities through Typified Participant Examples

This section demonstrates how classroom word definitions socialize students to cultural understandings of the majority language community by displaying and ascribing affective stances and social identities to L2 learners, who aligned with and at times resisted those ascriptions. Vocabulary explanations involved a discursive movement between the local and general explanatory levels. Abstract categories and generic meanings were extracted from the local level narratives. The teachers, when explaining and clarifying the referential and cultural meanings of new Swedish words, employed embodied demonstrations that were designed as participant examples where recognizable protagonists (co-present in the classroom) "animated" (Goffman, 1981) various typified narratives and displayed culturally significant affective stances. Shaped as embodied performances, these examples and short narratives referred to personalized, but also typical and recognizable, social situations. Local scenes were used to present exemplifications and lexical items from the perspective of prospective users. Demonstrations involving short narratives were embellished with embodied affective and moral stances (Goodwin, 1990; Ochs and Capps, 2001) that provided information about how the characters felt and how their feelings were affected by the events and actions of the short narrative. The participant example was then moved to a more general and abstract level. In this way, information provided in vocabulary explanations extended beyond information about the lexical item itself. By choosing the students or teachers as protagonists in the hypothetical but culturally characteristic narrative, teachers socialized the students into how they should feel and think about particular actions and events and cast participants in a kind of social typification that the words in question evoke in the broader sociocultural (Swedish) context. Such practices made explicit for the students the teachers' perspectives on the otherwise implicit cultural values and affective stances connected to the new words.

In Excerpt 6.2a, during a reading comprehension lesson (using textbooks written in simple Swedish that thematically dealt with Swedish children's everyday events), the students were reading a story about a girl, Lina, who wishes to have a pet and nags her mother to buy her a dog. In dictionaries, the Swedish word *tjata* 'nag' is defined as "to continuously and strenuously repeat the same demands and admonitions." It characterizes adult–child relations, where both parties can or need to nag each other to do things: children nag parents to buy them commodities, and parents nag children to comply with household tasks. In the family context, as egalitarian relations are celebrated in contemporary Swedish childhood, children frequently display an agency of resistance to authority in extended directive trajectories (Aronsson and Cekaite, 2011; Goodwin and Cekaite, 2018). During the lesson, some of the students appeared to be oblivious of the meaning of the verb *tjata* 'nag', and the teacher asks them to define it (line 01).

Excerpt 6.2a To Nag

01 Teacher: *vad är tjatar?*
                 'What is nags?'
02 Students: *tjatar?*
                 'Nags?'
03 Teacher: *hon tja:tar ofta på sin mamma.*
                 'She often na:gs her mother'. ((reads from the book))
04 Nura: ((raises her hand))
05 Teacher: *vad är tjatar?*
                 'What is nags?' ((points at Doy))
06 Doy: *e::h hon ha:r (1) hon säger (0.5) hon säger jättemånga gånger (.) om (.) ETT ord.*
                 'E:.h she ha:s (1) she says (0.5) ((repetitive gestures)) she says many many times (.) again (.) ONE word.' ((see Figure 6.1))

Figure 6.1 Doy says, 'She says many many times' while making a hand gesture

07 Teacher: *ju men om vi säger Nura! din mamma säger till dig Nura!* (1.0) *nu måste*
08   *du (.) gå lägga dig! (0.5) och du bara (.) taidadai dadai dadai.*
               ((nods)) 'Yes let's say Nura! your mom tells you Nura (1.0) Now you
               must go (.) to bed! And you just (.) tai dadai dadai dadai.' ((walks
               around, playfully gesticulating))
        ((unrelated talk omitted))
14 Students: *hahhaha*
15 Teacher: *nej men Nura. nu MÅSte du gå lägga dig.*
               'No but Nura. Now you MUST go to bed'.
16 Students: *haha*
17 Teacher: *och du bara tai dadai dadai dadai.*
               'And you just (go) taidadai dadai dadai.' ((walks around, playfully
               gesticulating))
18 Fatma: *det tja[tar?*
               'That nags?'
19 Teacher: [*'NURA! NU MÅSTE DU GÅR LÄGGA DIG!'*
               'NURA! NOW YOU MUST GO TO BED!'
20 Teacher: *då tja:tar mammor.=*
               'Then moms na:g.='
21 Nura: *=ah=*((smiling))
22 Teacher: *= hon får säga samma sak flera gånger.*
               = 'She needs to say the same thing many times.' ((gestures))
23 Nura: *ah.* ((smiling))
24 Teacher: *för att du inte gör det du ska (.) på en gång.*
               'Because you don't do what you should (.) immediately.' ((makes a
               disciplining gesture, leans toward Nura; see Figure 6.2))

Figure 6.2 Teacher makes a disciplining gesture, while leaning toward Nura

25 Nura: ((smiling, a nod))
26 Teacher: *det är att tjata!*
               'That is to nag!' ((mocks a disciplining gesture at Nura))
27 Fatma: *tjata.*
               'Nag.'
28 Nura: *tjata.*
               'Nag.'

When an adequate response is not forthcoming, the teacher provides a context for the word by reading a sentence from the text (line 03: 'She often nags her mother'). When some children raise their hands, the teacher solicits Doy's response. In his response, Doy uses verbal and nonverbal resources in a simple but adequate description of the word meaning, characterizing the iterative features of nagging (line 06: 'she says many many times again one word'; see Figure 6.1). The teacher acknowledges this definition, but goes on to elaborate its meaning, by initiating an extended instructional sequence that allows her to foreground her own extended version of the word meaning (lines 07–08, 15, 19, 20, 22, 24, and 26).

The design of the teacher's talk is typical of many vocabulary explanation sequences in these data. The teacher frames her explanation by using a hypothetical situation and presents a participant example that positions the students as protagonists in a narrative (lines 07–08). She begins her explanation by proposing a hypothetical scenario, as indicated by the introductory phrase 'let's say' and uses a familiar mode (pronoun 'you'). In that the story is concrete, detailed, and personalized, it allows the teacher to frame the explanation as relevant to the students' lives (Griswold, 2010, p. 479). While formulating the explanation herself, the teacher also actively pursues the students' alignment. In particular, she uses embodied "quotation" (Clark and Gerrig, 1990, p. 795), which invites "others to experience what it is like to perceive things depicted." In contrast to descriptions (cf. Doy's description of the target word meaning 'say the same word many many times'), Clark and Gerrig propose that, "in a quotation of a person's actions, the demonstrator usually takes that person's role. Quotations not only convey the propositional meaning of somebody else's utterances, they also may recycle the other's voice, nonverbal actions, and "depict his [or her] emotional state" (p. 769). Here, the teacher invokes a hypothetical but representative and concrete situation of Nura and her mother's encounter. This encounter depicts a conventional scene that characterizes the target word 'nag' and actualizes social typifications of related affect and generational identities. The teacher's embodied demonstration provides affective information, such as through varying volume and intonation, changing facial expressions, gestures, and bodily movements. She highlights the iterative sense of the verb 'nag' through a repetitive demonstration of the target word. In contrast to Doy's affectively neutral description (line 06), the teacher indexes a specific (playfully negative affective) stance on 'nagging' in parent–child relations (line 24; see Figure 6.2). The action of nagging and the concurrent display of affective stance are systematically tied to the relational category "child–mother." The teacher even describes a morally charged cause–effect relationship and displays a moral stance by using a conjunction 'because' and embodied affective resources (Goodwin et al., 2012) (line 24: 'because you don't do what you should immediately'). By selecting the student Nura (who has recently arrived from Iraq) as a protagonist in this narrative, the teacher presents the stances, identities, and social relations as omnirelevant, and not limited to the Swedish (or more generalized Western) society. In the process of explaining the word, the teacher shifts between the individual (supposedly lived experience) of a specific child's (Nura's) mother (line 19: 'Nura, now you must go to bed'; line 22: 'she needs to say the same thing many times') and a generic definition (line 20: 'then moms nag'), by recycling parts of Doy's earlier definition (line 06). She explains the target word by invoking a typification that nagging is related to being and acting as a child or parent in general.

The socializing potentials of word explanations are realized through affective and moral stances that the teacher builds into a typical situation and maps on to social identities and lexical items when she sets up and acts out participant examples and animates the nagging mother and her noncompliant daughter. In this vocabulary explanation, we can observe the movement between the personal/local and the general/abstract levels. The teacher extracts the definition from a concrete narrative situation, navigating between the (supposedly) lived experiences of Swedish children and the students, and general aspects of the lexical meaning of the Swedish word. The participant example, choreographed as an embodied demonstration that comprises a brief narrative, serves as a framework within which the children are expected to make sense of the lexical item and also participate in something that is amusing.

6.5.3   Negotiating Social Identities in the Dominant Language and Society

The socializing potentials of L2 vocabulary explanations were sedimented in their discursive organization. In addition to soliciting the students' own ostensive definitions, these explanations were also shaped as something the students were invited and expected to agree and align with. Vocabulary-related interactions served as sites for institutional and cultural socialization, stance-taking, and congruent alignment with the teachers' stances (Cekaite, 2012; Duff, 2011). If the teachers had treated children's learning of new words as a simple transmission of knowledge in a one-to-one mapping between the referent and the L2 form, the initial demonstrations and descriptions of the word meaning would have been sufficient to ensure students' understanding and potential learning. However, as demonstrated by the dialogic discursive organization, these interactional practices constituted mundane social sites for orienting to, inhabiting, and transforming the lifeworlds of the students and the teachers. The teachers shaped the children's understanding of Swedish words by using descriptions of situations and events in which they displayed typified affective stances (Ochs and Schieffelin, 1989) and suggested interpretations and feelings the children ought to have. In doing so, the teachers probed the children for congruent stances on various situations, phenomena and events.

Typifications (Schutz, 1970), stances (Goodwin et al., 2012), and identities connected to Swedish words were used to recast the abstract linguistic meanings into the action preferences and social identities relevant to and characterizing the dominant (Swedish) language community. Importantly, these perspectives were shaped as something to be agreed to and aligned with. The students' aligning or disaligning responses demonstrate that the children, rather than simply appropriating the teachers' norms and values, were actively engaging in a reciprocal meaning negotiating process, at times disagreeing with and resisting the teachers' ascription of stances and social identities. The distinction between the students' displays of understanding of a lexical item and their appropriation of relevant affective stances is demonstrated in Excerpt 6.2b (a continuation of Excerpt 6.2a), when the teacher ascribes a 'nagging' child identity to the students that is associated with common understandings of the "entitled" child in the Swedish cultural context. The students, however, resist this identity ascription.

Excerpt 6.2b To Nag
Continuation of Excerpt 6.2a

29 Teacher: *tjatar era pappor och mammor på er nån gång?*
                      'Do your dads and moms ever nag you?'
30   (2.0)
31 Fatma: *m. nej.*

'm. no.' ((headshake))

32 Teacher: <u>AL</u>drig Fatma?
               '<u>NE</u>ver Fatma?' ((facial expression of disbelief))

33 Fatma: nej.
             'No.' ((head shake))

34 Teacher: behöver inte din mamma <u>nån</u>sin tjata på dig?
             'Doesn't your mom <u>e</u>ver need to nag you?'

35 Fatma: [nej hehe
             'No hehe'

36 Doy: [ne::j. hon <u>al</u>drig tjatar med mig. (1.0) min pappa också.
             'No::j she <u>ne</u>ver nags with me. (1.0) my dad too.'

37 Teacher: (1.0) ((looks at Doy, demonstrating disbelief on her face))

38 Teacher: hur är det med Abdi? behöver nån tjata på di:g?
             'How about you Abdi? does anybody need to nag <u>you</u>:?'

39 Nura: a.
             'Yeah.'

40 Doy: hahaha

41 Abdi: lite.
             'A little.' ((smiling))

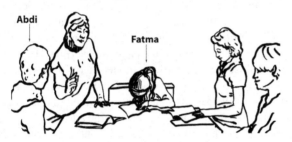

Figure 6.3 Teacher says, 'all parents <u>nag</u> their <u>chil</u>dren (.) <u>some</u> <u>time</u>'

42 Teacher: lite. lite sådär.((smiling)) jag tror att (0.5) det <u>al</u>la (.) föräldrar <u>tja</u>tar
43   nån <u>gång</u> (.) på sina <u>barn.</u>
             'A little. a little bit. I think that (0.5) all parents <u>nag</u> their <u>chil</u>dren (.)
             <u>some</u> <u>time</u>.' ((see Figure 6.3))

44 Fatma: tjata ( )
             'Nag ( )' ((to Nura))

45 Teacher: det har <u>jag</u> gjort med mina barn (.) i alla fall.
             '<u>I</u>'ve done that with my children (.) for sure.' ((seriously))

The teacher continues a vocabulary explanation by posing a question to the class (line 29: 'Do your dads and moms <u>nag</u> you?'). Her question incorporates the target vocabulary item in a new syntactic construction and also serves as a pedagogical strategy that allows her to encourage the students to use the target lexical item and to check their comprehension. The situation of parent–child relationships (including some aspects of gender identity) and mitigated parental authority is presented as given and evident, as it is in line with the child-centered socialization ideals of Swedish society that nourish child independence, negotiation, and resistant agency. Moreover, this categorization is treated as omnirelevant, in other words, as a common ground.

The teacher demonstrates concern with the children's understanding and aligning with these real-world and commonly shared categories and lexical meanings in her subsequent questions (lines 32, 34). These questions respond to several children's resistance to align (lines 31, 33, 35, 36) with the teacher's ascriptions of social identities and roles that portray the children as noncompliant and resistant social actors (Goodwin and Cekaite, 2018) whose parents have to nag them. The children's sense-making and alignment or resistance are revealed by their attentiveness, serious or smiling facial expressions, laughter, iconic gestures, and postures. The students and teacher engage in extended playful negotiations of relational gendered identities. The teacher defends her ascription of identities and affective stances, and some of the children articulate their resistance. The playful exchange continues when Nura makes a "piggybacking" (Goodwin, 1990) move on Abdi's turn. In particular, Nura "animates" (Goffman, 1981) Abdi's response in which she takes on an identity of a boy who is a righteous target of nagging. This noncompliant child identity is also adopted by Abdi, who verbally aligns and smiles (line 41: 'a little').

The children's resistance to aligning with the teacher's stance and identity ascriptions occasions the teacher's statement which, according to her, is omnirelevant (line 43: 'all parents nag their children some time'; see Figure 6.3). Following this statement, the teacher winds down this vocabulary explanation sequence by referring to her own actions and experiences (line 45: 'I've done that with my children for sure'). In this way, she concludes by making explicit the normative expectations concerning word meanings, indexing particular social identities and conduct, which are common to egalitarian adult–child relations and the expectance of child resistant agency (here manifested as nagging). The final part of the vocabulary explanation contains yet another evaluation of the word meaning as relevant for various contexts, including Sweden, and defines a generic characteristic of adult–child relations (lines 42, 43, 45).

On the whole, the teacher offers typifications of what the target word is connected to by invoking its social meaning and related social actions, and describing these actions as universally appropriate, in which she presents these expectations as a common ground (Clark, 1996) for the subsequent interactions. As demonstrated above, the vocabulary lesson was not aimed solely at teaching or instructing the referential or dictionary definition of a word, but also at socializing the children to stances and identities associated with the word as it is used, understood, and lived by members of Swedish society.

6.6   Concluding Discussion

By focusing on the sociocultural and interactional architecture of vocabulary explanations in a Swedish as a second language (L2) classroom for recently arrived immigrant students, this chapter has identified and explicated sociocultural issues that, thus far, have received little attention in studies on L2 vocabulary teaching and in language socialization studies of children in migration contexts. The chapter has demonstrated that Swedish classroom vocabulary lessons, in whatever form they take (e.g., the teacher picking out an ostensibly difficult word in a text and defining it with the students or responding to students' vocabulary comprehension questions) served as an important vehicle of L2 language socialization (e.g., Duff, 2011). The vocabulary explanation practices and definitional activities analyzed here were not neutral, semantically oriented activities. That is, the teachers not only mediated language forms but also socialized the children to values, norms, and affective stances associated with these words in new, majority communities of practice, and provided affordances for shaping the lifeworlds and identities of the L2 learners. They dealt with gender, generational identities, habits, and feelings in a broad range of normative areas, including children's roles in Swedish society and educational institutions. An underlying socialization message was related to fostering an understanding and appreciation of children's social agency and their ability to know, demand, and exercise their rights (Swedish National Curriculum for Primary School; Cekaite, 2017; Goodwin and Cekaite, 2018), which is assumed to be common ground and a part of the National Curriculum in Swedish educational institutions.

Common ground and shared knowledge are often assumed as a natural precondition in theorizing on lexical meanings in a first language (e.g., Linell, 2009). The present analyses have suggested that lexical instructions for and with Swedish language novices can provide insights into the processes through which L2 beginners relate words to the lifeworlds, perspectives, and expectations of the majority language community, and the language users' orientation to the cultural anchoredness of lexical meanings. Vocabulary explanations reveal that L2 teaching and learning focus on the need to establish shared meanings and to achieve a common ground between language novices and teachers. Such a process does not imply solely and simply conforming to abstracted identification of referents as they are defined in dictionaries. Rather, the definitions of word meanings were achieved through local exemplifications and spontaneous social typifications (e.g., participant examples) that anchored the meaning of words in concrete social situations, Swedish values and norms, and affects and desires (Kulick and Schieffelin, 2004).

By examining processes of language socialization into a particular community of practice, the present study demonstrates the methodological gains of interaction analysis. Employing a detailed interactional approach to recurrent language practices, it has uncovered and detailed language socialization templates that not only characterize the Swedish L2 classroom but are also found in cultural and language teaching settings in other societies (Griswold, 2010; Wortham, 1992). As demonstrated, in encounters with L2 novices, the teachers employed local typifications that allowed the learners to directly experience meanings and delve into the situations of uses of specific words. Generic vocabulary definitions were not sufficient in describing and disambiguating the lexical meaning potentials. Rather, the sense of particulars that specified the meaning of the word emerged from locally relevant examples: embodied demonstrations (Burdelski, Chapter 10 in this volume), hypothetical scenarios and narratives, and participant examples (Moore, Chapter 4 in this volume). The teachers embedded particular words in the phenomenal world and narratives with co-present protagonists. Definitions were offered in a dialogical situation by configuring a scene with the current participants (e.g., the students and teachers). The participants were thus looking at a general scene at the same time they were investigating various perspectives and identities. Importantly, the teachers usually built affective stances – characteristic of the children's L2 society – into these typical situations.

By means of a dialogic structure of vocabulary explanations and active interactional participation that is characteristic of the student-centered teaching that dominates Swedish educational institutions, the process of attribution of lexical meaning for the language novices was intimately related to the concrete, local, and experiential perspectives of language users. For the students in the language reception classroom, lexical knowledge of Swedish extended beyond abstract dictionary meanings, and semantics were accomplished interactively, when teachers defined and negotiated the uses of a word in the interactive field of the prospective users, the Swedish language, and cultural novices.

The teachers' use of social typifications in outlining general action preferences and normatively appropriate behavior patterns of Swedish society were instrumental as L2 discursive means for coordinating and establishing a common ground between the teachers and learners. According to Keane (2016), stances, when used across contexts and in relation to social typifications, can develop into routine-like knowledge about the lexical item itself, its social uses, and the network of associations between it, other items, and the lifeworld (Schutz, 1970) of the language users. In this way, the classroom vocabulary explanations deviated from formal vocabulary definitions as the teachers were socializing the students to everyday language use, where various facets of human experience such as motives, desires, emotions, values, cause–effect relations, and rights and responsibilities are likely to play a more central role than do paradigmatic relations within the language system (Churchill, 2008; Linell, 2009).

L2 language socialization practices did not automatically result in the students adopting congruent affective and moral stances on events, actions, objects, and phenomena (indexical of the norms and values in the majority language community). Similar to many other classrooms (see chapters by García-Sánchez, Friedman, and Klein, Chapters 2, 8, and 3 in this volume), the students at times actively resisted the ascription of specific identities and affective stances (Excerpts 6.2a and 6.2b). When viewed in terms of discourse-embedded identity work, L2 vocabulary explanations are instrumental in revealing multilingual identity negotiation processes (e.g., Cekaite, 2012, 2017; Duff, 2011). Becoming an accepted member of a majority language community is a complex and value-suffused process. Beyond the acquisition of target language forms and communicative competencies (i.e., the appropriation of interactional resources and comprehension of the underpinning socio-cultural values), it can involve the students' normatively expected congruent stances (i.e., affectively indexed appreciation of the values and ideologies that go along with discursive structures of educational activities in the majority language community). As demonstrated here, negotiation of the children's multilingual and multicultural identities – identities as a resistant or compliant child, adult–child egalitarian positioning, likes and dislikes, desires and emotions – was located at the very heart of recurrent and pervasive Swedish as L2 teaching practices, which have traditionally been seen as neutral, decontextualized, language form-focused pedagogical activities.

REFERENCES

Aronsson, K. and Cekaite, A. (2011). Activity contracts and directives in everyday family politics. *Discourse in Society*, 22(2), 1–18.

Cekaite, A. (2007). A child's development of interactional competence in a Swedish L2 classroom. *Modern Language Journal*, 91, 45–62.

Cekaite, A. (2012). Affective stances in teacher–novice student interactions: language, embodiment, and willingness to learn. *Language in Society*, 41, 641–670.

Cekaite, A. (2017). Emotional stances and interactional competence: learning to disagree in a second language. In G. Kasper and M. Prior (eds.) *Talking Emotion in Multilingual Settings*, (pp. 133–154). Amsterdam: John Benjamins.

Cekaite, A. and Aronsson, K. (2004). Repetition and joking in children's second language conversations: playful recyclings in an immersion classroom. *Discourse Studies*, 6(3), 373–392.

Churchill, E. (2008). A dynamic systems account of learning a word: from ecology to form relations. *Applied Linguistics*, 29, 339–358.

Clark, H. (1996). *Using Language*. Cambridge: Cambridge University Press.

Clark, H. and Gerrig, R. J. (1990). Quotations as demonstrations. *Language*, 66, 764–805.

Du Bois, J. W. (2007). The stance triangle. In R. Englebretson (ed.), *Stance in Discourse: Subjectivity in Interaction* (pp. 13–182). Amsterdam: John Benjamins.

Duff, P. A. (2011). Second language socialization. In A. Duranti, E. Ochs, and B. B. Schieffelin (eds.) *The Handbook of Language Socialization* (pp. 564–586). Malden, MA: Wiley-Blackwell.

Friedman, D. (2010). Speaking correctly: error correction as a language socialization practice in a Ukrainian classroom. *Applied Linguistics*, 31, 346–367.

Goffman, E. (1981). *Forms of Talk*. Cambridge: Cambridge University Press.

Goodwin, M. H. (1990). *He-Said-She-Said: Talk as Social Organization among Black Children*. Bloomington, IN: Indiana University Press.

Goodwin, M. H. and Cekaite, A. (2018). *Embodied Family Choreography: Practices of Control, Care and Creativity*. Milton Park, UK and New York, NY: Routledge.

Goodwin, M. H., Cekaite, A., and Goodwin, C. (2012). Emotion as stance. In A. Peräkylä and M-L. Sorjonen (eds.), *Emotion in Interaction* (pp. 16–41). Oxford: Oxford University Press.

Griswold, O. (2010). The English you need to know: the language ideology in a citizenship classroom. *Linguistics and Education*, 22, 406–418.

Hanks, W. (1996). *Language and Communicative Practices*. Boulder, CA: Westview Press.

He, A. (2011). Heritage language socialization. In A. Duranti, E. Ochs, and B. B. Schieffelin (eds.) *The Handbook of Language Socialization*. pp. 587–609. Malden, MA: Wiley-Blackwell.

Keane, W. (2016). *Ethical Life: Its Natural and Social Histories*. Princeton, NJ and Oxford: Princeton University Press.

Kulick, D. and Schieffelin, B. B. (2004). Language socialization. In A. Duranti (ed.), *Linguistic Anthropology: A Companion Reader*. Malden, MA: Blackwell.

Kusserow, A. (2004). *American Individualisms: Child Rearing and Social Class in Three Neighborhoods*. New York, NY: Palgrave Macmillan.

Lazaraton, A. (2004). Gesture and speech in the vocabulary explanations of one ESL teacher. *Language Learning*, 54, 79–117.

Linell, P. (2009). *Rethinking Language, Mind and World Dialogically: Aspects to Human Sense-Making*. Charlotte, NC: Information Age Publishing.

Moore, E. (2014). "You are children but you can always say ...": hypothetical direct reported speech and child–parent relationships in a Heritage language classroom. *Text and Talk*, 34, 591–621.

Nguyen, H. and Kellogg, G. (2010). "I had a stereotype that American were fat": becoming a speaker of culture in a second language. *Modern Language Journal*, 94, 56–73.

Ochs, E. (1996). Resources for socializing humanity. In J. J. Gumperz and S. C. Levinson (eds.), *Rethinking Linguistic Relativity* (pp. 407–437). Cambridge: Cambridge University Press.

Ochs, E. (2002). Becoming a speaker of culture. In C. Kramsch (ed.) *Language Acquisition and Language Socialization* (pp. 99–120). London: Continuum.

Ochs, E. and Capps, L. (2001). *Living Narrative*. Cambridge, MA: Harvard University Press.

Ochs, E. and Schieffelin, B. B. (1989). *Language has a heart. Text*, 9, 7–25.

Ochs, E. and Schieffelin, B. B. (2011). The theory of language socialization. In A. Duranti, E. Ochs, and B. B. Schieffelin (eds.) *The Handbook of Language Socialization* (pp. 1–22). Malden, MA: Wiley-Blackwell.

Persson Thunqvist, D. and Axelsson, B. (2012). "Now it's not school, it's for real!": negotiated participation in media vocational training, *Mind, Culture, and Activity*, 19, 29–50.

Poole, D. (1992). Language socialization in the second language classroom. *Language Learning*, 42(2), 593–616.

Rymes, B. and Pash, D. (2001). Questioning identity: the case of one second-language learner. *Anthropology and Education Quarterly*, 32, 276–300.

Schutz, A. (1970). *On Phenomenology and Social Relations*. Edited and with an introduction by H. R. Wagner. Chicago, IL: University of Chicago Press.

Talmy, S. (2015). A language socialization perspective on identity work of ESL youth in a superdiverse high school classroom. In N. Markee (ed.), *The Handbook of Classroom Discourse and Interaction* (pp. 353–368). Malden, MA: Wiley-Blackwell.

Watanabe, A. (2016). Engaging in an interactional routine in an EFL classroom. *Novitas-Royal*, 10, 48–70.

Willet, J. (1995). Becoming first graders in an L2: an ethnographic study of L2 socialization. *TESOL Quarterly*, 29(3), 473–503.

Wortham, S. (1992). Participant examples and classroom interaction. *Linguistics and Education*, 4, 195–217.

7   Making the Familiar Change
Language Socialization via Contrapuntal Interaction in a US High School Language Arts Class

Betsy Rymes and Andrea Leone-Pizzighella

7.1   Introduction

Looking both closely at interaction and broadly at social context is foundational to understanding processes of language socialization and to understanding classrooms. However, new curricula, teaching methodologies, and entire
schools have been built without close investigation of interaction in relevant
classrooms, or a mutual understanding between researchers and a classroom's
students, their teachers, and the surrounding community. Our work in classrooms has been an attempt to introduce curriculum, while also studying how
new material shapes the roles of students and teachers within the classroom
and the overall school community. Our approach is three-pronged: to introduce
Language Arts lessons that focus on what we call "Citizen Sociolinguistics"; to
understand the effects of this innovation on teaching and student participation;
and to share those findings in a way that leads to more curricular innovation,
now driven not only by the research team, but also by a developing local
community of practice. Our broad goal is to introduce changes in participation
that validate new voices, without damaging structures of learning that teachers
and students also value. We are using a language socialization approach to
conduct research in these classrooms because we want to identify how curricular innovations both adapt to classroom norms and invite new voices to be
full participants in Language Arts discussions. This chapter explores the
potential of this approach by analyzing the interplay between typical teacher-
fronted participation frameworks and other forms of participation, during a
discussion of *Hamlet* in a traditional honors English class in a high school in
the United States.

Language socialization provides a useful entry point for our study of
classroom interaction and curricular change because foundational studies in
language socialization address the interplay between societal norms and the
everyday interactions that make up an individual's life. Researchers have
examined, for instance, how dinner conversation in Western middle-class
homes builds gender expectations (Ochs and Taylor, 1996), how participation
in the *élema* routine in Papua New Guinea socializes children into a distinct

theory of other minds (Schieffelin, 1990), or how storytelling styles within Appalachian families develop different types of literacy practices (Heath, 1983). While language socialization studies generally attend to culturally organized routines and their structural features, such as recurring speech acts, turn-taking, repair, cohesion, or contextualization cues (Duff, 2002), language socialization is inevitably also the study of how individuals operate within (and subtly alter) these structures. Schools provide an everyday setting for the meeting of the structural and the individual as individuals socialize each other into the roles of student and teacher across diverse classroom activities.

Over the last three decades, there seems to have been a qualitative shift in thinking about how classroom teachers liaise between normative school expectations and students' less-predictable participation in class. Rather than silencing students to conduct a lesson, teachers frequently allow an undercurrent of student talk to provide a subtle counterpoint to teacher talk, even during otherwise "traditional" teacher-fronted lessons. Gutierrez, Rymes, and Larson (1995), Rampton (2006), and Rymes (2008) have illustrated the "contrapuntal" nature of teacher-directed classroom interaction through a focus on intersubjectivity and the search for shared meaning. Cazden (2001) has observed that classrooms are interesting discourse environments in part because they are full of potential speakers bidding for turns that are doled out by a single interlocutor: the teacher. Inevitably, when they are not participating in teacher-directed talk, overhearers generate "side talk" (Lemke, 1990) and participate in discussions that are in some way linked to their interpretations of the "official" classroom business, but that nonetheless occur in "unofficial" formats. Following Goffman (1961), Gutierrez et al. (1995) describe such peer-to-peer interaction in classrooms as "underlife" (described below) underlining the distinction between the official institutional activity and the unofficial activity that occurs in the gaps of institutional supervision. Important and complex identity work is accomplished during these side-interactions: important because these side discussions are often the only spaces where students make comments that are not quite fit for the main event (Blackledge and Creese, 2010), and complex because the side-discussions and the main event are never entirely separate from each other – for example, students may be performing both their friend-identity and their student-identity simultaneously. In our view, students are socialized into multiple classroom stances and demeanors – not simply one appropriate classroom self – through participation in this contrapuntal interaction.

To more precisely characterize processes of language socialization in late-modern classroom talk and to understand its effects on students' participation and engagement in school, this chapter analyzes the contrapuntal nature of language socialization among eleventh-grade honors students and their teacher as they negotiate their expertise and identities over the course of a single speech event: a teacher-led discussion of Shakespeare's *Hamlet*. We illustrate the role of individuals' diverse communicative repertoires in classroom language socialization by examining emergent, collaboratively constructed interactional sequences and participation frameworks, as well as the unique turns of teachers and students within those co-constructed interactional slots. In moment-to-moment negotiation of turns during different classroom activities, the roles associated with those turns become delicately intertwined. We posit that language socialization into a classroom's culture happens through participation in these delicate interweavings. Our research illustrates that students' and teachers' engagement with course material necessarily involves simultaneous use of standardized routines for participation *and* individual communicative repertoires. Paradoxically, students' repertoire displays, while perhaps done in ways that index counterpositions to structural prototypes of school behavior, also serve as points of classroom engagement. That is, while such displays may fall outside the range of what is officially condoned, they nonetheless serve as a means for students to engage – often on their own terms – with classroom life. Through an analysis of how an experienced teacher and gifted teens build classroom community and learn together through contrapuntal classroom discourse, we attend to the ways that structural norms of classroom talk afford and are affected by individual communicative repertoire exploration and development. Ultimately, this analytic approach will provide us a way to investigate changes in interaction and engagement, whether students are discussing Shakespeare's *Hamlet*, conducting independent research for our Citizen Sociolinguistics unit, or anything in between.

7.2   Theoretical Background

7.2.1   Shifting Participation Frameworks and Underlife

Language socialization often happens in both surveilled and "free" activities within the four walls of a school. We use the term "activities" here to de-emphasize the importance of physical places in the school and to emphasize the changing nature of participation throughout the school day and even over the course of a single lesson – or a single speech event. The courtyard and the cafeteria – typically thought of as relatively free spaces – cannot always be framed as "unofficial," nor can the entrance to the school or the front row of class always be "official." Classroom spaces can simultaneously be sites of official and unofficial activities, depending on the language practices of those inhabiting them. For example, in teacher-fronted lessons, a high-achieving student's "right answer" might be positively acknowledged by the teacher and simultaneously met with eye-rolls by her peers. This student will be socialized over time to mediate the way that she expresses what she knows and believes, depending on who is involved in the interaction. In class, students perform identities for the teacher that they do not perform for each other, and vice versa, but many learn how to manage both audiences at the same time through, for example, carefully couching their precisely correct answers as also ironic, or casting a sidelong glance at their buddies when skillfully reading aloud.

Goffman's concept of "participation framework" (and the potential for multiple and overlapping participation frameworks) captures this type of simultaneous activity. Goffman (1981, p. 226) defines the participation framework as "the circle, ratified and unratified, in which [an] utterance is variously received, and in which individuals have various participation statuses," with the condition that "when a word is spoken, all those who happen to be in the perceptual range of the event will have some sort of participation status relative to it" (p. 3). In the context of classroom discourse, one can easily see the relevance of shifting participation statuses: conversations overlap, run parallel to one another, and branch off from each other, all while a teacher is working through curricular objectives and seeking to make sure students are "getting it." Throughout these layered and connected interactions, interlocutors are shifting from one structural slot in an interaction to another, and back again; students may find themselves in conversations with each other where they are filling the structural slot of "teacher" in one moment, and of "partner-in-crime" in the next. Thus, analysis of in-class interactions among students and teachers potentially illuminates how small-scale mechanisms in classroom discourse provide sequential structures and participation frameworks within which students take up widely varied stances.

Our analysis also builds on another Goffmanian concept: "underlife" (Goffman, 1961). Goffman's observations of everyday life in a "walled-in organization" led him to assert that individuals within such institutions are not only subject to tight schedules and persistent surveillance, but also obligated "to be visibly engaged at appropriate times in the activity of the organization" (p. 176). He asserts that the more the participants' time is structured for them, the more likely there is to be divergence and resistance to the daily activities of this institution. There are those who become adept at engaging in the prescribed activity, pretending to engage in it, and entirely shirking their involvement in it. These various stances against the prescribed activity (both disruptive and contained) are termed "secondary adjustments" (p. 199). Underlife is defined as the collective secondary adjustments practiced in and sustained by an institution. In a United States high school, for instance, passing time (the five minutes during which students travel from one classroom to another) is rich in what we might call secondary adjustments: stalking your crush, scribbling something on the wall, or quickly finishing homework for the next class. Asking for a bathroom pass during class also serves several purposes, only some of which involve using the facilities. Most crucially for our purposes is the use of various planned or unplanned chunks of in-class time by students to socialize with their peers (e.g., taking advantage of the fact that the projector is taking a long time to warm up to share prom dress pictures with a desk-neighbor, or taking advantage of a teacher's end-of-a-long-week sigh just before the review of *Hamlet* to create a diversion by starting to tell jokes).

Over the course of the semester, students and teachers become more adept at designing their utterances for specific audiences and forms of participation – and to reading each other's utterances as specifically designed for one or another participation framework. These two types of participation (designing one's own action and reading that of others) are variable and develop over time – this give-and-take comprises the process of language socialization.

7.2.2   Language Socialization, Communicative Repertoire, and Indexicality in Counterpoint

In discussing processes of language socialization, Ochs (1990) has written that "the greatest part of sociocultural information is keyed implicitly, through language use" (p. 291). From this perspective, one learns how to be a "good student" and how that is different from being a "peer," not by being told directly, but by learning implicitly, largely through using the language associated with those roles. While Goffman does not fully articulate this point about language, negotiating participation as he describes it demands the implicit knowledge of language and communication described by Ochs. The secondary adjustments comprising underlife, for example, often involve nuanced "keying" (Goffman, 1974) in ways of speaking and word choice, as well as non-linguistic cues like gestures, posture, eye-movements, or subtle headshakes.

The forms of keying that Goffman describes are part of any individual's communicative repertoire (Rymes, 2010). Importantly, individuals come to the classroom with their own unique communicative repertoire which may, to varying degrees, overlap with the repertoires of other members of that classroom community. Some individuals may, for example, speak multiple languages or multiple varieties of a language. Some may have more "lacrosse" vocabulary, whereas others may know more about how to talk about the theater or be able to converse at length about late-night comedy. In classroom contexts, students and teachers with wide-ranging communicative repertoires are able to navigate different forms of participation, deftly moving between (or simultaneously acting within) underlife and more official activities. This is because these distinctive words, pronunciations, gestures, and postures – repertoire elements – are normatively associated with (that is, they *index*) certain lifeworlds.

Figure 7.1 Counterpoint across treble and bass clefs in Bach's
Invention #1 in C Major

As Burdelski and Cook (2012) have written, "the impact of indexicality on
the process of language socialization is immense, as indexical meanings are
typically not explicitly stated but are implicitly conveyed through language
use" (p. 175). People generally do not explicitly announce, "I'm a Lacrosse
player" or "I'm a theater person," but their communicative repertoire may
index those roles. Our analysis illustrates how the subtlety of such indexical
signaling is sustained within the contrapuntal nature of contemporary classroom discourse, affording the display of different stances, roles, and identities
simultaneously.

Drawing on a musical analogy illuminates the value of noticing "counterpoint" in classrooms. Counterpoint in a musical composition refers to two lines
occurring at the same time. Each line has its own integrity, but the interplay
between the two lines potentially creates the richness of a musical composition. J. S. Bach's *Two-Part Inventions* for piano provide a classical example:
One line starts, solo, in the right hand, noted in the treble clef, followed a few
notes later by a similar melody in the left hand, noted in the bass clef (see
Figure 7.1).

In classroom talk, a teacher and student engaging in a typical question and
answer sequence may form the first participation line, in place of the "treble
clef" line. In musical counterpoint, Anthony Tommasini, the classical music
critic for *The New York Times* has remarked, "when just one thing is
happening, you usually know counterpoint is coming" (2010). Similarly, in
classrooms, when just a teacher and a student are engaging in a single line of
question and answer, more voices inevitably emerge, often as underlife.
A teacher's question receives one official response, but this interaction also
sparks another, contrapuntal, interaction in the "bass clef". This "bass clef"
participation framework continues as its own line of talk, but, like musical
counterpoint, it interweaves with the initiating line of talk (see Figure 7.2).

Just as in musical counterpoint, where each line has a related but distinct
melody, in each of these lines of classroom counterpoint, students take on
related but distinct identities. In the teacher-initiated line of questioning, the
student may take on a formal key, indexing "good student" stance, but in the

𝄞 **"Treble Clef"**:   Teacher Question—Student Response—T Evaluation—T—S—T—S—T—S…

𝄢 **"Bass Clef"**:   Student Aside—S Response—S—S—S—S—S…

Figure 7.2 Counterpoint across participation frameworks in a classroom

student-initiated line of talk, students may speak more informally, indexing a wider range of peer-affiliated stances. As Tommasini has said of musical counterpoint, "the trick is to hear it as counterpoint. That's a challenge, but it is also part of the fun" (2010). Similarly, hearing counterpoint in what may seem like the cacophony of classroom interaction is a challenge, but it also illuminates the fun of classroom talk – and the myriad identities developing through language there.

7.2.3   A Note on Structure and Negotiation

Playing counterpoint is not easy. Remember the first time you sang a two-part round of *Row, Row, Row Your Boat* or *Frère Jacques*? It's easy to get thrown off when the second voice comes in. And each line may have to make subtle adjustments to keep the song from completely degenerating into a chaotic mess. Similarly, in classroom counterpoint, maintaining the "treble clef" of pedagogical talk involves continuous mindfulness of what the "bass clef" line of talk is up to. And both lines of participation subtly affect one another. Thus, even the stock "IRE (Initiation–Response–Evaluation)" routine (Mehan, 1979) of classroom recitation has to be fine-tuned to the nature of a particular classrooms' interactional context. Just as a melody line may fluctuate as different voices join in counterpoint, the form IRE takes in a classroom, while somewhat predictable, is also an emergent co-construction that gets stabilized through the skillful incorporation within a classroom culture over time. Seeing this as a continually negotiated routine gives a sense of the non-stop work that teachers do to bring off (more or less) collaborative action, which, like a round, if done well, does not look like work at all.

As we will illustrate in the analysis that follows, the continuously negotiated structure of typical question and answer sequences provides a first line of counterpoint in interaction between teacher and student, under which student lines of counterpoint unfurl in a new participation framework, or, as a form of "underlife." In music, counterpoint need not be limited to two voices, and the level of dissonance between lines can be minimal or extreme. Similarly, in classroom talk, while a teacher may initiate a relatively simple line of questioning to start a discussion, there are multiple lines of interaction and multiple participation frameworks – drawing on myriad forms of expression – that can emerge. The existence of a range of classroom repertoires, in counterpoint with the continuously negotiated question–answer sequence, also affords gradual changes in classroom norms. This is the type of incremental culture change that may be responsible for the characteristic "late modern" (Rampton, 2006) contrapuntal nature of much classroom talk today. Through participation across multiple lines of interaction or participation frameworks, students are socialized into both this contrapuntal practice and the types of selves they may inhabit within it. Part of the student socialization process, then, is about knowing how and when to participate in various lines of contrapuntal talk.

The student socialization process also involves learning when, where, and how particular ways of speaking fit into and influence the continually negotiated norms of classroom interaction. We draw on the concept of individual "communicative repertoire" (Rymes, 2010, 2014) to draw attention to the importance of individuals and the distinctive nature of individual utterances within the classroom socialization process. Looking at the role of communicative repertoire, or "the collection of ways individuals use language and other means of communication (gestures, dress, posture, accessories) to function effectively in the multiple communities in which they participate" (Rymes, 2010, p. 528) introduces the potentially creative role of the individual within even collaboratively constructed features of interaction such as greetings, leave-takings, summoning and responding, or, as we focus on particularly here, asking questions and answering them in classrooms. While each individual's repertoire is unique, effectively indexing stances and roles within these co-constructed events, in any social setting, draws on a substantially shared social history. In classrooms, assuming such a shared social history exists can lead to excluding certain voices from participation – or at least from participation that counts to the institution. Attending to individual voices and each voice's unique role within the complicated polyphony of classroom communication is central to our larger goal to follow the way curricular innovation affects patterns of participation. We want to understand how certain ways of speaking work and do not work within different types of classroom interaction. Ultimately, understanding how individual voices function within the negotiated culture of the classroom will help our research team work with teachers and administrators to address exclusionary patterns of ability tracking in this context.

7.3   Context

7.3.1   *Research Based on Mutual Concerns of Teacher and Researcher*

The interactions analyzed in the following section are a small slice of an ongoing research practice partnership between university researchers and the

teachers at Suburban High School.[1] For years, we have been working principally with Mr. Z, the language arts teacher, to develop lessons that bring
insights from linguistic anthropology and sociolinguistics to the Language
Arts curriculum. We have called these activities "Citizen Sociolinguistics"
(Rymes and Leone, 2014). Over the years, Mr. Z has grown accustomed to
sharing his space and ideas with a research team, sending out lessons to us
ahead of time, asking for input, encouraging us to present our own lessons and
to "jump in" during class discussions with relevant insights. In this regard, we
have developed a level of mutual trust that informs both how research proceeds
and what kinds of questions we ask.

Because of this ongoing mutualism, our Citizen Sociolinguistics curricular
development and research on classroom interaction have become intertwined:
inevitably, some Citizen Sociolinguistics projects seem to "work" in the
classroom and others just do not. What makes something intuitively count as
"working" or not? What is an effective lesson? Both Mr. Z and the research
team are interested in looking carefully at how forms of participation, and
associated roles and identities, change when we conduct class in certain ways,
and we are both committed to documenting that. Sometimes our curricular
changes fuel more discussion and student engagement, whereas at other times
the classroom discussion dies. Documenting how our curricular innovation
affects participation is crucial, especially because the students at Suburban
High School are highly tracked (or streamed), and classes are therefore socially
segregated. Eventually, we would like our research to inform pathways to
more socially inclusive classroom organization.

7.3.2   The Broader Context of Tracking at Suburban High School

Understanding this tracked environment requires a bit more background on the
school. Located in an affluent suburb of a major city in the northeastern United
States, Suburban High School's population of approximately 1,200 students is
79 percent White, 9 percent Black, 9 percent Asian, and 2 percent Hispanic,
with 14 percent of students considered to be economically disadvantaged. The
school serves students in grades 9 to 12, with a student–teacher ratio of less
than 11:1, and was recently ranked among the top 10 schools in its state for
standardized test scores. Students in each grade are tracked into one of three
ability levels: honors, college prep, or college and career prep. These three
"tracks" follow the same curriculum at different paces and with different
emphases, with some supplemental courses offered and/or required for
each track.

Our collaboration at the high school has given us an insider's view of the
experience of tracking in such an outwardly privileged context. We have seen
how the culture of excellence at the high school makes the tracking system

even more demoralizing by creating a set of students, those in the "Career and College Prep" (CCP) track, who have been designated as outsiders to that excellence. In sharing our Citizen Sociolinguistics work in the lower track classes, two matters have become clear: (1) These students demonstrate a facility for citizen sociolinguistics research on par with the students in other tracks; (2) These students have a perceptible malaise, qualitatively distinct from the higher track classes.

Despite the apparent appeal of the Citizen Sociolinguistics activities in all tracks, we began our work by piloting activities in the Honors track classes, primarily because of timing and logistics. But when we proposed this approach to additional teachers, there was also some hesitation to try Citizen Sociolinguistic projects with their non-honors classes, where they felt extra concern for meeting basic academic requirements and perceived less leeway for participating in any additional activities. Recent reports have put the district under considerable pressure to address the needs of these underperforming students, especially since they are disproportionately Black, Hispanic, and economically disadvantaged.[2]

We suspected, however, that these may be just the students for whom Citizen Sociolinguistics lessons may be most engaging. Gradually, we have now begun to work together implementing the activities with non-honors students. Although we have not been able to study the results in detail, our impression has been that student projects have been, on average, equally compelling across tracks, and the conversations around language as complex, if not more complex, than we have witnessed in the honors classes.

7.3.3   The Focal Classroom and Interaction

We have not yet analyzed materials from non-honors and blended tracks. However, the eleventh-grade Honors English course analyzed here provides a baseline for exploring how a language socialization approach can illuminate contrapuntal interaction, including the analysis of different student voices and variable forms of participation. In this class, four days per week, Mr. Z and his students would read and discuss the assigned texts according to the curriculum prescribed by Suburban High School's English Department and the State, and one day per week they would focus specifically on certain aspects of language that were particularly salient in or for those texts (e.g., translation, euphemism, gendered language). On those days, for 15 weeks, we gathered fieldnotes, observations, and class materials, and on our last two visits to Mr. Z's classes at the end of the semester, we recorded in-class discussions and conducted small-group interviews with the students. On the day in which the data for this chapter were collected, Mr. Z dedicated the first part of class to finishing up the class's work on *Hamlet*, reviewing the section of the play he had assigned for homework. We focus our analysis on eight segments of this five-minute class discussion, which resembled the typical discussion format in this particular class. The interplay between side-interactions and contributions to the main discussion was also common in Mr. Z's honors English class. While this interaction does not directly inform our Citizen Sociolinguistics lessons, it does provide us an opportunity for looking at the finer points of language socialization in classrooms in this high school. This preliminary analysis also provides a baseline for future comparisons as we begin to analyze how students participate and are socialized into certain classroom identities, across tracks, during Citizen Sociolinguistics lessons.

7.4   Analysis

We highlight the role of language and its indexical function to understand how teachers and students are socialized, to use language and through language, in contrapuntal classroom interaction. Slipping in and out of ways of speaking and forms of conduct that index "official" or "unofficial" classroom stances, individuals enact more "teacher-like," "student-like," or "peer-like" roles. While operating within structured interactional norms (like turn-taking), teachers and students also draw on their individual communicative repertoires to shift between official and unofficial classroom stances.

7.4.1   IRE and Repertoire: Know the Material, Use Your Own Words

In much of teacher-fronted classroom interaction one of the most recognizable turn-taking patterns is the IRE sequence (Mehan, 1979). In this three-part sequence, the teacher asks a known-answer question, a student provides a response, and the teacher evaluates it. Most generally, the IRE sequence provides predictable structural slots, constructing roles for teacher and student, as indicated in Table 7.1.

To participate effectively in classrooms, students must be able to predict when their responses will be expected within the IRE sequence. Some students, in fact, become so attuned to the rhythm of this pattern that they use it strategically – for example, stealing turns from others by sneaking in on the response slot. Erickson (1996) has even named these individuals "turn-sharks" for their ability to stealthily swim through the classroom interactional waters and strike the moment a teacher finishes the "Initiation," stealing the "Response" slot from any students who are not so attuned to the rhythm of the sequence. Other students use the rhythm of the IRE sequence to escape from ever having to give an answer and expose themselves as not knowing – timing a raised hand, for example, to shoot up precisely when it is clear someone else will be called on (Rymes, 2016). Rampton (2005) has

Table 7.1 *Roles indexed by each act in the IRE sequence*

Act in IRE sequence	Role typically associated with this slot	Example
Initiation	Teacher	"What is 2 + 2?"
Response	Student	"Four"
Evaluation	Teacher	"Good!"

documented how still other students slip ironic remarks into more pro forma classroom talk by coordinating their participation to the timing of IRE sequences. So, while the IRE sequence itself is a pedestrian classroom routine, one's command of the IRE sequence – a sense of its rhythm and timing and the types of utterances that can squeeze into each slot – allows one to imbue the structured sequence with individuality, drawing on unique elements of one's communicative repertoire, leveraging the potential to index a particular type of student (supersmart or eager) or peer (ironic or witty).

Taking up roles within an IRE sequence is thus a way of participating simultaneously in official (teacher-centered) and unofficial (peer-centered) classroom interactions, as well as doing other identity work. While a recognizable sequence of interaction creates a structural slot for a certain role (Obedient Student, for example, in the "Response" slot), the type of utterance one makes in that slot can simultaneously index a different role ("class clown," for example, when using irony in that same response). Our research illustrates how this simultaneity occurs in even the most orderly of interactions. The following unfolding discussion illustrates how explicit praise, in combination with implicit modeling of stance, socializes students into a specific way of discussing literature that Mr. Z values: Know the material. Use your own words.[3]

In Excerpt 7.1, Mr. Z (the teacher) initiates an IRE sequence during an honors English class discussion of Shakespeare's *Hamlet*. He asks students to recall the four pieces of advice that Polonius gives to his son Laertes before Laertes returns to Paris, referring to a reading guide he had given them in a previous class.

Excerpt 7.1 Make Friends But Don't Make Every Friend

In lines 01–07, Mr. Z explains that Laertes is "kind of, like, away at college" and has decided to give his younger sister some advice about her new boyfriend, Hamlet, before he leaves again.

```
08  Mr. Z:  Um, so he's going back and what does dad talk to
09          son about before he leaves? I say list four things
10          but don't worry about that right now.
```

```
11              Just what is the general idea?
12  Ava:        ((raising hand))
13  Mr. Z:      Ava.
14  Ava:        He gives him all sorts of like, friend advice,
15              like make friends but like don't make every
16              friend. He says something about like don't shake
17              every person's hand=
18  Mr. Z:      Yeah.
19  Ava:        =like establish who your friends are and then put
20              your trust in them=
21  Mr. Z:      Good. Good, good.
22  Ava:        =stuff like that.
23  Mr. Z:      Yeah, who to trust, who not to trust, right?
24              How to act.
```

As an experienced teacher, Mr. Z deftly opens the discussion by keeping his "Initiation" question broad (line 11: "Just what is the general idea?"). He does not risk shutting students down by holding them to precise expectations in their answers. Following this lead, Ava provides a "Response" turn that broadly paraphrases the ideas she remembers from Polonius' speech (lines 15–16: "like make friends but like don't make like every friend"). Her response draws encouragement from Mr. Z, (line 18: "yeah"), then a clearly positive "Evaluation" turn (line 21: "Good. Good, good") and affirmative, evaluative paraphrasing (lines 23–24: "Yeah, who to trust, who not to trust, right? How to act."). At this point, both Ava and Mr. Z are perfectly attuned to the IRE sequence. Through their participation in this sequence, they are taking on the roles of Teacher and Student, but they each have also kept the discussion of Shakespeare at the level of casual paraphrase. This is perhaps an intentional move by Mr. Z, as suggested by his framing of Polonius and Laertes as "dad" and "son," and could have been intended as a means of encouraging student participation. We suggest that this accomplishes not only active student participation, but it also gives students the chance to draw on their own individual repertoires to simultaneously index more nuanced social identities for themselves and still participate successfully in English,[4] as indicated in Table 7.2.

Immediately following this first IRE sequence, in Excerpt 7.2 Mr. Z calls on another student, Tim, whose hand was up while Ava was giving her answer.

Excerpt 7.2 Lend Your Ears to Many

```
25  Mr. Z:      Yeah. ((directed to Tim, who has his hand raised))
26  Tim:        He also says like lend your ears to
27              many but your mouth to few.
28  Mr. Z:      Yeah.
```

Table 7.2 *Ava and Mr. Z indexing social roles through a combination of IRE sequential acts and individual communicative repertoire*

Act in IRE sequence	Role indexed	Individual response	Simultaneous role indexed
Initiation question	Teacher	"Just what is the general idea?"	Teacher who knows the answers, but is open to general comments
Response	Student	"like make friends but like don't make like every friend"	Smart but not overly nerdy student
Evaluation	Teacher	"Good. Good, good."[5] "Yeah, who to trust, who not to trust, right?"	Chill/relaxed teacher who is accepting of casually phrased answers

```
29  Tim:    So like don't really be talking
30          as much as you're listening.
31  Mr. Z:  Right, be a good listener, right,
32          so not just like a blabbermouth.
```

Here, Mr. Z is still in the sequential slot of "teacher" in the IRE sequence. He has provided the initiation question (Excerpt 7.1, lines 08–11). Tim then takes up the response slot of "student." In contrast to Ava's response, Tim takes on a "quotation" tone of voice, providing an approximation of Shakespearian diction and "animating," in a Goffmanian sense, Polonius' advice to his son (lines 26–27). Though his exact words depart from the text (in the text, Polonius' line is "Give every man thy ear but few thy voice"), Tim seems to have some Shakespearean diction lodged in his individual repertoire and calls on it here. While he uses the word "like" a couple times here, his initial use differs from Ava's (setting up his quotes and summaries rather than peppering his utterances). Rather than Ava's repeated sprinkling of "like" ("like make friends but like don't make like every friend"), Tim uses the phrase "says like" to introduce and mark reported speech. The "says" introduces the quote, and the "like" seems to indicate "something to the effect of X." So, it seems the role "like" plays in Tim's repertoire is slightly different than the role it plays in Ava's. For Tim, it tempers his "direct quotation." By avoiding a more youthy "like" usage and instead using the "says like" combination to introduce something approximating Shakespearean language (e.g., line 26: "lend your ears") in his initial response, Tim has indexed a different stance than either Ava or Mr. Z did in the first IRE sequence. However, following with Mr. Z's paraphrase approach (and Ava's youth-indexical "like" diction), he then provides a gloss of his own quotation-like answer, rephrasing it as "so like don't really be talking as much as you're listening" (lines 29–30).

Table 7.3 *Tim and Mr. Z indexing social roles through a combination of IRE sequential acts and individual communicative repertoire*

Act in IRE sequence	Role indexed	Individual response	Simultaneous role indexed
Initiation question	Teacher	"Just what is the general idea?"	Teacher who knows the answers, but is open to general comments
Response	Student	"Lend your ears to many but your mouth to few" "so like don't really be talking as much as you're listening"	Smart student who also appreciates (and remembers) Shakespeare's language AND can paraphrase it in a suburban teen way
Evaluation	Teacher	"Right, be a good listener, right, so not just like a blabbermouth"	Chill/relaxed teacher who is accepting of casually phrased answers

While Mr. Z then takes up the typically teacher-occupied evaluation slot, he does not take up Tim's Shakespearean language at this point. He instead maintains the more casual tone of the initial IRE sequence with Ava and of Tim's self-paraphrase. In this way, he continues to index the role of teacher (through the predictable IRE sequence) but, through word choice, to simultaneously index "chill/relaxed teacher" who does not arbitrarily dole out praise for seemingly direct quotation and may even prefer a more down-to-earth rendering (e.g., lines 31–32). In turn, Tim's response highlights his individual communicative repertoire as not only a student who did the reading and who has some familiarity and appreciation for Shakespeare's language, but also, by paraphrasing, someone who understands what those words mean, and, by using the youth-indexical "like," a student at one with his suburban teenage friends (see Table 7.3).

Mr. Z continues to keep this discussion general, paraphrasing Shakespeare, rather than emulating exact wording. Mr. Z's repertoire – his tendency to paraphrase, his word choice ("blabbermouth"), and tag questions ("who not to trust, right?" [Excerpts 7.1 and 7.2] and "fatherly advice, right?" [Excerpt 7.3 below]) index a down-to-earth stance, and individual flair distinct from a more rigid teacher, who might be prone to restate students' answers in more "highfalutin" language. By indexing a more relaxed stance, Mr. Z may also invite students who do not share Tim's confidence with Shakespearean language into the sequence. In this way, his responses in the "Evaluation" slot each both (a) explicitly encourage students' participation through praise and (b) implicitly encourage more informal students' individual repertoire by matching their stance. This process suggests to us that students here are being socialized into a qualitatively distinct way of being students-discussing-literature: Know the material. Use your own words.[6]

This pattern continues. In Excerpt 7.3, after further contextualizing his paraphrase of Tim's self-paraphrase in the current line of questioning about Polonius' speech (lines 33–38), Mr. Z calls on another student, Olivia, who is raising her hand (line 39):

Excerpt 7.3 Don't Borrow Anyone's Money

33 Mr. Z:	A lot of – fatherly advice, right?
34	Again we said the last one, like big
35	brother telling little sister be careful who
36	you're dating, here's dad telling son,
37	here are some things to remember when
38	you go out into the world.
39 Mr. Z:	Yeah. ((to Olivia, who has her hand raised))
40 Olivia:	He also says like don't borrow anyone's
41	money because they always=
42 Mr. Z:	Good.
43 Olivia:	=and like don't lend out money.
44 Mr. Z:	Good, yep. Talking about financial advice,
45	friendship advice. A bunch of things that,
46	again, is that that far-fetched from what
47	we might hear from a parent when we go off
48	to college or something? Right? Probably not.

Departing from Tim's model, Olivia does not provide a direct Shakespearean quotation for this idea and neither does Mr. Z, despite this being one of the more quotable Shakespearean lines ("Neither a borrower nor a lender be"). Instead, Olivia, like Ava and Mr. Z, uses everyday phrasing. And, while still in the structural slot of "teacher," Mr. Z maintains his casual repertoire, continuing to paraphrase and make connections to familiar contemporary situations, big brothers and little sisters, dads and sons, and things that "we might hear from a parent when we go off to college" (lines 47–48). As the discussion continues, students follow in a similar manner.

A certain type of classroom language socialization is happening here. While scaffolded by the rigid structure of IRE sequences, individual communicative repertoires – and the stances and identities they index – emerge and recede. Some repertoire elements are acknowledged and praised, some are ignored. While students are abiding by the generic structuring of IRE, through their individual repertoires they enact stances that index different types of student identity. Similarly, over the course of this discussion, Mr. Z's consistent repertoire of paraphrase and his use of analogy to everyday situations generates a set of expectations for the types of responses he values and recognizes.

𝄞 "Treble Clef":   T: He says like lend your ears to many but your mouth to few. Yeah, so...

𝄢 "Bass Clef":   B: What does he say about money? A: What? B: Does he say.

Figure 7.3 Teacher-fronted IRE (treble clef) and Ava and Bea's discussion of *Hamlet* (bass clef)

While the IRE sequence creates a series of structural constraints, it simultaneously generates a slot within which individual communicative repertoires are displayed – and modified. Throughout the give-and-take, again, a particular way of being students-discussing-literature is being socialized through explicit evaluation and implicit stance-matching: Know the material. Use your own words.

7.4.2   Contrapuntal IRE

The sequential features of IRE also generate another simultaneous set of structural affordances for the expression of individuals' unique communicative repertoires: counterpoint. The IRE limits participation in a specific way, with the teacher doling out turns at talk, one student at a time. During this sequence, many students are left out and those "left out" students generally find other activity to engage in. Even in the orderly review discussion examined above, students engage in asides, constructing identities in side-conversations sparked by official classroom interaction.

While Tim was providing answers on the "treble clef" line of the classroom, in the prototypical IRE sequence, Ava and Bea continued their *Hamlet* discussion in the "bass clef" (see Figure 7.3).

To make the transcript more readable, in Excerpt 7.4 below we lay out the rest of the interaction in two columns.

Excerpt 7.4 Treble Clef and Bass Clef
Teacher/student exchanges repeated from Excerpts 7.2 and 7.3

𝄞 Teacher/student exchanges	𝄢 Student asides
26 Tim: He also says like lend your ears to	
27 many but your mouth to few	
28 Mr. Z: Yeah	Bea: ((to Ava)) What does he say about money?
29 Tim: so like don't really be talking	Ava: ((to Bea)) What?
30 as much as you're listening.	Bea: ((to Ava)) Does he say something
31 Mr. Z: Right, be a good listener, right,	

32	so not just like a blabbermouth.	about lending money?
33	A lot of – fatherly advice, right?	Ava: *((to Bea))* Yeah.
34	Again we said the last one, like big	
35	brother telling little sister be careful who	
36	you're dating, here's dad telling son,	
37	here are some things to remember when	
38	you go out into the world.	

There are any number of reasons that Ava and Bea may have started their side conversation as a new line of counterpoint (rather than engaging in Tim and Mr. Z's "treble clef" exchange). It may have been due to Tim's quotation-like response and pressure to approximate his repertoire. It may have been that Tim's use of the word "lend" made Bea remember the third piece of advice, asking Ava, "Does he say something about lending money?" (lines 31–32).[7] Or, it may have simply been structurally awkward to interrupt at this point in the IRE sequence. In any case, the activity on the initial line of questioning generates this new line of counterpoint. But this "bass clef" interaction, while complementary to the main line of questioning, is also distinct from it. In direct peer-to-peer talk, IRE sequences, anchored with teacher-like known-answer questions and evaluations, would be unusual. Instead (perhaps recognizing the expertise Ava just demonstrated in the official IRE sequence with Mr. Z), Bea asks Ava a "real" question (one to which she does not know the answer). In this interactional context a more conversational question and answer sequence provides the structural slots for participation. And since Bea seems to be checking on her answer before jumping into the official talk, this exchange indexes roles of "expert" and "novice" – Bea, as "novice," putting her friend, Ava, in the position of "expert." At the same time, this tiny side-interaction indexes a friendly collaboration between Ava and Bea as partners in the project of "doing school," rehearsing possibilities for the main stage (see Table 7.4).

Table 7.4 *Ava and Bea indexing social roles through a genuine question and answer sequence*

Act in IRE sequence	Role indexed	Individual response	Simultaneous role indexed
Genuine question	Novice	"Does he say something about lending money?"	Admirer? Friend?
Answer	Expert	"Yeah."	Helpful person? Friend?

The partnership between Ava and Bea, indexed by their offline collaboration, comes into relief when their re-entry to the official IRE sequence is headed off by another student. While Ava and Bea are discussing the money lending line from Polonius, Olivia raises her, and "steals" Bea's answer ("He also says like don't borrow anyone's money," lines 40–41 in Excerpt 7.5), evoking a soft sound of disappointment from Bea to which Ava responds with a soft sympathetic laugh:

Excerpt 7.5 Stealing Bea's Answer
Teacher/student exchanges repeated from Excerpt 7.3

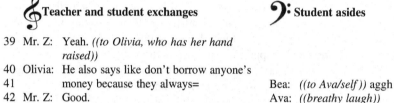

Teacher and student exchanges	Student asides

39	Mr. Z:	Yeah. *((to Olivia, who has her hand raised))*	
40	Olivia:	He also says like don't borrow anyone's	
41		money because they always=	Bea: *((to Ava/self))* aggh
42	Mr. Z:	Good.	Ava: *((breathy laugh))*
43	Olivia:	=and like don't lend out money.	
44	Mr. Z:	Good, yep. Talking about financial advice,	
45		friendship advice. A bunch of things that,	
46		again, is that that far-fetched from what	
47		we might hear from a parent when we go off	
48		to college or something? Right? Probably not.	

While Bea didn't get to enter the IRE sequence at this point, and while Ava and Bea, in the bass clef, seem to crumple a little, not having had a chance to state their version of "Neither a borrower nor a lender be," they may have developed some interactional solidarity. Bea's "aggh" (line 41) expresses her exasperation, and the light laughter from Ava (line 42) indicates Ava's humorous stance toward this exasperation.

Perhaps out of good-natured competition, out of defiance, or because she got confirmation from Ava that she was indeed on the right track with her answer, Bea gets her hand in the air for another new answer, is called on by Mr. Z (Excerpt 7.6), and re-enters the official IRE sequence:

Excerpt 7.6 Don't Pick a Fight

49	Mr. Z:	Yeah. *((to Bea, whose hand is raised))*
50	Bea:	He says like don't pick a fight but like,
51		once you get in one, stand your ground.
52	Mr. Z:	Very good. Yeah don't start fights, but if
53		something happens, show honor and stand up for
54		yourself.

55   (0.2)
56   Alright so there's a lot of uh, we'll look at it a
57   little more closely, and that's a famous speech.

After Bea provides this piece of advice from Polonius to Laertes (don't start fights), Mr. Z paraphrases Bea's contribution (lines 52–54) and then wraps up, signaling that he is ready to move on (lines 56–57). In summary, the students have come up with four "youthy" paraphrases of Polonius' distinct advice:

(1) "like make friends but like don't make like every friend" (Excerpt 7.1, lines 15–16)
(2) "like lend your ears to many but your mouth to few" (Excerpts 7.2 and 7.4, lines 26–27) and "so like don't really be talking as much as you're listening" (Excerpts 7.2 and 7.4, lines 29–30)
(3) "like don't borrow anyone's money" (Excerpts 7.3 and 7.5, lines 40–41) and "like don't lend out money" (Excerpts 7.3 and 7.5, line 43); and
(4) "like don't pick a fight but like, once you get in one, stand your ground" (Excerpt 7.6, lines 50–51).

At this point, while the students have given these four bits of Polonius' advice, in Excerpt 7.7 Mr. Z turns their attention to one more crucial line they haven't mentioned:

Excerpt 7.7 Unto Thineself Be True

58 Mr. Z: And there's that line in there above all else, unto thineself be true.
59   Above all else, be true to yourself because if you're not true to yourself,
60   you can't be true to anybody else.

Like Tim, Mr. Z here first uses quotation-like language (lines 58–59: "above all else, unto thineself be true"), indexing a Shakespearean realm (though the text of Polonius' speech reads, "This above all: to thine own self be true"), and he follows with a paraphrase of that Shakespearean-sounding bit (lines 58–59). In this way he straddles the teacher-indexical quotation-like representation of Polonius' speech and his own communicative repertoire to enact a more chill/relaxed stance. Then, as shown in Excerpt 7.8, he ends this discussion by reminding the students that Polonius' speech is important, both for the usual school-centered reasons, and for broader reasons.

Excerpt 7.8 Polonius Is an Interesting Guy

61 Mr. Z: Alright, we'll come back to that because Polonius is an interesting guy,
62   but that's a big line in this early part of the play.
63   (0.2)
64   Um, very good. You guys followed that great.

Mr. Z's own communicative repertoire emerges again here as he asserts that in addition to this being a "big line" (line 62) in the play, "Polonius is an interesting guy" (line 61). He not only stresses the importance of lines in this play as a literary artifact, but also the more general, relatable aspects of its characters. As a means of closing the review activity (and the series of IRE sequences through which it is accomplished), Mr. Z also makes one final, collective evaluative remark, sealing his role in the structural "Evaluation" slot as Teacher (line 64: "very good"), while maintaining his chill/relaxed stance through his characteristic "Mr. Z" repertoire (line 64: "You guys followed that great").

7.5   Discussion

In sum, just as literary form (like "the sonnet" or "haiku") provides a frame for infinite individual variation, generic interactional structures (IRE) have scaffolded some creative language use here (cf., Howard, 2009). Within recurring structures of classroom talk, Mr. Z and his students display their diverse individual communicative repertoires. Through consistent use of paraphrase, casual language, and tag questions, Mr. Z. invites students' informal repertoire into the discussion. They are not matching precisely his way of speaking. Mr. Z, for example, uses "like" tokens much less often than the students. He also draws on (what we, as Mr. Z's peers, recognize as) more old-fashioned language like "far-fetched" or "blabbermouth," which may not be in the students' repertoires. But the use of his own repertoire seems to invite students to call on theirs. He does not sanction their uses of "like," or their broad paraphrasing of Shakespeare. In no way does he espouse more erudite diction, even misquoting Shakespeare's lines himself.

This example of classroom discussion aligns with other language socialization work across classroom contexts that has illustrated varying ways IRE sequences provide a frame through which learners are socialized into locally distinct ways of "doing school" (e.g., Cook, 1999; Friedman, 2010; He, 2003). Mr. Z and the students are simultaneously accomplishing the work of school and the development of their own roles within the more rigid structural slots of traditional school participation. Throughout this interaction, several things are happening: Mr. Z is checking that students have grasped what he determined are the main points of the section that they read for homework; students are seeking to demonstrate their proficiency in the material to Mr. Z and to each other; and everyone in the class is being socialized into ways of talking about Shakespeare, or perhaps about literature more generally. Tim's and Mr. Z's practice of loosely quoting the text of *Hamlet* and then immediately following with a paraphrased version of the same idea illustrates how individual repertories can also turn into local patterns for doing school. One can imagine other English classrooms where students learn to simply quote text verbatim, or to memorize chunks of Shakespeare. In this classroom, however, responses that make the text relevant to life are consistently recognized and built on. There is always more to a discussion than simply reading a text and providing rote answers.

Students in Mr. Z's classroom do even more than attend to literature and make connections. Between peers, in addition to learning to be literate, they are also learning to balance friendly interaction and accountable classroom talk. In the behind-the-scenes interaction between Bea and Ava (Excerpt 7.4) they negotiate their own identities as experts and novices, friends and co-conspirators. Taken merely at face value, Bea is positioning Ava as more expert than herself (e.g., by asking her a question about the topic as preparation to volunteer an answer herself [possibly to save herself the embarrassment of providing a wrong answer in front of the class]). Ava apparently accepts this positioning by responding with a very sure-sounding answer to this question. In the broader context of the lesson and of the academic year, however, this exchange might be interpreted differently: not necessarily, or not only, as a means of Bea checking facts with Ava, but as a means of Bea seeking to ratify her position as a knower of information not only with Mr. Z but also with her fellow high-achieving peer. Ava was more likely to give sure-sounding answers to difficult questions, while Bea was often the one to say "I don't get it" during small group or pair work with Ava. Ava nearly always took the lead in their discussions. Perhaps, via both "public" and "private" discourse in the classroom, students are performing and witnessing ways of being an "honors" student. Since the "honors" designation goes beyond either working hard or being right, Bea and Ava are possibly socializing each other via their side-conversation to be more attuned to the ways that they take stances, make guesses, and give answers, developing notions of expertise and positions vis-à-vis the "honors" designation as they do so.

7.6   Conclusion: Making the Familiar Visible

7.6.1   Theoretical Implications

Language socialization has been repeatedly defined as "both socialization *through language* and socialization to *use language*" (Schieffelin and Ochs, 1986). That process is apparent in the speech event just discussed – as students and teacher socialized each other *through* the language of English class discussion and how to *use language* in an English class discussion about *Hamlet*. But one consistent critique of language socialization has been that, left at this minimal description, one might consider processes of language socialization to be not unlike those of behaviorism (see Kulick and Schieffelin, 2004). Though these processes may happen in subtler, implicit, socially indexical ways, children are rewarded through language for "appropriate" behavior and sanctioned for "inappropriate" language behavior. How is this different from a Skinner box? What is the role of the individual in what counts as "appropriate"? How do norms ever change? George Herbert Mead (1934) in *Mind, Self and Society* provided perhaps the original pragmatist's response to this type of critique. Individual minds are not simply biological organisms that react unthinkingly to positive and negative reinforcements. Instead, human minds, because they respond thinkingly as individuals to what happens around them, are a product of the interplay between self and society. The field of language socialization is an attempt to document what this process might look like.

In this chapter, we have framed our analysis as an illustration of precisely the role of the thinking self in the language socialization process. We have done so by examining the contrapuntal nature of classroom talk. Within classroom counterpoint, numerous stances and roles emerge as students are socialized into and help create a certain classroom culture.

As our analysis has shown, Mr. Z does not unthinkingly respond to the structural constraints of the IRE sequence, doling out questions, getting responses and reinforcing right and wrong answers with rote praise or condemnation. Instead, he has honed his individual repertoire within those structural slots. In the process, students are acting mindfully in response to both structural demands of the IRE sequence, and infinite other social factors in play, including Mr. Z's repertoire and the stance it indexes, their student identities and the stance they want to index vis-à-vis Mr. Z and the presence of their peers, and the different roles available to them in the underlife of the classroom. Documenting the negotiation across complex participation frameworks and the individual repertoires is one method of documenting the mindful behaviors of social actors as they practice their daily craft in unique ways.

7.6.2   Practical Implications

The contrapuntal nature of classroom talk we have discussed illustrates the presence of interactional mechanisms that afford more individual negotiation as teachers and students thinkingly engage with social structure while using their own unique communicative repertoires. In the interaction analyzed above, while working within the structural constraints of a quick-and-dirty homework review event, Mr. Z deftly invited more students into the discussion by engaging his own unique individual repertoire and welcoming the varied language of student responses. During the same discussion, in their contrapuntal talk, Ava and Bea were able to draw on each other as "expert" or "novice" as a way of engaging, even when they were not directly addressed by the teacher.

Now we want to use this form of analysis to evaluate interactions across different classrooms and activities. As discussed, this study is part of a much larger project the larger goal of which is to change a fundamentally unjust educational practice: ability tracking in language arts classrooms. Our three years working with teachers and eleventh-grade students in this context have shown us that all these students, at all ability tracks, engage uniquely in discussions about language. A lesson on "translation" for example (comparing multiple translations of *Siddhartha*), works as well in an Advanced Placement (AP) rhetoric class as it does with the CP and CCP classes, though the way students engage with the material varies widely. We as researchers have had the privilege of learning from students in all tracks. We have found that students' interactions with each other affect how they come to understand and talk about language and literature from numerous vantage points. They all have the potential to learn from one another. Yet, students remain segregated. Looking at these classroom interactions with a language socialization lens, tracking interactional counterpoint and other forms of participation, allows us to carefully document engagement, moving toward activities that blend tracks productively.

Now we will continue to work with teachers and students to analyze interactions in each of these classes and to assess the quality of engagement there and the degree to which certain activities work or flop and for whom. In the process, we will continue to hone analytic skills and interactional awareness among a community of teachers, students, and researchers. Our goal is to grant more power to individual voices so that they will be included in emergent classroom culture and this will only happen if we study these processes together. Once the emergent process of classroom language socialization becomes visible, once the implicit indexicality is made explicit, it becomes possible to share and develop each other's repertoires, and to make changes that enhance the experience of all students and teachers.

NOTES

1 Names are pseudonyms.
2 According to U. S. News and World Report, at Strath Haven High School 78.2 percent of disadvantaged students were proficient on the Keystone State Exams (calculated as "the weighted percentage of black, Hispanic and economically disadvantaged students that achieved proficiency or higher on state exit exams"), whereas 96.7 percent of non-disadvantaged students achieved proficiency. This is a difference of 18.5 percent.

3 Your "own words" being, technically, a locally socialized version of paraphrasing involving overlapping student–teacher repertoire, collaboratively arrived at through student–teacher interactions like these.

4 Thank you to an anonymous reviewer for this suggestion.

5 Mr. Z also puts his own unique repertoire stamp on the "Evaluation" slot with his use of a signature lilting "Good, good, good." By the end of this year, Mr. Z's "Good, good" was included on the students' underground "Teacher Catch-Phrase Bingo" card.

6 Again, with your "own words" being, technically, a locally socialized version of paraphrasing involving overlapping student–teacher repertoire, collaboratively arrived at through student–teacher interactions like these.

7 Thank you to an external reviewer for this idea.

REFERENCES

Blackledge, A. and Creese, A. (2010). *Multilingualism: A Critical Perspective*. London: Continuum International Publishing Group.

Burdelski, M. and Cook, H. M. (2012). Formulaic language in language socialization. *Annual Review of Applied Linguistics*, 32, 173–188.

Cazden, C. (2001). *Classroom Discourse: The Language of Teaching and Learning, 2nd Ed.* Portsmouth, NH: Heinemann.

Cook, H. M. (1999). Language socialization in Japanese elementary schools: attentive listening and reaction turns. *Journal of Pragmatics*, 31, 1443–1465.

Duff, P. A. (2002). The discursive co-construction of knowledge, identity, and difference: an ethnography of communication in the high school mainstream. *Applied Linguistics*, 23(3), 289–322.

Erickson, F. (1996). Going for the zone: the social and cognitive ecology of teacher–student interaction in classroom conversations. In D. Hicks (ed.), *Discourse, Learning, and Schooling* (pp. 29–62). Cambridge: Cambridge University Press.

Friedman, D. A. (2010). Speaking correctly: error correction as a language socialization practice in a Ukrainian classroom. *Applied Linguistics*, 31, 346–367.

Goffman, E. (1961). *Asylums: Essays on the Social Situation of Mental Patients and Other Inmates*. New York, NY: Anchor Books.

Goffman, E. (1974). *Frame Analysis: An Essay on the Organization of Experience*. Cambridge, MA: Harvard University Press.

Goffman, E. (1981). *Forms of Talk*. Philadelphia, PA; University of Pennsylvania Press.

Gutierrez, K., Rymes, B., and Larson, J. (1995). Script, counterscript, and underlife in the classroom: James Brown versus Brown v. Board of Education. *Harvard Educational Review*, 65(3): 445–471.

He, A. (2003). Novices and their speech roles in Chinese heritage language classes. In R. Bailey and S. R. Schecter (eds.), *Language Socialization in Bilingual and Multilingual Societies* (pp. 128–146). Clevendon, UK: Multilingual Matters.

Heath, S. B. (1983). *Ways with Words: Language, Life and Work in Communities and Classrooms*. Cambridge: Cambridge University Press.

Howard, K. M. (2009). Breaking in and spinning out: repetition and de-calibration in Thai children's play genres. *Language in Society*, 38(3), 339–363.

Kulick, D. and Schieffelin, B. B. (2004). Language socialization. In A. Duranti (ed.), *A Companion to Linguistic Anthropology* (pp. 349–368). Malden, MA: Blackwell.

Lemke, J. L. (1990). *Talking Science: Language, Learning, and Values*. Norwood, NJ: Ablex Pub. Corp.

Mead, G. H. (1934). *Mind, Self, and Society: From the Standpoint of a Social Behaviorist*. Chicago, IL: University of Chicago Press.

Mehan, H. (1979). 'What time is it, Denise?": asking known information questions in classroom discourse. *Theory into Practice*, 18(4), 285–294.

Ochs, E. (1990). Indexicality and socialization. In J. W. Stigler, R. A. Schweder, and G. Herdt (eds.), *Cultural Psychology: Essays on Comparative Human Development* (pp. 287–308). Cambridge: Cambridge University Press.

Ochs, E. and Taylor, C. (1996). The "father knows best" dynamic in family dinner narratives. In K. Hall and M. Bucholtz (eds.), *Gender Articulated: Language and the Socially Constructed Self* (pp. 97–120). New York, NY: Routledge.

Rampton, B. (2005). *Crossing: Language and Ethnicity among Adolescents*. Northampton, MA: Longman.

Rampton, B. (2006). *Language in Late Modernity: Interaction in an Urban School*. Cambridge: Cambridge University Press.

Rymes, B. R. (2008). The relationship between mass media and classroom discourse. *Working Papers in Educational Linguistics*, 23(1), 65–88.

Rymes, B. R. (2010). Communicative repertoires and English language learners. In M. Shatz and L. C. Wilkinson (eds.), *The Education of English Language Learners: Research to Practice* (1st ed.) (pp. 177–197). New York, NY: Guilford Press.

Rymes, B. R. (2014). *Communicating beyond Language: Everyday Encounters with Diversity*. New York, NY: Routledge.

Rymes, B. R. (2016). *Classroom Discourse Analysis: A Tool for Critical reflection, Revised 2nd Ed*. New York, NY: Routledge.

Rymes, B., and Leone, A. R. (2014). Citizen sociolinguistics: a new media methodology for understanding language and social life. *Working Papers in Educational Linguistics*, 29(2), 25–43.

Schieffelin, B. B. (1990). *The Give and Take of Everyday Life: Language, Socialization of Kaluli Children*. Cambridge: Cambridge University Press.

Schieffelin, B. B., and Ochs, E. (1986). Language socialization. *Annual Review of Anthropology*, 15, 163–191.

Tommasini, A. (2010). Counterpoint. www.nytimes.com/video/arts/1247468479041/counterpoint.html [Accessed June 23, 2017].

8 Negotiating Epistemic Authority and Co-Constructing Difference
Socializing "Nonnative Speaker" Teachers in a US Graduate Program in TESOL

Debra A. Friedman

8.1 Introduction

The field of Teaching English to Speakers of Other Languages (TESOL) conceptualizes language teacher education as a dialogue between the received knowledge of the profession, embodied in theories of second language (L2) acquisition and teaching methodology, and the commonsense knowledge that newcomers to TESOL classrooms have acquired from prior experiences as language users, learners, or teachers (e.g., Freeman and Johnson, 1998; Singh and Richards, 2009; Wright, 2010). Through engaging critically with research articles and reflecting on and questioning their own beliefs and teaching practices, teacher-learners are expected to acquire a body of disciplinary knowledge; to appropriate discipline-specific ways of thinking and talking about language, learning, and teaching; and to integrate both into their developing teaching practice (Hedgcock, 2002; Wright, 2010).

Yet this dialogue can also be a site for negotiation and contestation over the relative value of different kinds of knowledge (e.g., theoretical vs. practical) and the right to claim authority in key knowledge domains (e.g., Freeman and Johnson, 1998; Singh and Richards, 2009). One point of tension within TESOL has revolved around what counts as "knowledge about language" and who can claim access to this knowledge (Freeman and Johnson, 1998; Hedgcock, 2002). This issue is especially consequential for international TESOL students, who as "nonnative speakers" (NNSs) may be positioned (or position themselves) as less knowledgeable about English than their "native speaker" (NS) classmates and thus be constrained from full participation in classroom practices (e.g., Hedgcock, 2002; Morita, 2004; Singh and Richards, 2009) and from full recognition as TESOL professionals (Brutt-Griffler and Samimy, 1999, 2001; Doerr, 2009; Motha, 2006).

This chapter takes a language socialization approach to explore negotiation of "epistemic authority" (i.e., the right to claim certain kinds of knowledge) in language-focused TESOL classroom discourse as a locus for socializing "NS" and "NNS" newcomers into social identities as language teachers. Drawing

158

from data collected during an ethnographic case study of four international students during their first semester in an MA TESOL program at a US university, it focuses on two episodes in which students negotiated instructors' positioning of them as "NNSs" with limited knowledge of English in order to speak from positions of epistemic authority. I situate these episodes within discourses in circulation in TESOL that posit different competencies for "NS" and "NNS" teachers (Brutt-Griffler and Samimy, 1999; Doerr, 2009; Holliday, 2008) and consider their potential effects on students' socialization into distinct social identities as "NS teachers" and "NNS teachers" whose claims of expertise draw from different knowledge domains.

8.2   Background

8.2.1   Epistemic Authority, Classroom Discourse, and Language Socialization

Classrooms represent productive sites for the study of epistemic authority as they are typically viewed as spaces where such authority is largely predetermined by asymmetries of knowledge and power between "knowers" (teachers) and "unknowers" (students) and organized through discourse structures that allow teachers to determine what stances are made available to students and how these stances are evaluated (Jaffe, 2009). However, older children and adults bring to the classroom their expertise acquired from prior socialization experiences as well as established social identities as members of other communities and thus may have both the means and desire to exercise agency over their own socialization and to resist stances and identities that are institutionally ascribed to them (e.g., Duff, 2002; Duff and Anderson, 2015; Talmy, 2015; see also Cekaite, Chapter 6 in this volume). In addition, multicultural classrooms such as those featured in this study bring together individuals with diverse linguistic, social, and cultural backgrounds, thus creating an environment in which students may be positioned along a continuum as more or less "knowing" in a particular knowledge domain relative to each other and leading to diverse socialization outcomes, including possible exclusion from full community membership (e.g., Duff, 2002; Duff and Anderson, 2015). The study of classroom discourse can therefore contribute to ongoing discussions in language socialization regarding the nature of competence (e.g., Garrett and Baquedano-López, 2002) and expert-novice roles in socializing interactions (e.g., Lee and Bucholtz, 2015; Ochs and Scheiffelin, 2011).

Language socialization provides a rich theoretical and analytical framework for examining the situated, contingent, and ideological nature of expertise in classroom discourse (e.g., Jacoby and Gonzales, 1991; Lee and Bucholtz, 2015) and the role of epistemic stance-taking in mediating social identity (e.g., Ochs 1993, 1996). Part of the process of becoming a member of a community involves developing awareness of indexical meanings of linguistic signs as resources for performing social acts and enacting affective and epistemic stances that constitute community-recognized social identities (Ochs, 1993, 1996). Through what Ochs (1996, p. 417) calls "indexical valences" that create linkages across situational dimensions, ways of speaking and acting that index stance come to be associated with particular subject positions; for example, a social act involving use of metalanguage (e.g., identifying a noun phrase as a *direct object*) can index an epistemic stance as a "knower" about grammar, which can in turn index an identity as a language teacher. Conversely, claiming an identity as a language teacher involves performing social acts (e.g., explaining grammar rules) that entail demonstrating facility in certain ways of knowing and talking about language. As they participate in socializing interactions involving language-mediated displays of expertise, newcomers construct associations between particular ways of acting and speaking and particular identities (Ochs, 1996).

With its focus on the social and cultural underpinnings of everyday talk, a language socialization approach can also inform analyses of classroom discourse by foregrounding the regimes of knowledge that regulate classroom discourse at the microlevel and how these are bound up with discourses and ideologies operating at the macrosocial level (Duff and Anderson, 2015; Lee and Bucholtz, 2015; Ochs and Schieffelin, 2011). Although language socialization researchers have highlighted the fluidity of expertise within interaction (e.g., Jacoby and Gonzales, 1991), they have also recognized that claims of epistemic authority are mediated by power relationships that can constrain individual agency to take up certain stances or resist stances ascribed by others (Ochs and Schieffelin, 2011; see also Jaffe, 2009; Riley, 2011). As Ochs and Schieffelin (2011) have noted, the concept of experts socializing novices that is central to language socialization is predicated on asymmetries of knowledge and bound up with regimes of power and authority that favor certain kinds of knowledge as "ratified" (p. 6). For example, "ratified knowledge" in TESOL includes competency in Standard English, a variety spoken by an educated White elite from "Inner Circle" countries (e.g., Britain, North America) (Krachu, 1992). Restricting linguistic expertise to a single language variety marginalizes those who do not control this way of speaking (e.g., speakers of "nonnative" varieties) or who occupy identity categories (e.g., "Asian") perceived as incompatible with it (Motha, 2006).

8.2.2   *Epistemic Authority and "Nonnative Speakers" in TESOL*

Claiming authority as a TESOL professional in part involves demonstrating expertise in its subject matter, the English language. However, the nature of that expertise, who can claim it, and its relative value vis-à-vis other types of knowledge (e.g., how to translate linguistic knowledge into accessible lessons) is contentious (e.g., Freeman and Johnson, 1998; Hedgcock, 2002) and has contributed to an ongoing debate regarding the relative status of NS and NNS teachers within the profession (Moussu and Llurda, 2008).

The TESOL profession has traditionally granted authority to NS teachers on matters of language based on a belief that acquiring a language "naturally" as a first language (L1) from birth endows individuals with linguistic expertise (i.e., "NS intuition") not available to L2 speakers regardless of proficiency (e.g., Doerr, 2009; Rampton, 1990). However, over the past 30 years this belief has been subject to reappraisal, with questions about its relevance for teaching and arguments over its scientific validity. In a critique of the English teaching industry, Phillipson (1992) attacked "the native speaker fallacy" (p. 195) as a myth and argued that the competencies required of language teachers (e.g., language proficiency, cultural knowledge, teaching skills) can be acquired by NNSs. Others have declared the NS to be an ideological construct with little basis in reality and that the terms "NS" and "NNS" reference social categories in which membership is ascribed based on national origin (e.g., American), race (e.g., White), and subjective judgments of accent rather than objective criteria of linguistic competence (e.g., Brutt-Griffler and Samimy, 1999, 2001; Cook, 1999; Doerr, 2009; Holliday, 2008; Motha, 2006; Rampton, 1990). Critics have noted that the term "native speaker" is ill defined (Davies, 2003) and that capabilities said to characterize "NS competence" (e.g., fluency, ability to judge grammaticality) are not possessed equally by all NSs and may also be possessed by NNSs (Cook, 1999; Rampton, 1990). They further observe that NS competence is generally understood as competence in Standard English, and thus implicated in a post-colonialist project to ensure Inner Circle dominance over English language norms (e.g., Brutt-Griffler and Samimy, 2001; Motha, 2006; Phillipson, 1992).

Yet despite these critiques, the perception of an unequal status between NS and NNS teachers persists (see Moussu and Llurda, 2008), although it sometimes takes more subtle forms. Brutt-Griffler and Samimy (1999) have noted what they call the "difference approach" to NNS teachers in TESOL that emphasizes their positive attributes, such as providing models of successful L2 learning, explicit knowledge of the target language grammatical system, and ability to empathize with learners' struggles and identify their potential difficulties that compensate for their alleged linguistic deficiencies (e.g., see Medgyes, 1992). This approach has been seen as a means of countering the idealization of the NS teacher and opposing discrimination against NNS teachers and legitimating them as competent professionals. However, it has also been criticized as failing to address assumptions of NSs' linguistic superiority and "ownership" of English, thus reifying rather than challenging deficit discourses and contributing to the othering of NNS teachers (Brutt-Griffler and Samimy, 1999; Doerr, 2009; Holliday, 2008).

Language socialization research in TESOL classrooms has shown how deficit discourses interact with other identity categories to shape international students' ability to claim epistemic authority. In her study of MA TESOL students' socialization into doing oral presentations, Morita (2000) found that by drawing on other sources of knowledge (e.g., experience as learners or teachers), international students were able to overcome their presumed lack of linguistic competence and successfully negotiate epistemic authority with a (sometimes skeptical) audience to claim status as "knowers" of the texts they were presenting. Similarly, Ho's (2011) analysis of small group discussions in a TESOL methods course revealed how teaching experience, which all of the international students but few of the American students had, served as the primary resource for successful knowledge claims, thus allowing international students to position themselves as "experts" relative to their classmates.

However, other research has shown how ascribed identities as NNSs can limit international students' ability to participate in their academic community. In a longitudinal case study of female Japanese graduate students in Canada, Morita (2002, 2004) chronicled the experiences of two MA TESOL students, who, despite being seasoned English teachers, encountered difficulty negotiating epistemic authority in the program. Both expressed concerns about being viewed as less competent because of their "nonnative" English, a concern that was sometimes reinforced by instructors who commented negatively on their language proficiency. These concerns led them to withdraw from class discussions, although one of the two later began to question the deficit discourses behind the "NNS" label and to transform her own self-identification. Cho (2013), drawing from interviews with three Korean MA TESOL students in the United States, similarly made connections between students' varying degrees of success in integrating into their program communities and their ability to challenge their positioning as "NNSs" by demonstrating competence in English. However, she also noted the limits of this ability; for example, despite strong language skills, one participant found that her status as an "NNS" prevented her from obtaining an internship in the university's ESL program as part of her practicum.

This research has highlighted how the discourses and practices of the TESOL classroom interact with other factors, such as prior socialization experiences and perceptions of international students as less competent speakers of English, to facilitate or constrain students' ability to negotiate epistemic authority and challenge positioning as unknowers (see also Duff and Anderson, 2015). Yet although these studies have been critical of discourses that marginalize international students, they have not directly interrogated the underlying assumptions of the NNS construct itself and its potential effects on students' socialization into membership in the TESOL community outside of the classroom.

8.3   The Study

In common with much language socialization research, this study adopted an ethnographic approach that triangulated multiple sources of data (i.e., classroom observation and audio recording, interviews, collection of texts) and involved both micro and macro levels of analysis (e.g., Garrett and Baquedano-López, 2002; Ochs and Schieffelin, 2011). These data allowed me to construct a multilayered picture of the practices, ideologies, and social identities into which students were being socialized at the classroom level and how these were shaped by values operating at the level of the program and TESOL/applied linguistics communities.

8.3.1   Setting

The applied linguistics program of which the MA TESOL program was a part was housed in a linguistics department and also offered an undergraduate minor in TESOL and a Ph.D. in applied linguistics. The primary goal of the MA TESOL program was to prepare students to teach English as a second/ foreign language (ESL/EFL); however, it also aimed to enable students to ground teaching practice in theory and research and to prepare them for possible further graduate study. This dual focus was reflected in required coursework in linguistics, L2 acquisition, and research methods as well as teaching methodology and in program learning outcomes such as "understand and interpret current research as it applies to language teaching" (MA Student Handbook).

The teaching methods courses, TESL 515 and TESL 517,[1] that are the locus of this study were taken by MA TESOL students during their first semester and served as entry points into multiple communities of practice, including the program, graduate school, the TESOL profession, and the discipline of applied linguistics. Each course had two sections that met once a week for two and a half hours. Both instructors, Karen (TESL 515) and Jessie (TESL 517), spoke English as an L1 and had doctorates in applied linguistics and experience teaching ESL/EFL. TESL 515 was designed to prepare students for a practicum in which they worked in pairs to teach conversation courses for adult learners and focused on practical skills such as lesson planning, managing classroom interaction, and giving feedback. TESL 517 emphasized theory and developing students' ability to "read, understand, and think critically about current research pertaining to teaching methods and language teaching techniques to inform curriculum development" (TESL 517 syllabus). Both courses also aimed to introduce students to the TESOL field and to graduate-level academic discourse practices. For example, TESL 515 students kept notebooks of new terms they encountered in their academic reading, an assignment that Karen explained as helping them to gain deeper understandings of key concepts and avoid "us[ing] buzz words without really understanding what they mean" (Karen Interview). In TESL 517 Jessie scaffolded students' participation in whole-class discussions of research articles, pushing them to "think outside the bo:x (.) what else could the researchers have do:ne? ... What problems lie in the article that they don't really explain but you can uncover" (Jessie Interview).

8.3.2 Participants

Students in these classrooms largely overlapped; however, TESL 517 included four doctoral students not in TESL 515. The majority were female (75 percent) and international (60 percent in TESL 515, 70 percent in TESL 517). Four students from various Asian countries, three women (Flo, Linin, and Allie) and one man (Sy), volunteered as focal participants.[2] Although a convenience sample, they were representative of their cohort in terms of gender and region of origin (75 percent of the international students came from Asia; the remainder were from South America and Eastern Europe).

Two students, Sy and Flo, feature in the episodes in this chapter. Both had limited teaching experience (Flo had taken a five-month TESOL certificate course and taught English for a year in her home country; Sy had briefly taught his L1 as a foreign language) and were newcomers to US academia who had learned English as a foreign language. However, they positioned themselves differently regarding English expertise. Sy was confident about his English proficiency and seemed reluctant to adopt the NNS label, instead referring to himself in interviews as an "international student." His undergraduate major in English literature had given him considerable experience reading and writing in English, and he self-identified as a good writer who never sought help from the writing center or peers; comments that he received on assignments (e.g., "very well written") confirmed this self-assessment. Although he admitted struggling with assigned readings, he attributed this to his newcomer status in the TESOL/applied linguistics field rather than to English proficiency. In contrast, in interviews Flo frequently referred to herself as a nonnative speaker (NNS) and spoke from this position on assignments; for example, when evaluating a technique for teaching pronunciation she noted that it "could be demanding for nonnative teachers to teach" (Flo Article Presentation, TESL 517). She felt that writing was her weakest skill; she regularly went to the writing center for help with grammar and said that she appreciated the corrective feedback she received on written assignments. She also reported difficulty with readings, but unlike Sy she identified insufficient English vocabulary knowledge as one source of the problem.

8.3.3   Data Collection

The primary source of data comprises 38 hours of audio recordings and fieldnotes collected during teacher-fronted lessons[3] in both sections of TESL 515 and TESL 517. Although I was not a participant observer, I am an applied linguist and TESOL professional, and my insider status facilitated access to the classrooms and gave me insights into the culture of this academic community and the research and professional communities in which it was embedded. To triangulate my interpretations of socializing interactions, I interviewed each instructor at the end of the semester about her expectations for the course and the purpose of assignments and class activities and collected syllabi, assignment sheets, and handouts.

However, as a White professor, experienced ESL/EFL instructor, researcher, and L1 English speaker, I occupy a privileged position within the TESOL/ applied linguistics community that contrasted with the peripheral positions of the focal students and limited my ability to understand their lived experiences as newcomers and "NNSs." In an effort to bridge this gap, I interviewed each focal student at the beginning, middle, and end of the semester (approximately 45 minutes each) to discuss their expectations upon entering the program, what they were learning in their coursework, and whether the program was addressing their needs. These interviews have allowed me to incorporate voices and perspectives of focal students as individual social actors, each of whom brought a unique set of beliefs and experiences to the classroom, and to consider how these beliefs and experiences shaped their participation in classroom interactions.

8.3.4   Data Analysis

Research assistants provided rough transcriptions of audio-recorded data, which I used to identify episodes in which students' identities as "NSs" or "NNSs" were made relevant either explicitly (e.g., through use of these terms) or implicitly (e.g., asking "students from foreign countries" whether MA TESOL programs should provide English language support). I then prepared more detailed transcripts[4] of these episodes and analyzed them using a microanalytic approach informed by conversation analysis (CA), which is often used in language socialization research to enable a detailed and empirically grounded account of socializing interactions as they unfold moment-by-moment in talk (e.g., Garrett and Baquedano-López, 2002; Lee and Bucholtz, 2015). Attention to sequences of talk has allowed me to trace how claims of language expertise were co-constructed across turns and the extent to which students took up, resisted, or negotiated the epistemic stances and social identities that instructors ascribed to them.

The analysis is also informed by CA work on "epistemic status," defined as "the relative access to some [knowledge] domain of two (or more) persons at some point in time" (Heritage, 2012, p. 4). Although claims of epistemic status as "knowers" relative to a particular topic are subject to negotiation, validation, and contestation among co-participants, successful claims may also depend on external factors such as "the person's rights to know it in the first place [and] socially-sanctioned authority to know it" (Heritage, 2012, p. 5). Heritage (2012) further notes that some sources of epistemic status may be favored over others. For example, in MA TESOL programs, knowledge derived from empirical research tends to be valued over experiential knowledge derived from teaching practice (e.g., Freeman and Johnson, 1998). Although CA work on epistemic status is more concerned with how epistemic asymmetries structure interaction than with interrogating issues of power, the concept provides a useful heuristic for investigating how ascribed identities as NSs or NNSs support or undermine students' "rights and authority" to certain knowledge domains.

The episodes to be analyzed below involve performance of a social act, correcting language errors, that is associated with a language teacher identity and that entails claims of expertise regarding grammar. In selecting episodes from both classrooms that occurred at different points during the semester and involved different participants, I hope to illustrate how negotiations over students' epistemic status regarding language, although co-constructed in local interactional contexts, were also grounded in regimes of knowledge that operated across the program. In these episodes, multiple ways of knowing English – descriptive grammars of everyday usage, prescriptive grammars that govern formal usage, and explicit knowledge of grammar rules – were made relevant for membership in the TESOL/applied linguistics community. However, instructors unevenly attributed access to these ways of knowing in ways that shaped students' opportunities to take stances as knowers in classroom talk and naturalized the categories of "NS" and "NNS" as referencing functionally distinct users of English.

8.4   Negotiating Expertise

Officially the program made no distinction between American and international students; all took the same coursework, shared teaching duties equally in the practicum, and were eligible to teach in the department's Intensive English Program. However, tacit support for the existence of a dichotomy between NSs and NNSs was evident in the ways that faculty uncritically used both terms and in a departmental research culture that treated monolingual NS norms as a benchmark for measuring L2 acquisition. I never observed Karen or Jessie refer to individual students as "NSs" or "NNSs" or problematize students' language use in class. However, both routinely used the terms to refer to categories of students and linked these categories to different levels and types of expertise regarding knowledge of English. On the one hand, they represented NNSs as possessing superior metalinguistic knowledge (e.g., grammar terminology) as a result of learning English through formal instruction; for example, when students did an exercise in which they had to write sentences to illustrate terms such as "gerunds" and "phrasal verbs," Jessie advised them, "If you don't know [what the term means] ask one of the nonnative speakers because they probably do ... cuz they've learned it already" (TESL 517 Transcript). However, instructors also positioned them as deficient in other areas of language, such as vocabulary, colloquial language, and implicit (intuitive) knowledge of grammar.

8.4.1 Episode 1: "What's the Error?"

Literacy practices in the MA TESOL program included adherence to conventions of the *Publication Manual of the American Psychological Association* (2010), which are followed by most TESOL/applied linguistics journals and commonly referred to as "APA style." In the following episode in TESL 515 in mid-September, Karen presented an activity about what she characterized as "prescriptive grammar rules"[5] of APA style to introduce students to norms to be followed in their written work. She began by taking contrary stances toward what constitutes correct grammar that were grounded in different sources of epistemic authority: the descriptive grammar of everyday usage and the prescriptive grammar exemplified in APA style. After observing that APA grammar rules may be "really surprising to native speakers," Karen projected two sentences on a screen, describing them as "perfectly fine ... if you wro:te them nobody would probably ca:re," but adding, "but if you look at the APA manual each of them has a grammatical e:rror." She then invited students to align with her second stance and positioned them as potential knowers by directing them to "figure out what the error is."

In juxtaposing these perspectives, Karen encouraged students to shift their orientation on grammar from that of everyday users (for whom the sentences were "perfectly fine") to that of members of a disciplinary community that follows APA prescriptive rules. However, in attributing the affective stance of "surprise" regarding these rules exclusively to NSs, Karen ascribed to them a privileged epistemic status regarding (intuitive) language knowledge against which such rules can be compared. By naturalizing "NS intuition" as the basis for stance-taking toward the acceptability of a sentence, she ascribed a lesser epistemic status to the international students and implicitly questioned their right and authority to take such stances.

In Excerpt 8.1, Karen then called on volunteers to identify the error in the first sentence (see Text 8.1), which violates a rule stipulating *which* for nonrestrictive relative clauses and *that* for restrictive relative clauses (APA, 2010, p. 83).

Text 8.1
The students which were placed in the control group were not higher in language proficiency than those students in the two experimental groups.

Excerpt 8.1 What's the Error?

```
01  Karen:  Yeah u:m okay Annie what about the first one.
02  Annie:  Should it be the students who were placed?
03  Karen:  ((looks at sentence)) (1.3)
04          U::m (.) that would be (.) one option yeah. There's another option Rick?
05          (0.5)
06  Rick:   The students placed in?
07  Karen:  ((looks at sentence)) (1.0)
08  Rick:   The students placed in the control group-
09  Karen:  Well you could do that as we:ll there's a- but what's the er- there's an
10          actual e:rror. I mean those are both ways that would make it- that would
11          get rid of the error? but what's the error.
12          (0.4)
13  Karen:  What is the error itself.
            ((lines 14–21 omitted; another student identifies a problem with the
            sentence))
22  Karen:  No that's okay ac[tually yeah
23  Sy:                     [There should be a comma after students?
24  Karen:  ((looks at sentence)) (1.0)
25          Okay you're fixing it again not really okay if its- okay here's the thing.
26          (.) according to APA manual (.) if it's a restrictive relative cla:use (.) you
27          have to use that. Or who. Oka:y? You can't use which.
```

The first responses come from two American students, Annie (line 02) and Rick (lines 06 and 08), who attempt to claim status as knowers of two rules: (a) a preference in prescriptive grammars for *who* over *which* when referring to people (Annie) and (b) optional deletion of the relative pronoun and *be* in some relative clause constructions (Rick). Karen partially ratifies these claims as "ways ... that would get rid of the error" (lines 10–11). However, rather than closing the sequence as would be expected upon receipt of a correct response, she continues to pursue answers, thus indicating that these responses are insufficient. The problem seems to lie in a mismatch between how the students have oriented to the task and Karen's expectations regarding what kind of language knowledge is relevant. The students have located a potential problem with the relative clause and repaired it, thus indicating their understanding of the task as requiring them to make a correction. Karen, however, has asked them to "figure out what the error is," that is, to state which rule has been violated, a routine practice in the TESOL community in which a professional identity is indexed in part through the social act of drawing on metalinguistic knowledge to explain grammar rules to learners. With her question, "but what's the error" (line 11), Karen attempts to reorient students to speak from this teacher perspective and to ground their epistemic authority in APA-sanctioned grammar rules rather than their knowledge as language users.

Nevertheless, the next response (unclear on the recording) appears to correct another part of the sentence, and Karen negatively evaluates it on the grounds that the problem it proposes to fix is not a problem (line 22). At this point, Sy self-selects (line 23) and adds his voice to a discussion that thus far has involved only Karen and several American students. He thus engages in a social act, evaluating and correcting English usage, that seems inconsistent with the epistemic status implicitly ascribed to NNSs in Karen's prior talk and claims epistemic authority equal to that of his American classmates. Like Annie and Rick, Sy targets the relative clause as the source of the problem, but shifts the relevant knowledge domain from grammar to punctuation (i.e., relative clauses with *which* require a comma). Karen's consideration of Sy's response (line 24) ratifies his right to speak on this matter, and her use of "again" represents Sy's action ("fixing" the sentence) as equivalent to those of his "NS" classmates (line 25). However, in contrast with Karen's acceptance of Annie's and Rick's corrections as possible options, Sy's correction is rejected ("not really"). As Karen later explains, inserting a comma would change the restrictive relative clause to a nonrestrictive relative clause and alter the meaning of the sentence (omitted from this transcript).

It is unclear whether students' failure to accomplish the desired shift in perspective resulted from their inability to explain this grammar rule or inability to understand what Karen wanted. Karen's next turn (lines 25–27) addresses both possibilities, as she models an appropriate response to her question and an appropriate way of talking about grammar, including use of terminology such as "restrictive relative clause" (line 26) that is part of the metadiscourse and ratified knowledge of TESOL (Hedgcock, 2002).

Although he was unsuccessful in displaying the type of expertise that Karen was seeking, Sy accurately identified a problem with the relative pronoun and displayed knowledge of an APA (2010) rule, although it was not the appropriate rule to apply in this case. That is, his performance was essentially equivalent to those of his (also unsuccessful) "NS" peers, and he was recognized as a contributor to a discussion that was otherwise dominated by his American classmates. However, this recognition took place in an interactional context that privileged an epistemic domain ("learned" knowledge of prescriptive rules) that is theoretically available to "NNSs" over one that ostensibly is not

("NS intuition"). Sy's negotiation of epistemic authority therefore did not challenge Karen's assertion of "NS" superiority in matters of English usage generally, but was consistent with the discourse of difference that accords epistemic authority to NNSs within a limited set of knowledge domains, thus allowing Sy to speak from his recognized social identity as a "good writer" and knower of prescriptive rules governing academic English writing.

8.4.2   Episode 2: "Is That Hard to Find?"

The second episode arose in TESL 517 two months later (in early November) as Jessie was guiding students through a discussion of a research article (Chandler, 2003) that examined how different types of written error correction affected learners' revisions. The study found that "direct correction" (i.e., teacher corrects the error) and "underlining only" (i.e., teacher underlines the error) generated significantly more learner corrections than did "underline and describe" and "description only," with "description only" (i.e., teacher describes how to correct the error, but does not specify its location) being least effective. To get students to think critically about these results, Jessie directed them to examples of "description only" and took a stance toward the difficulty of finding errors under this condition, noting, "it's hard for a native speaker to go through there and find- oka::y you have to really think about it." In stressing "native speaker," Jessie implicitly contrasted the epistemic status of NSs with that of the learners in the study as a possible explanation for the ineffectiveness of "description only" (i.e., finding the errors would be difficult even for NSs). However, similar to the previous episode from TESL 515, she limits this expertise to a category of English users that excluded international students, thus implicitly questioning these students' epistemic status as knowers of English and their authority to identify and correct errors in learners' writing.

In Excerpt 8.2a, Jessie then challenged students to find the errors in the examples, in effect asking them to take the perspective of learners trying to make use of the feedback. This excerpt focuses on the second example (see Text 8.2), which had the description "delete" in the margin.

Text 8.2
(delete) Although the method hadn't worked yet, but I decided to try once more anyhow. (Chandler, 2003, p. 282)

Excerpt 8.2a Is That Hard to Find?

01 Jessie: What should get deleted?
02 Student 1: But
03 Jessie: But. Yeah you should delete but. Is that hard to find?

04	Ss:	*((slight laughter))*

04 Ss: *((slight laughter))*
05 Student 2:   (Yeah it's very hard)
06 Jessie: Ye:s especially the nonnative speakers are <u>l</u>aughing like, HA how
07   would I have ever found that right? And you're <u>su</u>per advanced
08   you're not le:arners you're u:sers of the language right? So (.) I think
09   it makes sense that one's really difficult.

The ease with which an unidentified student[6] answers the question "What should get deleted?" (lines 01–02) undermines Jessie's stance toward this task as difficult. Nevertheless, even as she validates this answer, Jessie continues to pursue agreement with her initial assessment (line 03). In response, several students laugh (line 04), and another student appears to align with Jessie (line 05; this hearing is uncertain). The meaning of the laughter is ambiguous, and following Student 1's demonstration that the error is not "hard to find," Student 2's words could be meant ironically. Regardless, Jessie construes both responses as alignment as evidenced by the "yes" with which she indexes agreement with Student 2 (line 06) and her characterization of the laughter. Using "like" to mark what follows as hypothetical reported speech (Romaine and Lange, 1991; see also Moore, Chapter 4 in this volume), she "animates" (Goffman, 1981) the "nonnative speakers" in the class as expressing incredulity that they would be able to locate the error ("HA how would I ever have found that," lines 06–07). Jessie thus claims access to an epistemic domain presumed to lie outside the scope of a speaker's knowledge, the thoughts of others that, with one possible exception (line 05), have not been openly expressed (Heritage, 2012). Through this ascription, she makes explicit the distinction between NSs and NNSs implied by her earlier statement, suggesting that although the task of error identification might be "hard" for NSs, it may be impossible for NNSs. She also blurs distinctions between the international students and the learners in Chandler (2003), classifying them as co-members of a homogenous group and reproducing views of NNSs as eternal language learners who will never achieve full language expertise (Brutt-Griffler and Samimy, 2001; Cook, 1999). Although Jessie somewhat repairs this representation to reposition these students as "super advanced" and as "users" rather than "learners" (lines 07–08), she nevertheless ascribes to them a status as unknowers on matters of correct usage relative to their American classmates.

Following a brief exchange about whether "description only" might work if the description were closer to the error, in Excerpt 8.2b (a continuation of Excerpt 8.2a) Jessie takes a stance toward "underline and description" as a superior form of error correction and moves to close this topic. Before she can do so, however, Flo enters the discussion.

Excerpt 8.2b Is That Hard to Find?
Continuation of Excerpt 8.2a
((lines 10-13 omitted))

14 Jessie: Yeah yeah or point it out (.) something like that. The underline and
15   description is much more clear. Right? Mm-hm. So it makes sense.
16   (.)
17 Jessie: Yeah.
18 Flo: Despite of the results of that result
19 Jessie: Uh-huh.
20 Flo: I still have a question about- between the underline and descri:be and (.)
21   just underline.
22 Jessie: Mm-hm?
23 Flo: Because they are so similar.
24 Jessie: Yeah.
25 Flo: Results are so different.
26 Jessie: Right. And they found the underline actually:
27 Flo: Ye:ah
28 Jessie: resulted in (.)
29 Flo: Yeah. [And for- for me: as a nonnative speaker, I think the underline and
30 Jessie: [fewer errors.
31 Flo: describe is (0.3) be:tter *((slight laugh))* [than just underlining (.) because
32 Jessie: [Uh-huh.
33 Flo: (0.3) i- underlining is so difficult? [to figure out?
34 Jessie: [Right right
35 Flo: to figure out?

As Flo takes the floor following Jessie's go-ahead (line 17), she takes a questioning stance toward another study result – the number of revisions generated by "underlining only" versus "underline and describe" (lines 23, 25), simultaneously aligning with Jessie's stance toward the preferability of "underline and description" and disaligning with Jessie's claim that the study findings "make sense." Jessie ratifies both Flo's right to speak and her stance by agreeing with her (lines 24, 26), and they co-construct a consensus that although some results (i.e., ineffectiveness of "description only") may "make sense," others (i.e., effectiveness of "underlining only" vs. "underlining with description") may not (lines 23–30).

Flo then makes explicit the subject position from which she enacts this stance – that of the "nonnative speaker" (line 29) – embracing both the social identity and its associations with limited linguistic competence (i.e., individuals who would have difficulty identifying an error without a description) that Jessie had earlier ascribed to the international students. However, she reconfigures this identity from a liability to an asset, positioning herself as someone qualified to comment on this issue because she shares the perspective of the language learners in the study. In drawing on her personal experience as an L2 writer,

Flo claims epistemic status as a knower in a domain unavailable to her American classmates (and to Jessie): insider knowledge about what learners might find challenging and what method of correction they might prefer. Evidence of her success in repositioning herself from an unknower about grammar to a knower about learners comes in the coda to this exchange (omitted here) in which Jessie agrees with Flo's position that these results are puzzling and suggests that Flo investigate this issue in her thesis, thus transforming a hypothesis based on personal experience into the empirical findings that comprise ratified knowledge within the TESOL/applied linguistics research community.

Flo was able to negotiate her initial positioning and claim the right to speak in part by performing two social identities that were valued in this classroom: the "good student" who has read and understood the article, and the "critical reader" who does not simply accept but questions its results. Yet she did so by accepting her positioning as a relative unknower about English grammar and using it as a resource to speak as an L2 writer with the right and authority to evaluate the effectiveness of written feedback. In doing so, she reproduced the discourse of difference that argues for "NNS" teachers' epistemic authority over "NS" teachers in matters related to understanding language learners.

8.5   Conclusion

These episodes illustrate how the instructors in TESL 515 and 517 sought to socialize newcomers into valued practices (e.g., explaining grammar rules, taking critical stances toward research findings) and ratified knowledge (e.g., APA style) of the program and TESOL/applied linguistics communities by scaffolding their participation in whole-class discussions, providing opportunities for them to display their expertise, and evaluating their knowledge claims. Yet as they were socializing students into social identities as competent language teachers, instructors clearly construed this competence differently for "NSs" and "NNSs," ascribing to them unequal epistemic status regarding knowledge of English. By routinely positioning "NSs" as having an inherent right to a knowledge domain ("NS intuition") that is by definition inaccessible to "NNSs," instructors conferred on NSs an authority that NNSs can never achieve and contributed to the reification of these deficit discourses.

As adult learners with expertise derived from prior experiences as English language learners and users, Sy and Flo were able to negotiate their epistemic status so that their voices could be heard and acknowledged. However, in drawing upon identities as "good writers" with knowledge of punctuation (Sy) or "L2 writers" with knowledge of learners' perspectives (Flo), they spoke from subject positions made available through a discourse of difference that grants NNSs epistemic authority in certain knowledge domains (e.g., prescriptive grammar rules, L2 learners' difficulties). And although instructors validated these students' right to speak as "experts" from these subject positions, they nevertheless continued to position "NNSs" as less competent in other areas of English language knowledge. Through interactions such as those illustrated in this chapter, instructors and students participated in the co-construction of difference (Duff, 2002) that reproduced and naturalized the existence of a dichotomy between NSs and NNSs and perpetuated ideologies of NS dominance in matters of language use, thus socializing students into separate identities as "NS" or "NNS" teachers whose competencies lay in distinct epistemic domains.

Taking a language socialization approach to the study of classroom discourse has drawn attention to the ways in which competence and expertise, although locally constructed in interaction, are also embedded in larger cultural systems that may constrain individuals' ability to negotiate epistemic authority, in this case, the culture and ideologies of TESOL regarding the relative value of different ways of knowing English and the relative status of "NSs" and "NNSs" vis-à-vis this knowledge. Students' ability to take epistemic stances as "knowers" in these episodes depended in part on locating their knowledge claims within a body of ratified disciplinary knowledge (e.g., APA grammar rules). Yet it also depended on social identities as "NSs" or "NNSs" that did not appear to be based on actual knowledge displays, but ascribed a priori based on students' status as "American" or "international," that is, on "who you are" rather than "what you know" (Rampton, 1990, p. 99). It thus both reflected and reproduced discourses in circulation in TESOL regarding the rights and authority of members of these categories to claim linguistic competence and expertise (see Holliday, 2008; Motha, 2006). While international students could, and did, draw upon their expertise in other knowledge domains to negotiate their epistemic authority, they did so within the confines of these discourses.

Bringing together classroom discourse analysis and language socialization has also highlighted how routine classroom talk can contribute to the reproduction of social inequality. The socializing messages conveyed in these classrooms provided students with information on not only how to perform the acts and stances associated with an identity as a competent language teacher, but also by whom these acts and stances could be performed. In positing differential access to certain knowledge domains for different categories of persons (i.e., "NNs" and "NNSs"), instructors were socializing students into understanding the NS–NNS dichotomy as a linguistic fact rather than an ideological construction and excluding "NNS" students from full membership in a professional community defined in part by mastery of Standard English norms. As they participated in these interactions, students were being socialized into the "NS" ideologies of TESOL as well through these ideologies into distinctive ways of speaking, being, and acting in the world as future TESOL professionals.

NOTES

1 Identifying information such as course numbers and instructors' names has been changed.
2 Focal students selected their own pseudonyms. To preserve confidentiality, I have not specified countries of origin.
3 At students' request, I did not record presentations and teaching demonstrations.
4 Transcripts follow transcription conventions outlined in Jefferson (1984).
5 Unless otherwise noted, quotations come from classroom transcripts.
6 I cannot definitively determine this student's status as American or international.

REFERENCES

American Psychological Association (2010). *Publication Manual of the American Psychological Association, 6th Ed.* Washington, DC: American Psychological Association.
Brutt-Griffler, J. and Samimy, K. (1999). Revisiting the colonial in the postcolonial: critical praxis for nonnative-English-speaking teachers in a TESOL program. *TESOL Quarterly*, 33(3), 413–431.
Brutt-Griffler, J. and Samimy, K. (2001). Transcending the nativeness paradigm. *World Englishes*, 20(1), 99–106.
Chandler, J. (2003). The efficacy of various kinds of error feedback for improvement in the accuracy and fluency of L2 student writing. *Journal of Second Language Writing*, 12(3), 267–296.
Cho, S. (2013). Disciplinary enculturation experiences of three Korean students in US-based MATESOL programs. *Journal of Language, Identity, and Education*, 12(2), 136–151.
Cook, V. (1999). Going beyond the native speaker in language teaching. *TESOL Quarterly*, 33(2), 185–209.
Davies, A. (2003). *The Native Speaker: Myth and Reality*. Clevedon, UK: Multilingual Matters.
Doerr, N. M. (2009). Introduction. In N. M. Doerr (ed.), *The Native Speaker Concept: Ethnographic Investigations of Native Speaker Effects* (pp. 1–10). Berlin: Mouton de Gruyter.
Duff, P. A. (2002). The discursive co-construction of knowledge, identity, and difference: an ethnography of communication in the high school mainstream. *Applied Linguistics*, 23(3), 280–322.
Duff, P. A. and Anderson, T. (2015). Academic language and literacy socialization for second language students. In N. Markee (ed.), *The Handbook of Classroom Discourse and Interaction* (pp. 337–352). Malden, MA: Wiley.
Freeman, D. and Johnson, K. E. (1998). Reconceptualizing the knowledge-base of language teacher education. *TESOL Quarterly*, 32(3), 397–417.
Garrett, P. B. and Baquedano-López, P. (2002). Language socialization: reproduction and continuity, transformation and change. *Annual Review of Anthropology*, 31, 339–361.
Goffman, E. (1981). Footing. In E. Goffman, *Forms of Talk* (pp. 124–159). Philadelphia, PA: University of Pennsylvania Press.

Hedgcock, J. S. (2002). Toward a socioliterate approach to second language teacher education. *Modern Language Journal*, 86(3), 299–317.

Heritage, J. (2012). Epistemics in action: action formation and territories of knowledge. *Research on Language and Social Interaction*, 45(1), 1–29.

Ho, M. (2011). Academic discourse socialization through small-group discussions. *System*, 39(4), 437–450.

Holliday, A. (2008). Standards of English and politics of inclusion. *Language Teaching*, 41(1), 119–30.

Jacoby, S. and Gonzales, P. (1991). The constitution of expert–novice in scientific discourse. *Issues in Applied Linguistics*, 2(2), 149–181.

Jaffe, A. (2009). Introduction: the sociolinguistics of stance. In A. Jaffe (ed.), *Stance: Sociolinguistic Perspectives* (pp. 3–28). New Y, NY: Oxford University Press.

Jefferson, G. (1984). On the organization of laughter in talk about troubles. In J. M. Atkinson and J. Heritage (eds.), *Structures of Social Action: Studies in Conversation Analysis* (pp. 346–369). Cambridge: Cambridge University Press.

Krachu, B. (1992). *The Other Tongue: English across Cultures*. Urbana, IL: University of Illinois Press.

Lee, J. S. and Bucholtz, M. (2015). Language socialization across learning spaces. In N. Markee, (ed.), *The Handbook of Classroom Discourse and Interaction* (pp. 319–336). Malden, MA: Wiley.

Medgyes, P. (1992). Native or non-native: who's worth more? *ELT Journal*, 46(4), 340–349.

Morita, N. (2000). Discourse socialization through oral classroom activities in a TESL graduate program. *TESOL Quarterly*, 34(2), 279–210.

Morita, N. (2002). "Negotiating participation in second language academic communities: a study of identity, agency, and transformation." Unpublished doctoral dissertation, University of British Columbia, Canada. https://open.library.ubc.ca/media/download/pdf/831/1.0078209/1

Morita, N. (2004). Negotiating participation and identity in second language academic discourse communities. *TESOL Quarterly*, 38(4), 573–603.

Motha, S. (2006). Racializing ESOL teacher identities in US K-12 public schools. *TESOL Quarterly*, 40(3), 495–518.

Moussu, L. and Llurda, E. (2008). Non-native English-speaking English language teachers: history and research. *Language Teaching*, 41(3), 315–348.

Ochs, E. (1993). Constructing social identity: a language socialization perspective. *Research on Language and Social Interaction*, 26(3), 287–306.

Ochs, E. (1996). Linguistic resources for socializing humanity. In J. J. Gumperz and S. C. Levinson (eds.), *Rethinking Linguistic Relativity* (pp. 407–437). New York, NY: Cambridge University Press.

Ochs, E. and Schieffelin, B. B. (2011). The theory of language socialization. In A. Duranti, E. Ochs, and B. B. Schieffelin (eds.), *The Handbook of Language Socialization* (pp. 1–21). Malden, MA: Blackwell.

Phillipson, R. (1992). *Linguistic Imperialism*. Oxford: Oxford University Press.

Rampton, M. B. H. (1990). Displacing the "native speaker": expertise, affiliation, and inheritance. *ELT Journal*, 45(2), 97–101.

Riley, K. (2011). Language socialization and language ideologies. In A. Duranti, E. Ochs, and B. B. Schieffelin (eds.), *The Handbook of Language Socialization* (pp. 493–514). Malden, MA: Blackwell.

Romaine, S. and Lange, D. (1991). The use of like as a marker of reported speech and thought: a case of grammaticalization in progress. *American Speech*, 66(3), 227–279.

Singh, G. and Richards, J. C. (2009). Teaching and learning in the course room. In A. Burns and J. C. Richards (eds.), *Cambridge Guide to Second Language Teacher Education* (pp. 201–208). New York, NY: Cambridge University Press.

Talmy, S. (2015). A language socialization perspective on identity work of ESL youth in a superdiverse high school classroom. In N. Markee (ed.), *The Handbook of Classroom Discourse and Interaction* (pp. 353–368). Malden, MA: Wiley.

Wright, T. (2010). Second language teacher education: review of recent research on practice. *Language Teaching*, 43(3), 259–296.

Part III

Language Socialization and Ideology

9 The Morning Assembly
Constructing Subjecthood, Authority, and Knowledge through Classroom Discourse in an Indian School

Usree Bhattacharya and Laura Sterponi

9.1 Introduction

This chapter leverages insights from language socialization and critical discourse analysis to unpack the discursive shaping of subjectivity and epistemic ideology in an Indian school. We focus on a lynchpin daily event in the instructional experience of young Indian children: the Morning Assembly. Therein, different dimensions of authority and subjecthood are performed and invoked, via the differentiation of forms of knowledge and the articulation of distinctive mechanisms of learning. Although the formation of subjecthood and knowledge might be conceptualized as independent processes, in the context of schooling they are deeply entangled and, in fact, mutually constitutive.

The ritual of the Morning Assembly, the distinctive start to an Indian school day, has long been ingrained within the educational system. It normally encompasses dissemination of news, patriotic and devotional songs in multiple languages, as well as edifying lectures (see Section 9.5) whereby students are exposed to and engaged in a variety of texts and genres such as prayers, songs, pledges, *mantras*, and lectures. It is also a daily ritual meant for developing character, and is considered instrumental in conditioning children into ethical living (Duesund, 2013; Kumar, 1990). In this capacity, it serves as a medium for the inculcation of moral values regarding, among other aspects, patriotism, citizenship, and spiritual growth (Benei, 2008; Duesund, 2013; Kumar, 1990; Sarangapani, 2003; Subramaniam, 2000; Thapan, 2014). Our analysis reveals that the language practices of the Morning Assembly reflect and enact two "regimes of truth" (Foucault, 1980): two paradigms of knowledge/power relations that both justify and undermine the schooling experience of Indian children.

This study builds on the limited research on this ritual by scholars, principally Sarangapani (2003), who argues that the Morning Assembly socializes students into particular learner stances that draw on traditional Hindu religious and cultural scripts. Crucially, ideologies about teachers' authority are pivotal within this socialization process, achieved chiefly through keying into "ancient truths" (Sarangapani, 2003, p. 407). The traditional *guru–shishya* (master–disciple) relationship figures most prominently within this discourse. This dyadic relationship, while an integral aspect of Indian custom, also encodes certain elements of subversion. Not only does it compete "in Indian folklore with the mother–child relationship for idealization and reverence" (Sarangapani, 2003, p. 406), but it also disrupts strictly regulated hierarchical relationships based on caste and gender. The casting of the contemporary teacher and student in the traditional mold of *guru* and *shishya* endows teachers with authority because of the absolute primacy of that model of educational relationship since ancient times (Sarangapani, 2003).[1] This chapter expands on Sarangapani's analysis in two fundamental ways: (1) We detail how different components of the ritual of the Morning Assembly enact different forms of authority and subjectivity; (2) We discern the relationship between authority and knowledge. More specifically we delineate how authority is predicated upon knowledge, which in turn legitimizes deployment of disciplinary technologies (e.g., surveillance, classification, regulation) (Foucault, 1977) aimed at promoting different dispositions toward learning among students.

After establishing the theoretical backdrop, the chapter describes the context, participants, and procedures that relate to the collection and analysis of data. We then present three representative excerpts that illuminate how authority, knowledge, and subjecthood are co-articulated within and through the ritual of the Morning Assembly. A complex picture emerges, in which the traditional *guru–shishya* relationship is invoked and at the same time displaced by the teacher–student model promoted within the modernist educational agenda of the postcolonial Indian state. This tension also manifests in the epistemological sphere, with the juxtaposition of traditional and modern forms of knowledge and pedagogical practices. In the conclusion, we consider how the Morning Assembly – a site of layered authority and subjecthood – may contribute to the reproduction of socioeconomic inequalities within Indian education.

9.2   Theoretical Framework

The investigation employs the theoretical lens of language socialization, which is centrally concerned with the socialization of cultural novices into and through language (Schieffelin and Ochs, 1986). A key tenet of the language socialization paradigm is that everyday communicative practices are a locus of production, reproduction, and transformation of culture. Routines in particular, punctuating the everyday experience of community members, function as central sites of cultural learning (Baquedano-López, 2008; Rogoff et al., 2007). Often quite simple and formulaic, and rooted in "bodily hexis" (Bourdieu, 1984), routines are indexical of broad and complex sociocultural orientations (Schieffelin and Ochs, 1986). The routine of the Morning Assembly, for instance, organizes Indian children's normative positions vis-à-vis learning, knowledge, and authority.

As a result of the "criticalist" (Watson-Gegeo and Bronson, 2013) orientation of our scholarship, we also utilize a critical discourse analysis (Fairclough, 1989) lens to unpack the ritual of the Morning Assembly. This allows us to sharpen our focus on power, hierarchy, and inequality, drawing largely on Althusser's and Foucault's theorizations on ideology, discourse, discipline, subjecthood, and education (e.g., Fairclough, 1989; Hall, 2001; Luke, 1995). Althusser (1971) posits that systems of power, notably the State, deploy ideology to ensure their reproduction by incorporating individuals into power structures. The State utilizes "ideological state apparatuses," such as educational institutions, to shape subjectivities that will be fitting to the dominant power matrix (Althusser, 1971). In a similar fashion, Foucault conceives of schooling as a core element in the production of subjecthood, principally via disciplinary techniques. According to Foucault (1977), discipline does not intervene on a pre-existing subject but rather brings this subject into being in the very moment it imposes onto him/her/them conditions for recognition.

In a Foucaldian perspective, it would be misleading to consider disciplinary interventions as a purely oppressive mechanism of subjugation. Modern pedagogies foster primarily "technologies of the self," "which permit individuals to effect by their own means or with the help of others a certain number of operations on their own bodies and souls, thoughts, conduct, and way of being, so as to transform themselves and attain a certain state of happiness, purity, wisdom, perfection, or immortality" (Foucault, 1988, p. 18). Subjects are educated to become the master of their own ethical self-constitution.

The pedagogues – fashioned as technicians or sages – draw students to disciplinary practices that, while steeped in societal and cultural values, are ultimately to become individual regulations and aspirations.[2]

9.3   Data, Methodology, and Focal Event

Language socialization researchers document how sociocultural and linguistic patterns are saturated with cultural content, sedimented over time (Schieffelin and Ochs, 1986). Language socialization research adopts an ethnographic perspective characterized by longitudinal study design, field-based data collection, and conversation/discourse analysis of a substantial corpus of audio and video recorded naturalistic interaction (Garrett and Baquedano-López, 2002). Conforming to these methodological principles, this study brings together a range of data to provide a complex and holistic picture of the ritual of Morning Assembly. Part of a broader investigation of young boys at an *anathashram* (orphanage) in suburban New Delhi spanning nine years, this study draws on data from eight months of ethnographic fieldwork conducted by the first author at a village school the boys attended, between December 2010 and August 2011. The boys were between the ages of five and 14 during the data collection period. The data collection process entailed participant observation in the *anathashram*, supplemented with audiovisual recordings of semi-structured informal interviews with the boys, and nearly 100 hours of classroom observations (approximately four to six hours per week when school was in session). The focal subjects were eight children from the *anathashram* and five teachers at the school, though each classroom had approximately 30 students. Written artifacts that offered additional insight included the children's school diaries, textbooks across subjects from nursery through Class VIII (eighth grade), homework, schoolwork, Unit Tests, Midterms, final exams, and *anathashram* records.

9.3.1   The Research Site

SCB School[3] is located in Madhupur Village (within the city of Noida), home to approximately 3,500 inhabitants, a mostly floating population of migrant workers. Noida is one of the cities comprising the National Capital Region, a conurbation of New Delhi and several urban agglomerations. An ethnically, culturally, linguistically, and socially heterogeneous city, it has about 650,000 inhabitants. The languages of state administration, business and commerce, and schooling are English and/or Hindi, although many inhabitants speak other languages at home (e.g., Punjabi and Urdu). SCB School, a co-educational semi-private institution, had approximately 250 students and was in session Monday through Saturday, from 8 a.m. until 1 p.m. The teachers (including the school principal), in their thirties and forties, had grown up in nearby towns and villages and held postgraduate degrees in various disciplines from regional universities.[4] The school principal also taught English, Hindi, and social science to several of the classes. The school itself was made up of a series of rooms connected with half-walls, with each classroom and teacher serving concurrently two or three grade levels. Each classroom was packed with small desks, two to three children to a desk, and each classroom was separated by a narrow aisle. As a result of the spatial constraints, each classroom was run as a multi-grade context. During the Morning Assembly, the children, in their uniformed attire, would stand or sit at their desks, and the teachers would walk back and forth across aisles in each classroom and also across the open corridor connecting all the rooms. Thus, as a result of the open plan of the school (see Figures 9.1, 9.2, and 9.3), all the children participated together in the ritual of Morning Assembly.

Figure 9.1 Standing in the aisle of a classroom, *Bade* Sir reads and chants from the *Hanuman Chalisa*, while the children repeat after him. Sixth graders are on the right of the aisle, and seventh graders are on the left.

Figure 9.2 Students recite the School Pledge, with their hands outstretched. Fourth grade students are on the right of the aisle, and sixth graders are on the left.

Figure 9.3 Students are chanting the *Gayatri Mantra*, standing with their hands folded in the *namaste* pose and their heads slightly bowed.

9.4   Analytic Procedures

At the start of this investigation, we were broadly interested in examining the dialectical relationship between traditional and contemporary Indian educational practices, particularly with reference to processes of authority and subjectivation. As we mined the data, the Morning Assembly ritual – with its juxtaposition of languages and textual practices (see Section 9.4.1 for a detailed description) – emerged as an especially rich site from which to examine these intersections.

In the course of this research project, the first author has reflected deeply on her own religious and educational experiences and been sensitive to the ways in which they have framed, informed, and shaped the collection and analysis of data. She grew up 13 miles away from the village school, in a similar linguistic landscape to that inhabited by the children. Her educational history also entailed Morning Assemblies similar to the ones under analysis. Her personal and academic background as an Indian, a New Delhi native (where she spent the first 22 years of her life), as a married Hindu Bengali woman in her thirties (at the time), playing the multiple roles of *didi* (Bengali, 'elder sister') and researcher, a product of the Indian K-12 system, an academic within US higher education, and someone specifically interested in the processes of schooling and language socialization, have potentially influenced the nature of the data collected and analysis conducted and also provided an additional source of reflection on the data.

9.4.1   Focal Event

At SCB School, every day commenced with the Morning Assembly. It is comprised of devotional, inspirational, and patriotic songs and prayers (in Hindi, English, Awadhi, and Sanskrit), followed by choral recitation of the School Pledge, and ending with the singing of the Indian national anthem. Meditation is also integrated into the assembly most days. The Morning Assembly would follow a similar format on every school day except on the auspicious days of Tuesdays and Saturdays, when students would recite the *Hanuman Chalisa*, an extended devotional hymn spanning 40 verses dedicated to Hanuman, a Hindu deity. The duration of the morning assembly varied from half an hour to over two hours, depending on what else was going on that day (such as exams or festival celebrations).

On a typical day, the Morning Assembly began with the children being given a teacher's drill commands "Attention!" and "Stand at ease!" several times, in English. The children would stiffen and relax their bodies according to the orders, and the cement floor would reverberate with the sound of their feet hitting the ground in time with the commands. The teachers would watch the children carefully to make sure that they all remained silent while moving in unison. During this process, the children would be given specific instructions (involving code-switching between Hindi and English) that ranged from regimenting the distance between their heels (down to the exact centimeter) during the "Attention" pose; the straightness of their backs; and how precisely their hands should be clasped behind their backs when "At ease." Normally Swaraj Sir, who had trained as a cadet in his youth, would be in charge of giving these commands to the children. In a way that recalls Mauss' descriptions of "techniques of the body" (Mauss, 1973 [1935]), these commands target explicitly and exclusively the child's body, imparting instructions on proper posture and gait (see also Burdelski, Chapter 10 in this volume). After faithfully following the commands several times, the children would be told to start with prayers.

While chanting the *Gayatri Mantra*, an important Vedic hymn, the children would be instructed to stand erect, hands clasped in a *namaste* pose, with their heads bowed down in devotion (see Figure 9.3). For the School Pledge, the students would keep their right hand outstretched, their backs straight and gaze looking firmly ahead (see Figure 9.2). For the national anthem, their right hands would be against their right temples forming a salute, their bodies steady. For the extended chanting of the *Hanuman Chalisa* (see Figure 9.1), the students would sit in their seats, their backs straight, with most students clapping along in rhythm to the chants. Finally, they would meditate (with "eyes and mouths closed," as they were ordered to do) for a few minutes, after which they would listen (relatively) quietly as a teacher (most often the principal, *Bade* Sir) lectured. After the lecture finished, the students would be instructed to remain seated silently with "straight backs, straight waists," their eyes closed shut. A couple of minutes later they would be told to open their eyes, and, with the Morning Assembly drawing to a close, teaching would commence.

9.5   Authority, Subjecthood, Knowledge, and Education in the Morning Assembly

In this section, we analyze three representative excerpts that illuminate situated notions of authority, subjecthood, knowledge, and education, as they emerge during the ritual of the Morning Assembly at SCB School. We begin by closely examining the pledge and show how its textual and performative dimensions call specific dimensions of subjecthood into being, situating each individual child into a social matrix of both communion and hierarchical order. The second and third excerpts, segments of lectures delivered by the principal on separate days, illustrate how submission to teachers' authority is articulated

Figure 9.4 School Pledge in the children's school diary. The pledge is written in English at the top of the page on the left, and its Hindi version at the bottom (the two versions are separated by a prayer). On the right of the page is the Indian national anthem, which is a Bengali song that is written here in Devanagari (Hindi) script.

and socialized through ideological processing of epistemic differentiation and valorization of tradition.

9.5.1   The National Pledge as Interpellation

Once the devotional singing draws to a close, the children prepare to recite the School Pledge. They stand with their right hand outstretched in front of them, their bodies erect. One or two children are selected to lead the school in reciting the pledge. They enunciate a segment of the pledge, roughly a prosodic unit (not all mapping onto a full sentence), with loud voice and staccato rhythm, and then the rest of the children repeat the segment in unison. As such, the pledge recitation can be likened to formulaic language practices that language socialization scholars have documented as central to "socializing novices to social dimensions such as politeness, hierarchy, and social identities including social roles and statuses, and relationships" (Burdelski and Cook, 2012, p. 173).

The pledge appears in both an English and a Hindi version in the children's school diary, but the one recited during Morning Assembly is the English version (Excerpt 9.1). The original English text of the pledge follows (Figure 9.4):

Excerpt 9.1 School Pledge
India is may (*sic*) country. All Indian (*sic*) are my brothers and sisters. I love my country and I am proud of its rich and varie (*sic*) heritage. I shall always strive to be worthy of it. I shall always give my parents teachers and elders respect and treat every one with

courtesy. To my country and my people I pledge my devotion, In (*sic*) their well being and prospeeity (*sic*), lies my happiness.

The pledge is recited quickly, with most of the breaths drawn sharply at the end of prosodic units. The errors in written text are, on the instances observed by the researcher, preserved in the oral recitation. Additionally, depending on how well the selected child or children remember the text, minor variations are introduced during the recitation (e.g., fragments would be repeated or left out). We would like to suggest that the pledge functions as an interpellation act, in an Althusserian sense (i.e., as a process of calling individuals into ideologically saturated subject positions) (Althusser, 1971). Althusser offers the simple but effective example of a police officer shouting out "hey, you there!" in public. When an individual, upon hearing the exclamation, turns toward the officer "by this mere one-hundred-and-eighty-degree physical conversion, he becomes a *subject*" (Althusser, 1971, p. 174). In the act of responding, if only nonverbally to the officer's hailing, the individual accepts that it is he who is addressed. This way subjects take on their subjecthood, one that was made possible for him by the officer's exclamation, and, as such, one that is inherently situated in a power relationship.

In having the children enunciate the pledge (with proper accompanying body posture) the authority figures in the school recognize them as individual subjects. By inhabiting vocally the "I" of the pledge, the child accepts the conditions for this recognition of subjectivity, the stipulations that shape her/him/them as subject. We argue that the pledge is a textual technology that interpellates children into subjecthood predicated on reverence for adults and relatedness with all fellow Indians.

The pledge operates as interpellation at two levels: the performative and the referential. As a performative act, the pledge enacts affiliation and closeness. Repeating verbatim after a leading prompt instantiates agreement, alignment, and alliance. Repeating in unison is an enactment of togetherness. Thus, as the children perform the pledge every morning they subscribe to conditions of being that root them deeply in an experience of belonging and mutual interdependence. At the referential level, the pledge establishes students' sense of ownership in their homeland ("may [sic] country"). Mirroring in part the performative, the pledge also situates Indians within a familial network ("brothers and sisters"). It then iterates students' pride in Indian tradition, which students must "always" endeavor to prove "worthy of." These lines show how children are not just socialized into a sense of patriotism, but also taught that patriotism is entwined with personal responsibility. Attendant to these notions is the emphasis on showing respect to "parents teachers and elders." Significantly, this grouping treats parents, teachers, and elders as if they comprise one category. We suggest that the absence of commas within this sentence, instead of merely reflecting missing punctuation, symbolically naturalizes the three groups as peers within a single unit. By explicitly classifying the three together, teachers are able to tap into a tradition of respect, deference, and obedience accorded to parents and elders that has been the cornerstone of Indian society for thousands of years (e.g., Gokhale 2003; Srinivasan and Karlan, 1997). These themes also emerge, as we see next, in the lectures given by the principal.

9.5.2   Forms of Knowledge and Hierarchical Order

Excerpt 9.2 offers a clear illustration of the SCB educators' epistemic ideology. Categorization and hierarchical ordering of forms of knowledge were repeatedly discussed in the principal's lectures, thereby constituting a salient socialization domain for the children in the school. The excerpt reveals tension between what the principal professes to be the most valuable knowledge and what the children are taught in the school.

Excerpt 9.2 Bade Sir's Lecture
(March 7, 2011) The prayers completed, the principal, *Bade* Sir, begins his lecture by invoking the upcoming examinations, a cause of great stress and anxiety among the children that day.

01   हम यह जो शिक्षा ग्रहण करने के लिए यहाँ पर आये हैं,
    'This education that we have come to acquire here,'

02   इन किताबी शिक्षा का एक आपके सामने अभी जो आने वाला है दस दिन में पांच
    दिन, में जो परीक्षा होने वाली है,
    'This examination that will happen of the bookish education that is in front
      of you in coming ten days, five days,'

03   यह इस किताबी ज्ञान का इम्तेहान है. बाक़ी हमारे जीवन में हर रोज़ इम्तेहान,
    'This is an exam of this bookish knowledge. The rest [of it] in our life
      everyday [there are] exams,'

04   और उस ही इम्तेहान में हम लोगों को वही देते हैं जो हमारे पास होता है.
    'And in that exam we can give only that which we [already] have.'

05   हम अपने व्यवहार द्वारा जीवन में दुसरे लोगों को वही देते हैं जो हमारे पास हुआ
    करता है,
    'In our life we through our behavior towards other people [we] can give only
      that which we already have,'

06   [. . .]

07   हमारे अंदर विद्वता है तो दूसरे को भी विद्वता देंगे. हमारे अंदर मूर्खता है तो दूसरों
    को भी मुर्ख बनाएंगे मूर्खता देंगे उनको भी.

'If we have erudition within us then we can also give erudition to others.
If we have stupidity in us then we will make fools of others, we will
also give stupidity to others.'

08 तो शिक्षा का क्षेत्र मात्र इतना नहीं है कि हमारे सिलेबस में जो books लगी हों

उनकी ( ) को पढ़ें, उनके पीछे जो question answer दिए हैं उनके answer

रट लें,

'Then the field of education is not only limited to that we () the books in
our syllabus we study, the question answers at the end we memorize by rote,'

09 कॉपी में लिखाएं और समाप्त हो जाये बात.

'Get written in the notebook and the matter is finished.'

10 शिक्षा का उद्देश्य है हम जीवन में "how to behave," दूसरों के साथ कैसा

व्यवहार करना है,

'The meaning of education is how to behave in life, how to behave with
others,'

11 शिक्षा की जो parameter है इतना छोटा नहीं है,

'The parameter of education is not this small,'

12 शिक्षा के parameter में वो तैयारी की जाती है कि हम जीवन में, अपने जीवन

को उत्कर्ष की और ले जाने के लिए हम क्या क्या करें,

'In the parameter of education the preparation is done that in our lives, what
all we must do for going towards progress in life,'

13 तो हम दूसरों के साथ दूसरों को क्या देंगे, यह depend करता है की हम अपने-

मेरी-जेब में क्या है,

'Then what we do with others, what we give depends on what we-our
own-have in our pockets,'

14 मेरी जेब में जो है वही मैं दूसरों को दे सकता हूँ.

'What is in my pocket that is only what I can give to others.'

15 [. . .]

16 यह पीढ़ी व पीढ़ी चलने वाली व्यवस्था है,

'This is an arrangement happening generation after generation,'

17 हमने अपने शिक्षकों से, पेरेंट्स से, अपने बड़े बुजुर्गों से जो चीज़ें सीखीं है,

'We from our teachers, our parents, our elders those things that we have
learned,'

18 वही हमारे पास हुआ करती है.

'That only is with us.'

In this excerpt from *Bade* Sir's lecture, students are invited to see an expanded 'parameter of education' (line 11). This perspective extends the scope of education beyond 'bookish education' (line 02) and encompasses learning 'how to behave' (line 10). *Bade* Sir's description of book learning captures prototypical literacy practices at the school: the children study books assigned in the syllabus, learn by rote (Moore, 2006) answers to questions provided at the end of lessons, and copy answers into their notebooks. In fact, this lecture was immediately followed by these same activities during that particular school day. In redefining education as going beyond these activities, *Bade* Sir not only leans on traditional ideals of respect for India's heritage and elders – as articulated in the pledge – but also invokes a commercial metaphor, by mentioning what is in one's pocket. Thus, virtuous knowledge (that is, knowledge of virtues) is commodified and likened to money. It is given a transactional value. It is what one 'has' to offer to others and previously had to take from key adult figures. Indeed, the adults may also be seen to be investing in the children. Moreover, *Bade* Sir adds historical scope to his comments by claiming, 'This is an arrangement happening generation after generation' (line 16). This serves to establish that his statements are not merely his perspective: They convey an understanding of education with long roots in Indian history. Furthermore, as in the pledge, we find 'teachers, ... parents, ... elders' (line 17) classified together. Through this deliberate discursive move, teachers are removed from the more technical sphere of academic pedagogy – which is strictly related to books, schoolwork, and testing – and are again elevated into the sacred and venerated space in Indian tradition that parents and elders have occupied for millennia. This also attempts to recast the present-day teacher into the same venerated space as the ancient *gurus*. Moreover, the adverbial qualifier *only* in the statement 'That only is with us' (line 18) drives home the point that 'bookish knowledge' (line 03) is not as lasting or as virtuous knowledge, which plays a more powerful role in defining how students should live their lives.

The ideological work that *Bade* Sir's words do is complex and significant: the principal categorizes forms of knowledge, differentiating bookish knowledge from erudition. This distinction is made through the articulation of a hierarchical order between forms of knowledge, with knowledge acquired (in school) for the school test not deemed as important as that acquired for virtuous conduct in life. A key aspect of the epistemic ideology transmitted in the lecture is the differentiation between sources of knowledge: schoolbooks are not authoritative sources of knowledge; elders and parents are, by tradition. The teacher is thus aligned to elders and parents, the more valued sources of knowledge, to gain ultimate authority over pupils. Furthermore, different forms of knowledge are associated with different pedagogies and mechanisms of learning: written questions that rephrase textbook information and rote repetition are dominant teaching/learning methods within the academic domain. As for erudition, it is acquired in everyday interaction, by observance and observation, best modeled by older adults. Through epistemic ideology children are thus also socialized to differentiate between forms of knowledge and to relate differently to different knowledge sources. The sources affirmed as authoritative are those that are linked to Indian tradition, toward whom, consequently, the children are expected to submit themselves.

9.5.3   Student–Teacher Relationship Steeped in Tradition

Through the analysis of Excerpt 9.3, we unpack further the authority construct in the Morning Assembly rituals and how students are positioned vis-à-vis the educational figures in the school.

Excerpt 9.3 Student–Teacher Relationship
(March 13, 2011). This lecture followed the group recitation of *Hanuman Chalisa*, which was recited in tune, punctuated by the rhythm of timed applause. The children were then told to sit still and meditate, their backs erect (with repeated orders, in English, of 'Straight [sic] your back!'), eyes closed, and no talking allowed. After the meditation was over, they opened their eyes, but continued sitting with straight backs, listening (mostly) quietly as *Bade* Sir lectured.

01   ध्यान की पद्धति इस लिए है, कि हमारी जो बिखरी हुई चेतना है, (.)
      'Path of meditation is so, that our scattered thinking,'

02   उस में एकाग्रता आये.
      'In that concentration arrives.'

03   वह सारी की सारी जो बिखरी हुई चेतना हैं,
      'All that scattered thinking,'

04   इधर उधर की बातों में जो लगी हुई है,
      'That is focused on matters here and there,'

05   उसको हम एक जगह एकत्र कर सकें.
      'We can accumulate in one place.'

06   और एकत्र करने के बाद, उसको किसी उद्देश्य में लगाया जा सके.
      'And after accumulating, put it in the service of some purpose.'

07   जो हमारा उद्देश्य हैं. (.) उद्देश्य कुछ भी हो सकता हैं
      'That which is our purpose (.) our purpose can be anything at all,'

08   अभी आपका उद्देश्य सिर्फ़ पढ़ना हैं, education प्राप्त करना हैं, शिक्षा प्राप्त करना है.
      'Right now your purpose is only studying, obtaining education, obtaining education.'

09 तो उस में शिक्षा प्राप्ति के उद्देश्य को आप भली भाँति साकार रूप दे सकें इस लिए आवश्यक हो

'Then in that for you to be able to give proper shape to the aim of obtaining an education it is necessary that,'

10 कि आप के अंदर एकाग्रता हो. और एकाग्रता के लिए अनिवार्य है की आप (.)

'That in you there will be concentration. And for concentration it is mandatory that you,'

11 ध्यान करे, ध्यान. (?) आँखें बंध कर के ध्यान कराया जाता है.

'Do meditation, meditation. With closed eyes meditation is gotten done.'

12 यह सब इस लिए कराये जाते हैं की आप के मन की जो चिंता (चिंतुता) है

'These all, for this reason are gotten done. That the anxiety that is in your mind,'

13 वह दूर हो. मन जो बार-बार भागता है, आपको लेकर इधर-उधर, भागता है,

'That is removed. The mind that again and again runs, taking you, runs here and there,'

14 उसको रोकने के लिए ध्यान कराया जाता है.

'To stop it meditation is gotten done.'

15 मैं (.) हमारी जो prayer, morning prayer होती है, उस morning prayer में

'Me (.) our prayer, morning prayer that happens, in that morning prayer,'

16 हनुमान चालीसा, या अन्य प्रार्थनाएं जो भी हैं, गायत्री मंत्र (.)

'Hanuman chalisa, or other prayers that are there, Gayatri Mantra,'

17 गायत्री मंत्र छोटी-मोटी वस्तु नहीं है.

'Gayatri Mantra is not a small thing.'

18 गायत्री मंत्र जितने भी हमारे चारो वेदों में मंत्र है उनका, उन सब का मुख्य एक मंत्र है,

'Gayatri Mantra all the four Vedas in, in those it is the premier mantra,'

19 इस लिए उसका उच्चारण कराया जाता है. चारो वेदों में,

'That is why its recitation is gotten done. In four Vedas,'

20 जो जितने भी मंत्र हैं उनका एक सबसे मुख्य मंत्र है,

'Whatever mantras are there it is the premier mantra,'

21 इस लिए केवल इसी का सुबह पांच बार जाप कराया जाता है,

'That is why only this one chanting is gotten done in the morning five times.'

22 जिससे कि हमें चारो वेदों के मन्त्रों के जाप का फल प्राप्त हो सके.

'So that we can get the fruits of the chanting of [all] four Vedas.'

23 हम जो हनुमान चालीसा पढ़ते हैं हनुमान चालीसा-हमारी भारतीय संस्कृति में ऐसी परंपरा है,

'That we read Hanuman Chalisa. Hanuman Chalisa-our Indian culture has such a tradition,'

24 शिक्षा प्राप्त करना, हम यह नहीं समझते कि हम कोई वस्तु खरीदने जा रहे हैं बाज़ार से,

'Obtaining an education, we do not think that we are buying a thing in the bazaar,'

25 टीचर को फीस दो, education मिल जाएगी. ऐसी हमारी मान्यता नहीं है,

'Give the teacher fees [and] get an education. That is not our belief,'

26 हमारी मान्यता है गुरु शिष्य के बीच का एक ऐसा पवित्र सम्बन्ध है,

'Our belief is that (.) There is such a pure relationship between guru and student,'

27 जहाँ पर समर्पण के बाद इस वस्तु को हासिल किया जा सकता है.

'Where after surrender this thing can be achieved.'

28 गुरु गोविन्द दोनों खड़े काके लागु पाँय?

'If Guru and Govind [Krishna/God] are standing [there] whose feet do I touch[5]?'

29 बलिहारी गुरु आपनो गोविन्द दियो मिलाये.

'Guru's feet first, since he introduced you to God.'

30 इसमें गुरु का स्थान है वो ईश्वर से भी बड़ा होता है.

'In this the place of the guru is even bigger than God.'

31 कवीराज ने गुरु का जो स्थान है ईश्वर से भी बड़ा बताया है.

'The poet king [Kabir Das] has said the role of the guru is bigger than God.'

The principal's lecture opens with a lengthy explanation of why it is important that students meditate. It is noteworthy that the students just completed a meditation session. The explanation is thus provided after the students are directed to engage in the activity and not before. In a similar manner, this lecture includes an explanation of why students chant the *Gayatri Mantra* and the *Hanuman Chalisa*, after the ritual chanting has been completed. We argue here that the sequential order, of activity (first) and (then) justification for the activity, where students are imparted instructions and expected to be obedient, socializes them to follow unconditionally the authority figure of the teacher.

The explanation proper provides additional detail about the subject position students are to assume in the educational context, specifically in relation to authority figures. As in Excerpt 9.2, reference is made again to market transaction. Here, however, it serves to set the teacher–student relationship in contrast to a commercial relationship and to place it instead in the "pure" mold of the traditional *guru–shishya* dyad (lines 26–27). As such the teacher–student relationship is imbued with powerful cultural, spiritual, and religious overtones.

Conditions for obtaining an education and a learning trajectory are also alluded to by *Bade* Sir's words: necessary to undertaking and then achieving education is an act of surrendering to a *guru* and submitting to his guidance (line 27). The reverence that the student is to give to the teacher cannot be overestimated. Quoting a well-known *doha* (couplet) by the famous fifteenth-century mystic and poet Kabir Das, *Bade* Sir posits that the *guru* is greater than God because it is through the *guru* that God becomes known. In fact, this notion is invoked three times (lines 29–31) in the span of the four lines: first within the *doha*; then in the explanation following the couplet; and finally during *Bade* Sir's assertion that Kabir himself had articulated this. The repetitions reinforce the hierarchy, thus discursively reifying the primacy of the instructor.

9.6   Concluding Remarks

This chapter has extended Sarangapani's scholarship (2003) on the pivotal Indian schooling ritual of the Morning Assembly by demonstrating how it contributes to the subjectivation of Indian pupils through participation in a set of regimented disciplinary activities. Employing both language socialization theory and critical discourse analysis, we illustrated how school discourse within this ritual component recruits the child into a subject position steeped in tradition and subservient to authority.[6]

The School Pledge, recited at the beginning of the ritual, warms up, so to speak, the children's disposition to obedience, at both the referential and performative levels, which unarguably is essential for the smooth running of the instructional operations to follow. The chanting of the *mantras* and the silent meditation, as "technologies of the self" (Foucault, 1980), foster each child's submission to tradition. The moral lectures often invoke tradition explicitly, through reference to sacred texts, religious figures, and spiritual guides, notably the *guru*. To him – ultimate authority exceeding that of God, as articulated by Kabir – is due absolute submission.

The Morning Assembly is also a site where the subject position of teachers is articulated. Our analysis has revealed that for teachers as well, tradition is a chief reference. Their authority is claimed and legitimized through discursive acts of alignment with elders and parents, who are long-established authoritative figures in Indian society.

In doing that, however, a tension emerges between domains of knowledge and pedagogical strategies linked to the traditional *guru–shishya* relationship and those associated with the contemporary schooling institution. We suggest that this tension can be characterized as the coexistence of two distinct regimes of truth, that is two sets of institutionally produced and approved truths that govern sanctioned and desirable ways to think, act, and feel (Foucault, 1980). On the one hand, we have wisdom and moral growth, which are apprehended through observation of and participation in virtuous practices of parents, elders, and *gurus*, whereas on the other hand, we have academic education, chiefly literacy skills, acquired through textbook exercises and rote learning. Both seem to undergo some form of commodification, but the mechanisms of transmission within the two regimes of truth remain significantly different.

In closing, we wish to bring attention to an important implication: juxtaposing the schooling regime of truth to the traditional regime of truth inevitably undermines the former and the emancipatory potential of education. Children are being socialized into stances that not only put a premium on obedience but also redirect their aspirations away from academics and toward good behavior. For underprivileged children, for whom literacy skills and academic success may be the only way out of poverty (Dreze and Sen, 2002; Mohanty, 2008), this form of socialization can be especially consequential, ultimately leading to the reproduction of existing socioeconomic inequalities within Indian education.

NOTES

1 Sheshagiri (2010) traces the ascendancy of the *guru* in Indian civilization to the Upanishadic times, between 800 and 500 BC. There, the *guru* served as intellectual mentor, requiring from the pupils the "exercise of reason rather than exercises in submission and blind conformity" (p. 468). It was only in the *Bhakti* period, around the seventh century, when this understanding of the *guru*'s role underwent a sea change. During that time, "devotional surrender" to the *guru* became critical to the acquisition of knowledge (ibid.). This conception held sway until colonial mechanisms reshaped the learning context, rendering the *guru* as the instructor, or "meek dictator" (Kumar, 1991) in the classroom. The tensions we articulate below map onto these different historical trajectories of the term.

2 Indeed, Foucault (1987) points out that "if I am interested in fact in the way in which the subject constitutes himself in an active fashion, by the practices of self, these practices are not nevertheless something that the subject invents by himself. They are patterns that he finds in his (*sic*) culture and which are proposed, suggested and imposed on him by his culture, his society and his social group" (p. 11).

3 Names of people, the village school, and the village have been changed to protect participants' identities.

4 Teachers were typically referred to by their first names followed by the title "Sir." However, one exception was the principal, who also taught in the school and was referred to as "*Bade* [big] Sir."

5 The touching of elder's feet is a core aspect of broader Hindu culture, and symbolic of the respect and authority accorded to one's elders.

6 While we have focused exclusively on disciplinary technologies and authority, we do not assume those to be solely oppressive and children's agency insignificant. While we did not witness overt resistance during the Morning Assembly, we observed children exercising subtle subversive tactics like mumbling words or merely mouthing words instead of reciting them, and slouching when required to sit erect. Children's tactical maneuvering within regimented spaces would indeed deserve more careful investigation.

REFERENCES

Althusser, L. (1971). Ideology and ideological state apparatuses (notes towards an investigation). In *Lenin and Philosophy and Other Essays* (translated by B. Brewster) (pp. 127–186). New York, NY: Monthly Review Press.

Baquedano-López, P. (2008). The pragmatics of reading prayers: learning the Act of Contrition in Spanish-based religious education classes (doctrina). *Text & Talk: An Interdisciplinary Journal of Language, Discourse Communication Studies*, 28(5), 581–602.

Benei, V. (2008). *Schooling Passions: Nation, History, and Language in Contemporary Western India*. Stanford, CA: Stanford University Press

Bourdieu, P. (1984). *Distinction: A Social Critique of the Judgement of Taste*. London: Routledge.

Burdelski, M. and Cook, H. M. (2012). Formulaic language in language socialization. *Annual Review of Applied Linguistics*, 32, 173–188.

Dreze, J. and Sen, A. (2002). *India: Development and Participation*. New York, NY: Oxford University Press.

Duesund, K. (2013). Is there a potential for Norway to learn from the ethics education in the educational system of India? *Nordidactica: Journal of Humanities and Social Science Education*, 2, 142–164.

Gokhale, S. D. (2003). Towards a policy for aging in India. *Journal of Aging & Social Policy*, 15(2–3), 213–234.

Fairclough, N. (1989). *Language and Power*. London: Longman.

Foucault, M. (1977). *Discipline and Power: The Birth of the Prison*. Harmondsworth: Penguin Books.

Foucault, M. (1980). *Power/Knowledge: Selected Interviews and Other Writings, 1972–1977*. New York, NY: Pantheon.

Foucault, M. (1987). The ethic of care for the self as a practice of freedom. In J. Bernhauer and D. Rasmussen (eds.), *The Final Foucault* (pp. 112–131). Boston, MA: MIT Press.

Foucault, M. (1988). Technologies of the self. In L. H. Martin, H. Gutman, and P. Hutton (eds.), *Technologies of the Self: A Seminar with Michel Foucault* (pp. 16–49). Amherst, MA: University of Massachusetts Press.

Garrett, P. B. and Baquedano-López, P. (2002). Language socialization: reproduction and continuity, transformation and change. *Annual Review of Anthropology*, 31(1), 339–361.

Hall, S. (2001). Foucault: power, knowledge and discourse. In M. Wetherell, S. Taylor, and S. J. Yates (eds.), *Discourse Theory and Practice: A Reader* (pp. 72–81). London: SAGE.

Kumar, K. (1990). Hindu revivalism and education in north-central India. *Social Scientist*, 10(10), 4–26.

Kumar, K. (1991). *Political Agenda of Education: A Study of Colonialist and Nationalist Ideas*. New Delhi: SAGE.

Luke, A. (1995). Text and discourse in education: an introduction to critical discourse analysis. *Review of Research in Education*, 21(1), 3–49.

Mauss, M. (1973 [1935]). Techniques of the body. *Economy and Society*, 2, 70–88.

Mohanty, A. K. (2008). Perpetuating inequality: language disadvantage and capability deprivation of tribal mother tongue speakers in India. In W. Harbert, S. McConnell-Ginet, A. Miller, and J. Whitman (eds.), *Language and Poverty* (pp. 102–124). Clevedon, UK: Multilingual Matters.

Moore, L. C. (2006). Learning by heart in Qur'anic and public schools in northern Cameroon. *Social Analysis*, 50(3), 109–126.

Rogoff, B., Moore, L., Najafi, B., Dexter, A., Correa-Chavez, M., and Solis, J. (2007). Children's development of cultural repertoires through participation in everyday routines and practices. In J. E. Grusec and P. D. Hastings (eds.), *Handbook of Socialization* (pp. 490–515). New York, NY: Guilford Press.

Sarangapani, P. (2003). Childhood and schooling in an Indian village. *Childhood*, 10 (4), 403–418.

Schieffelin, B. B. and Ochs, E. (1986). Language socialization. *Annual Review of Anthropology*, 15(1), 163–191.

Sheshagiri, K. M. (2010). A cultural overview of education in Hindu civilization. In Y. Zhao, J. Lei, G. Li, M. F. He, K. Okano, N. Megahed, D. Gamage, and H. Ramanathan (eds.), *Handbook of Asian Education: A Cultural Perspective* (pp. 463–480). New York, NY: Routledge.

Srinivasan, B. and Karlan, G. R. (1997). Culturally responsive early intervention programs: issues in India. *International Journal of Disability, Development and Education*, 44(4), 367–385.

Subramaniam, B. (2000). Archaic modernities: science, secularism, and religion in modern India. *Social Text*, 18(3), 67–86.

Thapan, M. (ed.). (2014). *Ethnographies of Schooling in Contemporary India*. New Delhi: SAGE.

Watson-Gegeo, K. A. and Bronson, M. C. (2013). The intersection of language socialization and sociolinguistics. In R. Bayley, R. Cameron, and C. Lucas (eds.), *Oxford Handbook of Sociolinguistics*, (pp. 111–131). New York, NY: Oxford University Press.

10 Embodiment, Ritual, and Ideology in a Japanese-as-a-Heritage-Language Preschool Classroom

Matthew J. Burdelski

10.1 Introduction

In communities across the globe, classrooms are sites for socializing children's bodies in culturally specific ways. As the sociologist Chris Shilling (2012 [1993]) observes, "schools are not just places which educate the minds of children, they are also implicated in monitoring and shaping the bodies of young people" (p. 19). From more mundane actions and activities such as raising a hand before speaking or standing to recite prayers (Bhattacharya and Sterponi, Chapter 9 in this volume) to more exceptional ones such as participating in school ceremonies, children are socialized to "techniques of the body" (Mauss, 1973 [1935]) as part of their "habitus," defined as "a set of *dispositions* which incline agents to act and react in certain ways" (Bourdieu, 1991, p. 12). This socialization occurs in part through classroom interactions with teachers and peers who may model, instruct, and correct children's corporeal behaviors in ways that are informed by and convey beliefs and ideas about how language ought to be used (e.g., Riley, 2011). As language socialization concerns the process of how less competent members are socialized both *to* and *through* language (Schieffelin and Ochs, 1986) – that is, how they are socialized *to use* language and how they are socialized *through the use* of language into familiarity with the ways of thinking, acting, and feeling as members of their social group – the body is a central resource in this process. Often co-occurring with linguistic features, bodily acts can index an array of sociocultural meanings in situated interaction (Bucholtz and Hall, 2016). Although language socialization theory has long been concerned with the body, such as the cultural variability of "corporeal arrangements of social interactions involving children" (e.g., Ochs, Solomon and Sterponi, 2005, p. 556), we have less understanding of the body as a social indexical resource and object of explicit socialization in classrooms, which have their own goals, "participation frameworks" (Goffman, 1981), and activities, and how this socialization is mediated by and conveys culturally specific "language ideologies" (see Section 1.2.3 in the Introduction to this volume).

This chapter explores embodied socialization in a Japanese-as-a-heritage-language (JHL) preschool classroom in the United States. Previous research in preschools in Japan has focused on children's bodies within various activities (e.g., Ben-Ari, 1997; Burke and Duncan, 2015; Hayashi and Tobin, 2015), such as sleeping, bathing, mealtime, and play. While that research has primarily examined informal routines, or "everyday rituals" (Enfield, 2009), such as greetings and expressions of appreciation (for a meal), this chapter focuses on a formal ritual, or "ritual exchange" (Bourdieu, 1991, p. 72): a *preschool graduation ceremony* (see Peak, 1991: pp. 116–125 on the opening ceremony) that requires children's use of a specific sequence of bodily moves in presenting a "public self" (Cook, 1996). It builds on previous research on Japanese preschools (e.g., Holloway, 2000; Tobin, Wu, and Davidson, 1989) through micro analysis of a specific ritual. Despite its relative infrequency (occurring at the end of the school year), this ritual, I contend, is a powerful vehicle of socialization in this JHL preschool in ways that reflect and construct culturally specific ideologies of the body. Specifically, the ritual entails a good deal of preparation and rehearsal *prior* to the actual performance (see Jaffe, Chapter 5 in this volume); this preparation and rehearsal is carried out through explicit and implicit references to "correct" bodily comportment and tactile guidance in socializing children to an ideology concerned with the importance of paying attention to the details of (embodied) form. The goals of the chapter are thus to examine how teachers instructed children's bodies in preparing them for this ritual, and how this instruction conveyed to children norms of their heritage language and culture.

10.2   Setting, Participants, and Methods

The data for this study are drawn from linguistic and ethnographic research conducted over four months (during the 2011 school year) in a preschool classroom at a Japanese-as-a-heritage-language (JHL) school (*nihongo hos-huujugyookoo*, literally 'Japanese supplementary school classroom') in the United States. JHL schools across the globe, primarily located in large cities and metropolitan areas, play an important role in educating Japanese-speaking children and adolescents living outside of Japan, by developing not only their language and literacy skills but also their broader cultural practices (e.g., Doerr and Lee, 2010), typically with the aim of preparing them to (re-)adjust to schooling in Japan (Goodman, 2012). Although located in the United States, this preschool classroom can be described in terms of what Holloway (2000) calls a Japanese "role-oriented preschool"[1] in which the basic curriculum consists of "group-oriented instruction in academic skills" (p. 19). Similar to many other JHL schools, this school holds classes on Saturdays from preschool to high school. The mission statement for the preschool, which is divided into three classes based on age (three, four, and five-year-olds), is in reality both social and academic: for children to get along as members of a social group and to read and write *hiragana* and *katakana* (the two phonetic lettering systems). According to the school principal, whom I spoke with, the primary reason that Japanese parents cited for sending their child to this school was so that their child would experience cultural events similar to those that the parents had experienced when they were children, suggesting that parents were centrally concerned that their children engage in cultural activities.

The analysis draws upon ten hours of audiovisual recordings in the upper-level preschool classroom (five-year-olds). In this classroom, there were 21 children and three teachers (all in their thirties; Teacher-1 [head teacher], Teacher-2, and Teacher-3), who rotated among the other preschool class-rooms. All of the children were JHL speakers who used the language with one or both parents at home. According to the principal, about half of these children were from families who had been relocated to the United States by their Japanese employers for a fixed period, and the other half were from mixed families (one parent a US citizen and the other a Japanese national) who were permanently residing in the United States. In addition to lessons that often focused on reading and writing Japanese, as with other preschools in Japan, part of the year is spent participating in cultural events, such as a graduation ceremony, sports day, and a performing arts festival. At the time of the research (in the winter, or toward the end of the Japanese academic year in February and March), I observed preparation for the preschool graduation ceremony in the classroom, which revealed cultural and pedagogical practices surrounding attention to detail of form and modeling/imitation that I had observed in other activities in this classroom as well as in prior research on children's language socialization in homes and a preschool in Japan (Burdelski, 2010, 2011). This classroom rehearsal functioned, in Goffman's (1959) sense, as a "backstage" space where "correctness" and attention to form was highlighted in preparation for the later "front stage" public performance.

The graduation ceremony was to be held at the school auditorium with the ceremonies for the other classes (elementary to high school), and attended by school staff and family members. It seems to represent a crucial event that is among the kinds of experiences that parents had in mind for sending their children to this school, and thus the preparation for the event was selected for an analysis of language socialization. In classes at my university back in Japan, college students displayed a familiarity with the graduation ceremony and the rehearsal it entails, which suggested to me that there is a degree of continuity between schools in Japan and this heritage-language school in the United States.

10.3   Ideology as Attention to Details of Prescribed 'Form' (*Kata*) and Modeling and Imitation in Japanese Society

In preparing the children on how to receive the graduation certificate, teachers expended a great deal of energy in encouraging them to attend to "techniques of the body" (Mauss, 1973 [1935]) in displaying a social demeanor – being respectful and deferential – and presenting a public self to the school principal (who would offer them the graduation certificate) and the audience composed of parents, teachers, and other children. Attention to the details of prescribed 'form' (*kata*) is a central ideology in Japanese society, and has been traditionally observed in the performing, graphic, and martial arts (e.g., DeCoker, 1998). Instruction and learning of prescribed form are often carried out through modeling and imitation, a method that has deep roots in Japanese history. During the Edo period (1603–1868), the *iemoto* system (literally, 'family foundation') structured ways in which skills and techniques were transmitted across generations (e.g., Smith, 1998). An ideological principle of this system was an emphasis on direct instruction,[2] which "consisted essentially of demonstration by the teacher without explanation, and then of minute imitation by the pupil" (O'Neill, 1984, p. 636). During this same period, the Confucian philosopher Ekiken Kaibara argued that bodily habit formation is central to children's development. He suggested that "the decisive factor in the formation of character in early childhood is the 'power of imitation,' through which the child comes to resemble what is imitated through the repetition of what is seen and heard by the eyes and ears" (Tsujimoto, 2014, p. 151). According to Tsujimoto (2014), Kaibara's theory can be considered as reflective of "the process of study and learning that was generally in practice at the time" rather than as something Kaibara formulated out of the abstract (p. 142).

Despite a criticism from some circles that modeling and imitation lead to a "stifling of spontaneity and creativity" (Smith, 1998, p. 32), in current Japanese society this method is widely used not only in the arts but also in other settings such as service industry training, business etiquette training for new company employees (Dunn, 2018), and company retreats with the goal of developing employees' 'minds/hearts/souls' (*kokoro*) and their bonds as a social group (Kondo, 1990). Modeling as well as imitation is also a method of early childhood socialization in homes and preschools in Japan. For instance, in encouraging children to exchange greetings, make apologies, and express thanks, Japanese caregivers often use "elicited imitation" (Hood and Schieffelin, 1978), by modeling an utterance for a child followed by a directive to repeat it verbatim (e.g., *gomennasai tte* 'I'm sorry, say') (Burdelski, 2011). In previous research (Burdelski, 2011), I frequently observed parents and preschool teachers modeling for children what to do with their bodies (such as putting the hands together while saying *itadakimasu* 'I humbly accept this meal'), and physically guiding children's bodies to perform social actions with others (such as pressing a hand on the child's back to encourage bowing). Japanese caregivers also used such verbal and embodied strategies with children within more formal rituals, such as praying at shrines. They also used elicited imitation as a kind of error correction, to reformulate children's utterances that were grammatically correct but pragmatically "incorrect" (e.g., impolite/rude, or not gender appropriate) (Burdelski, 2015). In other research, Peak (1991) has observed how Japanese preschool staff instruct children to attend to their seated postures by telling them to sit upright during the preschool opening ceremony. In these ways, Japanese caregivers and teachers foster children's public social skills in ways that reflect cultural models of teaching and learning (Burdelski, 2011).

In this JHL classroom, attention to prescribed form was integral to the pedagogy that informed the activities and was not limited to learning merely bodily moves for the graduation ceremony. For instance, in instructing children to write the Japanese syllabaries (*hiragana* and *katakana*), teachers emphasized that each character had to be written with a certain 'stroke order' (*kakijun*). Moreover, in engaging the children in craft projects, teachers often conveyed relatively fixed ways of doing things, such as folding the paper during origami lessons and pasting decorated paper dolls on colored construction paper in a specific location (e.g., male on left and female on right as an index of hierarchy). Also, in reciting formulaic expressions at the start and end of lunchtime (e.g., *itadakimasu* 'I humbly accept this food'; *gochisoosamadeshita* 'Thank you for the meal'), teachers directed the entire class to redo these routines if their "collective voice" lacked 'energy' (*genki*). In encouraging children to reproduce various semiotic forms that involve the body (including the vocal tract), teachers tacitly conveyed to them the importance of doing things in prescribed ways, similar to others, as a member of a social group.

10.4   Preparation on How to Receive the Preschool Graduation Certificate

An activity to prepare the children on how to receive the graduation certificate was conducted in the classroom several weeks prior to the actual ceremony. This preparation occurred once in the classroom and once again (two weeks later) on the auditorium stage. Here, I examine the preparation in the classroom, as this is the first time the children rehearsed it.

Similar to educational activities observed in other communities, such as learning to read Qur'anic texts among the Fulbe of Northern Africa (Moore, 2006), preparing the children in the classroom on how to receive the graduation certificate consisted of what can be described as three stages: (1) announcement and description, (2) modeling, and (3) rehearsal. These

Table 10.1 *Summary of principal's and child's verbal and bodily actions in giving/receiving the graduation certificate*

Principal's actions	Child's actions
1. Calls out child's full name.	1. Raises hand while gazing toward audience and saying *hai* 'Yes.' Turns and walks with upright posture toward principal, and stops a few feet away.
2. Bows toward child while holding out graduation certificate toward him or her.	2. Bows toward principal.
3. Says child's full name a second time, followed by the phrase, 'Congratulations on graduating from preschool' (*sotsuen omedetoo gozaimasu*).	3. Steps forward and takes certificate with both hands.
4. Holds out certificate toward child with both hands.	4. Steps backward (left foot first and then right foot).
5. Bows a second time.	5. Bows a second time, and then puts certificate under left arm and walks away with upright posture.

stages can be considered heuristic in the sense that they were not mutually exclusive. For instance, teacher modeling on what to do (stage 2) also occurred during individual rehearsal (stage 3). Moreover, in each of these stages, the teachers conveyed direct instructions to the children on what to do (e.g., during stage 1: *ojigi o suru* 'You will bow'; during stage 3: *ojiji* 'Bow').

In the first stage, Teacher-1 announced the graduation ceremony where she told the children that the way of receiving the certificate is 'fixed/decided in advance' (*morau yarikata ga kimatte imasu*). She then described a series of verbal and embodied actions between the school principal and each child (Table 10.1). Among these actions, the school principal's use of honorifics (in bold) in the set phrase, *sotsuen omedetoo **gozaimasu*** 'Congratulations on graduating from preschool' and the deep bowing (twice) by the school principal and student indexes a formal "register" (Agha, 2001) through linguistic and embodied practices.

Having briefly outlined the first stage above, in the following sections I focus on the second and third stages of this preparation, as these stages were where the teachers fully deployed their bodies through pointing, touch, haptic correction, and other physical acts in shaping children's bodies to perform the ritual.

10.4.1   Modeling: "Good" and "Bad" Examples

In the second stage of the preparation for the graduation ceremony, the teachers modeled the ritual for the children using a role-play in which one teacher assumed the role of "school principal" and the other the role of a "child." Similar to findings in a preschool in Japan (Burdelski, 2011) and a public-speaking course for Japanese adults (Dunn, 2016), these teachers framed the children's performance of the ritual in relation to morality, by juxtaposing "good" and "bad" examples for children to observe and evaluate. More specifically, after the teachers modeled the ritual for the first time, several children expressed a negative affective stance by saying, 'No way' (*iya da*) and 'embarrassing' (*hazukashii*). In response, Teacher-1 told the children that she would now 'show the embarrassing way to do it' (*hazukashii yarikata misete ageru yo*), and slumped her shoulders and made sad and funny-looking faces while walking up and taking the certificate from Teacher-2 (who was playing the "school principal"). In Japanese society, the feeling of 'embarrassment' (*hazukashisa*) as well as 'shame' (*haji*) is a powerful regulator of social behavior and a strategy of early childhood socialization (e.g., mother to misbehaving child: "You will be laughed at by people," Clancy, 1986, p. 236). Although the teacher's model of the 'embarrassing way' to do the ritual generated a great deal of positive affective stance as laughter from the children, it allowed the teacher to emphasize to them the correct and incorrect ways of performing the ritual by harnessing the children's displayed heightened attention. Immediately following the children's responses to the 'embarrassing way' to do the ritual, the teacher reused the adjective *hazukashii* 'embarrassing' by reframing this lexical "assessment" (e.g., Goodwin and Goodwin, 1992; Moore, Chapter 4 in this volume) *from* individual (negative) feelings about performing the ritual in front of an audience *to* the group's (negative) feelings that can arise from doing the ritual in a way that displays improper bodily comportment. The teachers followed this "bad" example by modeling another "good" example, which Teacher-1 prefaced by referring to it as the 'correct way to do it' (*tadashii yarikata*). In these ways, the teacher used metapragmatic, or what can be specified here as "meta-corporeal language" (i.e., commentary and assessment on bodily acts), in modeling for the children what to do and what *not* to do. In the process, the teachers socialized the children to pay attention to the details of prescribed bodily movements as an index of a social demeanor and a public presentation of self.

10.4.2   Rehearsal: Corrective Feedback

In the third stage of preparation on how to receive the graduation certificate, the teachers had the children line up (in order of last name) and engaged them in individual rehearsal. Similar to the modeling described earlier between the two teachers, this rehearsal was also done as a role-play in which Teacher-1 adopted the role of "school principal." Teacher-2 observed from the side and attended to the children waiting in line by adjusting their postures or turning their bodies to prepare them to face the imaginary audience (Figure 10.1).

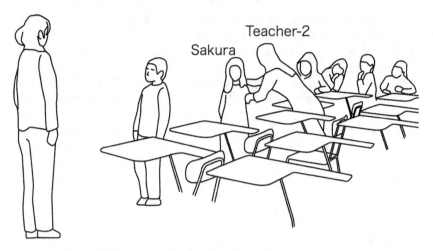

Figure 10.1 Teacher-2 (right) adjusts the bodily posture and direction of a girl (Sakura), who is waiting for her turn to receive the certificate, and then tells her to 'face this way' (*kocchi muite*). (Line drawings from video still frames by Hiroyuki Mae.)

During the rehearsal, one of the main instructional practices that emerged during the analysis was "corrective feedback." According to Ellis (2012), corrective feedback refers to a "specific move that corrects a learner error" (p. 135). Research on classroom interaction has traditionally examined the linguistic aspects of corrective feedback, including how it is initiated, carried out, and responded to by learners as "uptake" (Lyster and Ranta, 1997). More recently, studies of language socialization (Friedman, 2010; García-Sánchez, 2010; Howard, 2009; Klein, Chapter 3 in this volume; Moore, 2011) and related perspectives (Razfar, 2005) have examined the cultural organization of corrective feedback by relating it to ideologies concerning the use of language as an index of identity. For instance, in a Northern Thai village, Howard (2009) observes that a commonsense notion about language – stipulating that speakers use Standard Thai honorific forms over the local vernacular (Kam Muang) when displaying respect to people in institutionally powerful positions – is socialized in classroom discourse at an elementary school. Howard shows how a teacher engaged children in "correction routines" by instructing them to re-say their utterances that were addressed to teachers using Standard Thai politeness particles. In some communities, corrective feedback is deployed to socialize children's bodily comportment during on-going activities. Moore (2011) observes that teachers in a Northern African Fulbe school "paid close, corrective attention to children's bodies" as they were learning to recite French and Arabic text "because pointing, eye gaze, body position, and other forms of embodiment were believed to be both signs of and means for developing the desired skills, knowledge, and orientations that were associated with the two languages" (p. 214).

Similarly, in this JHL preschool classroom, teachers used their bodies to provide immediate corrective feedback on children's bodily moves. This feedback, I contend, was mediated by a language ideology centered on the importance of attending to the details of "correct" bodily form. This ideology was explicitly conveyed to children through the metalinguistic and meta-corporeal expression, *tadashii yarikata* 'the correct way to do it' as discussed above, and implicitly conveyed to them through practices of correction that involved pointing, gaze, and touch and other haptic acts (Kern, 2018), as described in the next sections.

10.4.2.1 Pointing and Gaze: Directives for Action In providing the children with corrective feedback on their embodied movements during the rehearsal, teachers often used pointing and gaze. As a "situated interactive activity" (Goodwin, 2003), pointing together with gaze and talk functioned as a "directive," or an action "designed to get someone else to do something" (Goodwin, 1990, p. 67). At the beginning of the ritual, the child whose name is called is expected to raise his or her hand and say *hai* 'yes' while orienting his or her body toward an imaginary audience, and then walk toward Teacher-1 (who is playing the role of "school principal"). Although Teacher-1 had earlier modeled these embodied practices and Teacher-2 adjusted the bodily orientation of children at the head of the line (Figure 10.1), they had not given the children explicit instructions on this bodily direction and gaze, which may have made it difficult for some of the children to "notice" (cf. Schmidt, 2001) in order to put into immediate action. In Excerpt 10.1, the teacher employs pointing and gaze together with verbal language to initiate corrective feedback on Ken's bodily orientation at the start of the ritual. (In addition to transcription symbols outlined at the beginning of this volume, the following markers are used to indicate: ⇒ child's trouble source: → teachers' corrective feedback: * child's response/ uptake).

Excerpt 10.1 Beginning of the Ritual
Child #2 (Ken Suzuki: male)

```
01      T-1:   [((picks up paper as a prop for a "graduation certificate"))
02      Ken:   [((nodding head))
03      T-1:   SUZUKI KEN.
               'Ken Suzuki.'
04  ⇒   Ken:   [hai. ] ((raising hand and walks toward Teacher-1; see Figure 10.2))
               'Yes.'
```

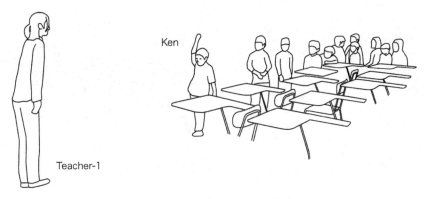

Figure 10.2 Child (Ken) says *hai* 'yes' while raising his hand and walking toward Teacher-1 (in role of "school principal").

05 → T-1:   [( )] *moo ikkai*
               '( ) once more.'
06 → T-1:   *mukoo* [*mite. saisho kara.*
               'Look that way. From the beginning.' ((pointing toward imaginary audience; see Figure 10.3))
07   Ken: [((stops, turns, as in Figure 10.3, and walks back to front of line))

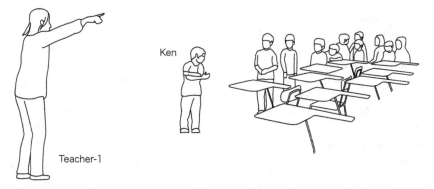

Figure 10.3 Teacher-1 (as "school principal") gazes and points toward imaginary audience while saying, 'Look that way.'

08   (1.2)
09   T-1:   *dare ga ichiban joozu ka na::*
               'I wonder who will be the most skillful?'
10   (0.2)
11   T-1:   *SUZUKI KEN.*
               'Ken Suzuki.'
12 * Ken: [*hai* ((raising hand while gazing toward imaginary audience; see Figure 10.4))
               'Yes.'

Figure 10.4 Child (Ken) says *hai* 'yes' while raising his hand and looking toward the imaginary audience.

13   T-1:   *ai*
               'Yes.'
14 *   Ken: ((turns and walks toward Teacher-1))
15   ((ritual continues, see Excerpt 10.3))

In Excerpt 10.1, when Ken responds to hearing his name called by walking toward Teacher-1 while raising his hand and saying *hai* 'yes' (line 04 and Figure 10.2), Teacher-1 shifts "footing" (Goffman, 1981) by stepping out of the fictive role of "school principal" to initiate corrective feedback. In particular, she points and gazes toward the empty chairs and beyond them (toward the windows in the back of classroom) while issuing a directive to Ken to 'look that way' (line 06 and Figure 10.3). In doing so, she encourages Ken to present himself first to an imagined audience and then to the fictive school principal (played by the teacher). Then, by issuing a directive to Ken to do the ritual 'from the beginning' (line 06), she supplies him with the opportunity to re-do this series of prescriptive actions, which he does "correctly" on the second attempt (line 12 and Figure 10.4) as implied by the teacher's continuation of the rehearsal.

In carrying out corrective feedback, teachers also used other verbal strategies that function in instructing children's bodies in culturally specific ways. Here, immediately following her feedback to Ken, Teacher-1 says, 'I wonder who will be the most skillful' (line 09), which can be heard as addressed to the entire class in framing this rehearsal as a competition among the children.

(At the end of the entire rehearsal with all of the students, Teacher-1 named a child who she deemed the most skillful.)

By using different multimodal resources such as pointing and gaze laminated with talk to do "explicit correction" (Lyster and Ranta, 1997) of children's corporeal acts, the teacher conveyed to the children the importance of attending to the details of the body in displaying a social demeanor and a public self during the formal ritual.

10.4.2.2 Haptic Acts: Control Touch, Guided Manipulation, and Intertwined Bodies

In addition to pointing and gaze, the teachers also employed "haptic acts" (Cekaite, 2015) of "control touch" (Goodwin and Cekaite, 2018) and "guided manipulation" (Kassing and Jay, 2003) in initiating and carrying out corrective feedback on children's bodies. In their discussion of embodied forms of correction in dance classes, Kassing and Jay (2003, p. 76) define guided manipulation as a "teacher's physical handling of a student's body or body part," which asserts authoritative power and control as an expert. As with other non-verbal actions, haptic correction is mutually elaborated upon by the accompanying talk in ways that elucidate its meaning as social action. During the middle of the ritual when the child approaches Teacher-1 as "school principal," who is holding the "graduation certificate" while saying 'congratulations on your graduation from preschool,' the child is expected to respond by performing another series of bodily actions that include taking hold of the certificate, stepping back, and bowing deeply. Several children had trouble with performing this part of the ritual, particularly the hand and footwork. As illustrated in Excerpt 10.2, Teacher-2, who had been standing to the side, comes over to assist in the corrective feedback initiated by Teacher-1 by engaging in haptic correction.

Excerpt 10.2 Stepping Back after Taking the Certificate
Child #9 (Yuri Toyota, female)

01	T-1:	*Toyota Yuri, sootsuen omedetoo.* ((holding "certificate" as
		if reading it))
		'Yuri Toyota, congratulations on graduating from preschool.'
02	T-1:	((offers "certificate" to Yuri))
03	Yuri:	((takes certificate "correctly" with right hand first, then left hand))
04	T-1:	( ) (0.4) °*kocchi*°
		'This side.'
05	T-1:	((begins to take a step back))
06 ⇒	Yuri:	((takes step back "incorrectly" with her right foot;
		see Figure 10.5))

Yuri

Teacher-1   Teacher-2

Figure 10.5 Child (Yuri) takes a step back "incorrectly" with her right foot first

07 → T-1:   >*hantai*<
               'The opposite.'
08 ⇒ Yuri: ((takes step back with left foot))
09 → T-1:   >*hantai*<
               'The opposite.'
10 → T-2:   *kocchi de morattara* (0.3) ((touching Yuri's left arm and hand))
               'When you receive it with this side (=left hand)'
11 → T-2:   *kocchi de ima moratta desho, saigo.* ((pushing on Yuri's back))
               'You received it now with this side (=left hand) didn't you, lastly?'
12 → T-2:   >*moo ikkai.*< ((T-2 positions her body directly behind Yuri))
               'Once more.'
13   T-1:   (0.4)
14 → T-2:   °>*moo ikkai*< ( )°
               'Once more ( ).'
15 → T-2:   >*massugu itte goran.*<
               'Try going straight.'
16   T-1:   ((0.5: taking "certificate" from Yuri in order to re-start the ritual))
17   T-2:   *iku desho.*
               'You'll go, okay' ((brings Yuri's hands together))
18   (0.4)
19 → T-1:   *ko*[*cchi de morattara* ( )]
               'When you receive it with this side [=left hand],'
20 → T-2:   [*kocchi de* ((moving Yuri's right hand)) *mo<u>r</u>attara* ((moving Y's left
               hand))]
               'When you receive it with this side [=right hand then left hand],'
21 → T-2:   *ko*[*cchi no ashi.*] ((touching Yuri's left leg))
               'This leg (=left leg).'
22 → T-1   [*kocchi no ashi.*] ((makes a hand gesture toward Yuri's left leg:
               Figure 10.6)) 'This leg (=left leg).'

23 ⇒ Yuri   ((begins to takes step backward "incorrectly" with her right foot, as
             Teacher-1 continues to gesture and T-2 continues to touch Yuri's left
             leg; see Figure 10.6))

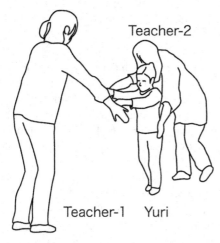

Figure 10.6 Teacher-2 takes hold of child's (Yuri's) right arm while touching
the child's left leg

24   T-1:   [n h [h]
                'Mm h.'
25 *   Yuri: [((brings right foot forward and moves left foot back; see Figure 10.7))

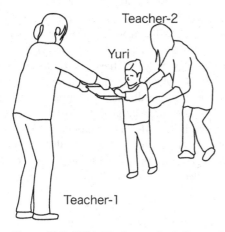

Figure 10.7 Child (Yuri) steps back "correctly" with her left leg first

26   T-2:   [*soo.*]
                 'Correct.'
27   T-1:   *soo.*
                 'Correct.'
28   T-2:   *muzukashii ne.*
                 'It's difficult, isn't it.'
29   ((ritual continues))

In Excerpt 10.2, after Yuri takes a step back "incorrectly" with her right foot first (line 06 and Figure 10.5), Teacher-1 initiates corrective feedback by telling Yuri it is 'the opposite' (lines 07 and 09). When Yuri does not correct this footwork on her own, Teacher-2 comes over to assist. She approaches Yuri from behind and wraps her body around Yuri's body (Figure 10.6) in a way that creates an "intercorporeality" (Merleau-Ponty, 1962; Meyer, Streeck, and Jorden, 2017) of "intertwined bodies" (see Goodwin and Cekaite, 2018, on hugs). From this position the teacher assumes an "embodied formation of control" (Cekaite, 2010, p. 7) in which she encourages Yuri to do the hand and footwork 'once more' (lines 12 and 14). In guiding Yuri to re-do this part of the ritual, Teacher-2 takes hold of Yuri's right arm and physically moves Yuri's arm to receive the proffered certificate while touching Yuri's left leg (which is the leg Yuri is expected to step back with first) and says 'this leg' (line 21). Yuri responds to this coordinated feedback from the teachers by beginning to step back "incorrectly" with her right leg first (line 23 and Figure 10.6), but stops this action midway through in order to self-correct and successfully complete the required footwork (line 25 and Figure 10.7). As they often do in response to children's correct uptake, here the teachers produce evaluations, or assessments (see Moore, Chapter 4 in this volume), that function as encouragement in the form of praise (line 26 and 27: *soo* 'correct/so/right') or account for the child's error (line 28: *muzukashii ne* 'It's difficult, isn't it'). Also, by using words such as *soo* 'correct/so/right,' teachers implicitly convey a language ideology of "correctness" of bodily moves.

This excerpt has shown ways in which teachers used touch and guided manipulation in sequences of corrective feedback on a child's bodily moves during individual rehearsal on how to accept the graduation certificate. In using touch and guided manipulation, Teacher-2 added a haptic modality to the corrective feedback that was initiated and carried out by Teacher-1 through a different combination of modalities (talk + gesture). As a result, through their coordinated and collaborative efforts, the teachers socialized children to the importance of attending to the details of bodily moves in this ritual.

10.4.2.3 Participation Frameworks: Children as Observers Classroom discourse and socialization are an inherently multiparty endeavor. Thus, corrective feedback and other instructional practices occur within multiparty "participation frameworks" (Goffman, 1981; see also, Goodwin and Goodwin, 2004; Karrebæk, Chapter 11 in this volume; Rymes and Leone-Pizzighella, Chapter 7 in this volume), which refers to situated interaction that consists of different kinds of "speakers" (e.g. animator, author) and "recipients" (e.g., addressee, observer, bystander). In rehearsing the ritual for receiving the certificate, teachers overtly positioned the children standing in line (waiting for their turn) as "observers" (e.g., Gaskins and Paradise, 2009; Philips, 1983) in ways that promoted their "learning through keen observation and listening, in anticipation of participation" (Rogoff et al., 2003, p. 176). Similarly, in drawing upon Lave and Wenger's (1991) theory of "peripheral participation," Hayashi and Tobin (2011) propose that Japanese preschool teachers promote children's "active watching" of their peers, such as in cases of children's fighting in which teachers tended not to intervene so as to encourage children to resolve conflicts on their own, which can attract an audience of peer onlookers. They argue that this non-interventionist approach fosters children's social skills in becoming a communicatively competent member of a social group. In this JHL preschool classroom, the teachers encouraged the children's active watching of the rehearsal in various ways, such as by directing the children waiting for their turn to 'look at' (*mitete yo*) their peers.

These also used embodied resources (their own and others' bodies) together with verbal directives in promoting the observers' active watching. In Excerpt 10.3 (continuation of Excerpt 10.1), while she engages in embodied corrective feedback of an individual child's (Ken) handwork, Teacher-2 turns and instructs the children waiting in line to observe the correct order of hands when receiving the certificate.

Excerpt 10.3 Taking Certificate with Right Hand First
Continuation of Excerpt 10.1
        Child #2 (Ken, male)

15   T-1:   *Suzuki Ken* ((holding up "certificate")), *sotsuen omedetoo*.
                'Ken Suzuki, congratulations on graduating from preschool.'
16   T-1:   ((holds out "certificate"))
17 ⇒ Ken: ((reaches out with both hands toward "certificate"; see Figure 10.8))

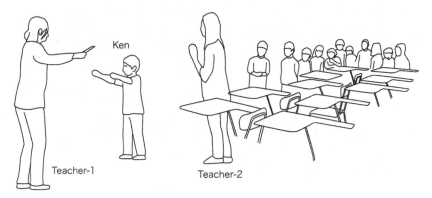

Figure 10.8 Child (Ken) reaches out "incorrectly" with both hands to take the "certificate"

18 → T-1: >*junban da yo.* ((reaching out toward Ken's right hand))
'The order (of hands).'
((lines skipped as Teacher-2 clarifies with Teacher-1 that the right hand
goes first))
29 → T-1: [*MIGITE KARA   ] MORAU N DA YO.*
'(You) receive it from the right hand.'
30 → T-1: [((holding out her right arm))]
31 → T-1: [[((holding out "certificate" toward Ken))]]
32 → T-2: [[((touches Ken's left shoulder and arm, and then his
right side))]]
33 → T-1: <*migite:*>
'Right hand.'
34 → T-2: ((takes Ken's right hand/arm and holds it up to receive
"certificate"))
35   (0.3)
36 → T-2: *kocchi-* ((moving Ken's right hand to take the "certificate" from
Teacher-1))
'This side-'
37 → T-2: *MINNA NE* ((turns to address children standing in line;
see Figure 10.9)) *SHOOJOO MORAU TOKI MITETE YO.*
'Everyone, when receiving the certificate, watch.'

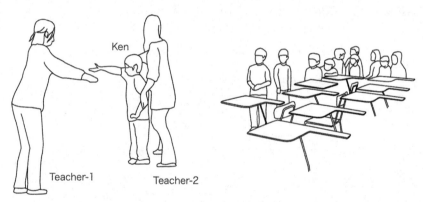

Figure 10.9 While guiding child's (Ken's) body, Teacher-2 turns her torso
and addresses the children waiting in line

38 → T-1: *MI[GI TE.*
'Right hand.'
39 → T-2:   [*KOCCHI* ((holds Ken's right hand up)) *TE* ((releases
Ken's hand))
'This hand [= right hand].'
40 → T-2: ((raises her right hand up high; see Figure 10.10))

Figure 10.10 Teacher-2 raises her right hand up high

41 → T-2:   *<KOCCHI NO TE DE>* (0.3)
            'With this (right) hand.'
42 → T-2:   *HITO:TSU ZUTSU.* ((lifts up Ken's left arm))
            'One (hand) at a time.'
43   (0.8)
44 → T-2:   *BI::* ((moving Ken's left arm to receive "certificate"))
            (("bi" is an onomatopoetic form expressing movement))
45   T-1: [((*sa:ga:*[*ru*   ] ((takes one step backward))
            'Step back.'
46   Ken: [((takes "certificate" into his hands))
47   T-2:   [>*sorede*<]*sagaru* ((takes a step back while holding Ken))
            'And then step back.'
48   T-2: °*migi* [*sagaru*°
            'Step the right (foot) back.'
49   T-1: [((bows deeply))
50   Ken: ((bows deeply))
51   T-2: °( ) *ne*°
            '( ), okay.'
52   Ken: ((puts "certificate" under left armpit, and walks away))
53   T-2: *s::o::: so, joozu da.*
            'Correct, correct, correct, skillful.'
54   (0.9)
55   T-2: *so.*
            'Correct, correct.'

In Excerpt 10.3, when Ken reaches for the proffered certificate "incorrectly" with both hands (Figure 10.8), Teacher-1 shifts out of the "school principal" role to initiate haptic correction by invoking 'the order [of hands]' (line 18). Following an aside with Teacher-2 in which she confirms that the certificate should be taken with the right hand first, Teacher-1 uses a loud voice to address the children who are waiting in line for their turn (line 29: '[You] receive it from the right hand'). In aligning with this multiparty framework, Teacher-2 comes over to assist in the corrective feedback by first guiding Ken's body to take the certificate with his right hand first and then by turning her torso to address the children waiting for their turn (line 37: 'Everyone, when receiving the certificate, watch' and Figure 10.9). The teacher's torso turn represents a "body torque" (Schegloff, 1998). In contrast to typical body torque that represents "involvement in *more than one* activity or course-of-action" (Schegloff, 1998, p. 544; italics mine), here the teacher uses body torque within *a single* activity involving multiple participants. More specifically, as she guides Ken's handwork, she twists her upper torso and directs the other children (waiting in line) to observe this handwork (Figure 10.9); in addition, she demonstrates the handwork to them by manipulating Ken's body as a "puppet," in order to prepare these children for their own upcoming rehearsal. In elaborating on this demonstration, Teacher-2 turns back to her original "home" position and uses her own body to model for the observing children what to do by raising her right arm high while saying 'this hand' (lines 39–40 and Figure 10.10). In these ways, while she momentarily puts the guided manipulation of Ken's body on hold, the teacher uses body torque, modeling, and accompanying verbal instruction to address the other children in encouraging them to closely observe the "correct" bodily actions. This strategy makes Ken's error publically available for the other children to observe as they prepare for their own rehearsal.

Excerpt 10.3 has built upon those that preceded it by examining ways in which teachers used verbal and embodied strategies to evoke different kinds of participation frameworks in engaging the children in rehearsal on how to receive the graduation certificate. In showing how the teachers instructed the children in prescribed bodily techniques during the classroom rehearsal, it suggests that the children were socialized through the culturally preferred method of modeling and imitation into the cultural norms of attending to the details of embodied practices for indexing a social demeanor in presenting a public self during the formal ritual.

10.5   Summary and Conclusion

This chapter has explored embodied socialization in a Japanese-as-a-heritage-language (JHL) preschool classroom in the United States as it is linked to ideologies of "correctness" and paying attention to the details of 'form' (*kata*) in Japanese society. In focusing on a specialized activity – preparing children for their graduation ceremony – it has shown how teachers used their bodies to instruct children on corporeal acts for performing a formal ritual that is valuable to membership in the preschool and other Japanese-speaking educational institutions. It has suggested that this instruction is tied to language ideologies of correctness concerning the formulaic use of bodily actions (e.g., bowing, receiving something with two hands) in specific contexts, and in the process conveys to children norms and values of their heritage culture. These norms included attending to the details of prescribed form as techniques of the body to index a social demeanor in presenting a public self. They also included modeling and imitation as a culturally preferred way of teaching and learning prescribed form. Having taking into consideration that attention to the details of prescribed form was not unique to this particular activity or classroom, this preparation can be considered as one of a constellation of activities through which Japanese-speaking children are socialized in (and outside) the classroom to attend to the details of prescribed form and become familiar with preferred paths to acquiring social skills and cultural competencies. Although I have not been able to examine the actual performance here, children did "successfully" receive their certificates on the auditorium stage, and thus demonstrated their *acquisition* (Kulick and Schieffelin, 2004) of the practices that they were socialized to in the classroom. The corrections and attention to form done during rehearsal in the classroom weeks earlier (and once on the actual stage) allowed the yearly ritual event to run smoothly, seemingly allowing parents and other family members to experience the joy and satisfaction of having their own child graduate from preschool as a member of group.

In conclusion, this study has shed light on the potential of language socialization for examining classroom discourse, and the potential of classroom discourse for contributing to language socialization theory. In comparison to studies of Japanese-speaking preschool classrooms that tend to gloss over the details of language and embodiment, taking a language socialization perspective has enabled us to not only examine the details of embodied instruction, such as meta-corporeal comments and explicit directives for embodied action, but also to consider how these practices index socio-culturally meaningful realties related to ideologies, demeanors, and personhood. This study has gone beyond the analysis of linguistic and sequential features of discourse to consider ways in which bodily acts participate in the process of reproducing socio-cultural meanings. While there has been a long tradition of concern in language socialization with non-verbal resources and other communicative channels, this study underscores that socialization involves "fully embodied actors" (Goodwin and Goodwin, 2004, p. 226) who engage in social activities and social actions with others. Classrooms are thus sites of socializing bodies in culturally specific ways. Yet, children are not merely objects of this socialization, but also agents who along with teachers provide models of embodied behavior to peers, and, in turn, socialize others.

NOTES

1 In addition to the "role-oriented preschool" Holloway (2000) categorizes two other kinds of Japanese preschools: (1) "relationship-oriented": "provide an enticing intro- duction to group life that focused on building the children's ability to form relation- ships with peers and learning basic classroom activities" (p. 18); (2) "child-oriented": "Most of the day was devoted to free play, with few group activities and no direct instruction" (p. 20).

2 According to O'Neill (1984), in addition to direct instruction, four other key ideolo- gies within the *iemoto* system included: (1) hereditary succession, (2) strict division between professional (teacher) and non-professional (student), (3) hierarchical organ- ization, and (4) strong sense of duty and obligation (p. 635–637).

REFERENCES

Agha, A. (2001). Register. In A. Duranti (ed.), *Key Terms in Language and Culture* (pp. 212–215). Malden, MA: Blackwell.

Ben-Ari, E. (1997). *Body Projects in Japanese Childcare: Culture, Organization and Emotions in a Preschool.* London: Curzon.

Bourdieu, P. (1991). *Language and Symbolic Power* (translated by G. Raymond and M. Adamson). Cambridge: Polity Press.

Bucholtz, M. and Hall, K. (2016). Embodied sociolinguistics. In N. Coupland (ed.), *Sociolinguistics: Theoretical Debates* (pp. 173–197). Cambridge: Cambridge University Press.

Burdelski, M. (2010). Socializing politeness routines: action, other-orientation, and embodiment in a Japanese preschool. *Journal of Pragmatics*, 42(6), 1606–1621.

Burdelski, M. (2011). Language socialization and politeness routines. In A. Duranti, E. Ochs, and B. B. Schieffelin (eds.), *The Handbook of Language Socialization* (pp. 275–295). Malden, MA: Wiley-Blackwell.

Burdelski, M. (2015). Reported speech as cultural gloss and directive: socializing norms of speaking and acting in Japanese caregiver-child triadic interaction. *Text & Talk*, 35(5), 575–595.

Burke, R. S. and Duncan, J. (2015). *Bodies as Sites of Cultural Reflection in Early Childhood Education.* New York, NY: Routledge.

Cekaite, A. (2010). Shepherding the child: embodied directive sequences in parent- child interaction, *Text & Talk*, 30(1), 1–25.

Cekaite, A. (2015). Coordination of talk and touch in adult-child directives: touch and social control. *Research on Language and Social Interaction*, 48(2), 152–175.

Clancy, P. M. (1986). The acquisition of communicative competence in Japanese. In B. B. Schieffelin and E. Ochs (eds.), *Language Socialization across Cultures* (pp. 213–250). Cambridge: Cambridge University Press.

Cook, H. M. (1996). Japanese language socialization: indexing the modes of self. *Discourse Processes*, 22(2), 171–197.

DeCoker, G. (1998). Seven characteristics of a traditional approach to learning. In J. Singleton (ed.), *Learning in Likely Places: Varieties of Apprenticeship in Japan* (pp. 45–67). New York, NY: Cambridge University Press.

Doerr, N. and Lee, K. (2010). Inheriting "Japanese-ness" diversely: heritage practices at a weekend Japanese language school in the United States. *Critical Asian Studies*, 42(2), 191–216.

Dunn, C. D. (2016). Creating "bright, positive" selves: discourses of self and emotion in a Japanese public-speaking course. *Ethos*, 44(2), 118–132.

Dunn, C. D. (2018). Bowing incorrectly: aesthetic labor and expert knowledge in Japanese business etiquette training. In H. M. Cook and J. S. Shibamoto-Smith (eds.), *Japanese at Work: Politeness, Power, and Personae in Japanese Workplace Discourse* (pp. 15–36). London: Palgrave Macmillan.

Ellis, R. (2012). *Language Teaching Research and Language Pedagogy*. Cambridge: Cambridge University Press.

Enfield, N. (2009). Everyday ritual in the residential world. In G. Senft and E. B. Basso (eds.), *Ritual Communication* (pp. 51–80). Oxford: Berg Publishers.

Friedman, D. (2010). Speaking correctly: error correction as a language socialization practice in a Ukrainian classroom. *Applied Linguistics*, 31(3), 346–347.

García-Sánchéz, I. M. (2010). The politics of Arabic language education: Moroccan immigrant children's language socialization into ethnic and religious identities. *Linguistics and Education*, 21(3), 171–196.

Gaskins, S. and Paradise, R. (2009). Learning through observation in daily life. In D. F. Lancy, J. Bock, and S. Gaskins (eds.), *The Anthropology of Learning in Childhood* (pp. 85–117). Lanham, MD: AltaMira Press.

Goffman, E. (1959 [1956]). *The Presentation of Self in Everyday Life*. New York, NY: Doubleday.

Goffman, E. (1981). *Forms of Talk*. Philadelphia, PA: University of Pennsylvania Press.

Goodman, R. (2012). From pitiful to privileged? The fifty-year story of the changing perception and status of Japanese returnee children. In R. Goodman, Y. Imoto, and T. Toivonen (eds.), *A Sociology of Japanese Youth: From Returnee to NEETs* (pp. 30–53). Abingdon, UK: Routledge.

Goodwin, C. (2003). Pointing as situated practice. In S. Kita (ed.), *Pointing: Where Language, Culture and Cognition Meet*. Mahwah, NJ: Lawrence Erlbaum.

Goodwin, C. and Goodwin, M. H. (1992). Assessments and the construction of context. In A. Duranti and C. Goodwin (eds.), *Rethinking Context: Language as an Interactive Phenomenon* (pp. 147–190). Cambridge: Cambridge University Press.

Goodwin, C. and Goodwin, M. H. (2004). Participation. In A. Duranti (ed.), *A Companion to Linguistic Anthropology* (pp. 222–244). Malden, MA: Blackwell.

Goodwin, M. H. (1990). *He-Said-She-Said: Talk as Social Organization among Black Children*. Bloomington, IN: Indian University Press.

Goodwin, M. H. and Cekaite, A. (2018). *Embodied Family Choreography: Practices of Control, Care, and Mundane Activity*. Abingdon, UK and New York, NY: Routledge.

Hayashi, A. and Tobin, J. (2011). The Japanese preschool's pedagogy of peripheral participation. *Ethos*, 39(2), 139–164.

Hayashi, A. and Tobin, J. (2015). *Teaching Embodied: Culture Practice in Japanese Preschool*. Chicago, IL: University of Chicago Press.

Holloway, S. D. (2000). *Contested Childhoods: Diversity and Change in Japanese Preschools*. London: Routledge.

Hood, L. and Schieffelin, B. B. (1978). Elicited imitation in two cultural contexts. *Quarterly Newsletter for Comparative Human Development*, 2(1), 4–12.

Howard, K. M. (2009). "When meeting Khun teacher, each time we should pay respect": standardizing respect in a Northern Thai classroom. *Linguistics and Education*, 20(3), 254–272.

Kassing, G. and Jay, D. M. (2003). *Dance Teaching Methods and Curriculum Design*. Champaign, IL: Human Kinesics.

Kern, F. (2018). Correcting bodily conduct in adult–child interaction. *Research on Children and Social Interaction*, 2(2), 213–234.

Kondo, D. (1990). *Crafting Selves: Power, Gender, and Discourse of Identity in a Japanese Workplace*. Chicago, IL: University of Chicago Press.

Kulick, D. and Schieffelin, B. B. (2004). Language socialization. In: A. Duranti (ed.), *A Companion to Linguistic Anthropology* (pp. 349–368). Malden, MA: Blackwell.

Lave, J. and Wenger, E. (1991). *Situated Learning: Legitimate Peripheral Participation*. Cambridge: Cambridge University Press.

Lyster, R. and Ranta, L. (1997). Corrective feedback and learner uptake: negotiation of form in communicative classrooms. *Studies in Second Language Acquisition*, 20 (1), 37–66.

Mauss, M. (1973 [1935]). Techniques of the body. *Economy and Society*, 2, 70–88.

Merleau-Ponty, M. (1962). *Phenomenology of Perception* (translated by C. Smith). London: Routledge and Kegan Paul.

Meyer, C., Streeck, J., and Jordan, J. S. (2017). *Intercorporeality: Emerging Socialities in Interaction*. New York, NY: Oxford University Press.

Moore, L. C. (2006). Learning by heart in public and Qur'anic schools in Marous, Cameroon. *Social Analysis: The Interactional Journal of Culture and Social Practice*, 50(3), 109–126.

Moore, L. C. (2011). Language socialization and repetition. In A. Duranti, E. Ochs, and B. B. Schieffelin (eds), *The Handbook of Language Socialization* (pp. 209–226). Malden, MA: Wiley-Blackwell.

Ochs, E., Solomon, O., and Sterponi, L. (2005). Limitation and transformations of habitus in child-directed communication. *Discourse Studies*, 7(4–5), 547–583.

O'Neill, P. G. O. (1984). Organization and authority in the traditional arts. *Modern Asian Studies*, 18(4), 631–645.

Peak, L. (1991). *Learning to Go to School in Japan: The Transition from Home to Preschool Life*. Berkeley and Los Angeles, CA: University of California Press.

Philips, S. U. (1983). *The Invisible Culture: Communication in Classroom and Community on the Warm Springs Indian Reservation*. New York, NY: Longman.

Razfar, A. (2005). Language ideologies in practice: repair and classroom discourse. *Linguistics and Education*, 16(4), 404–424.

Riley, K. C. (2011). Language socialization and language ideologies. In A. Duranti, E. Ochs, and B. B. Schiefflin (eds.), *The Handbook of Language Socialization* (pp. 493–514). Malden, MA: Wiley-Blackwell.

Rogoff, B., Paradise, R., Arauz, R. M., Correa-Chávez, M., and Angelillo, C. (2003). Firsthand learning through intent participation. *Annual Review of Psychology*, 54, 175–203.

Schegloff, E. A (1998). Body torque. *Social Research*, 65(3), 535–596.

Schieffelin, B. B. and Ochs, E. (1986). Language socialization. *Annual Review of Anthropology*, 15, 163–191.

Schmidt, R. (2001). Attention. In P. Robinson (ed.), *Cognition and Second Language Instruction* (pp. 3–32). Cambridge: Cambridge University Press.

Shilling, C. (2012 [1993]). *The Body and Social Theory, 3rd Ed.* London: SAGE.

Smith, R. J. (1998). Transmitting tradition by the rules: an anthropological interpretation of the *iemoto* system. In J. Singleton (ed.), *Learning in Likely Places: Varieties of Apprenticeship in Japan* (pp. 23–34). New York, NY: Cambridge University Press.

Tobin, J. J., Wu, D. Y. H., and Davidson, D. H. (1989). *Preschool in Three Cultures: Japan, China, and the United States.* New Haven, CT and London: Yale University Press.

Tsujimoto, M. (2014). The somaticization of learning in Edo Confucianism: the rejection of body–mind dualism in the thought of Kaibara Ekken (translated by B. D. Steben). In C.-C. Huang and J. A. Tucker (eds.), *Dao Companion to Japanese Confucian Philosophy* (pp. 141–164). Dordrecht: Springer.

11 Talking about Lunch
Diversity, Language, and Food Socialization in a Danish Kindergarten Classroom

Martha Sif Karrebæk

11.1 Introduction

This chapter offers a language socialization view on everyday experiences with food in a kindergarten classroom in Copenhagen. As across Europe, many schools in Copenhagen are ethnically diverse, and this is relevant to the themes of food experiences and language socialization in various ways. Food is a domain in which people regularly encounter differences between their own and others' everyday practices and displayed understandings. In Danish schools, most children bring food prepared at home, making lunch an activity where norms of home and school meet in congruent or conflicting ways. Food norms of the school typically go unnoticed, especially when they are followed. However, children with immigrant backgrounds may bring lunches that suggest norms other than those considered appropriate by teachers. This may have discursive consequences and socializing potentials. Teachers' and peers' assessments of food brought to school are based on culturally embedded systems of beliefs and ideas, or ideologies. Such assessments are often moral, as they concern what is "right" and "wrong," targeting not only food but also people (Coveney, 2006; Fader, 2011; Iacovetta, 2006; Paugh and Izquierdo, 2009). Although food and food practices are based on different ideologies and are reflexively motivated in different ways, we find two common themes: national traditions and health. Whereas tradition is clearly culturally loaded, health is typically regarded as objectively verifiable and thus culturally and ideologically neutral. This however is a misconception (Bradby, 1997; Margetts et al., 1997). In the case analyzed in this chapter, the cultural embedding is reflected in the obligation for students to bring rye bread for lunch, because this is considered "healthy" and therefore morally appropriate.

Many language socialization studies analyze meetings between *educational systems*, which propagate state-sanctioned, hegemonic language and cultural ideologies, and *young people* with different minority backgrounds (for an overview, see García-Sánchez and Nazimova, 2017). Such studies discuss how a particular socio-political situation forms the experiences of young people, what shapes processes of belonging and marginalization, and how children struggle with, follow, manipulate, subvert, and challenge the social orders they encounter (Cekaite and Aronsson, 2004; Karrebæk, 2012; Pallotti, 2002). Several studies demonstrate that educational settings do not merely target academic skills. Children are socialized to become "good students" or "good citizens" through a focus on social behavior considered mainstream and "normal" in a range of domains (Cekaite, 2012; Wortham, 2006). The present study continues this line of research.

In the following I examine discursive encounters that take place between teachers and children during the social activity of lunch, primarily focused on the topic of rye bread. I analyze the ways in which teachers, children, and parents are positioned, using Goffman's (1981) "production format" in order to understand how teachers and children occupy different speaker positions and how the teacher attempts to socialize parents through the children. While the teacher is an "author" and a responsible "principal" of messages, children become "animators" by relaying these messages to parents, and parents are introduced through discourse and become conversational "figures". Furthermore, I look at "accounts," or discursive ways of engaging with unexpected and (often) dispreferred actions (Austin, 1961; Scott and Lyman, 1968; Sterponi, 2003). The children presented accounts in numerous cases (e.g., when not bringing rye bread), yet these were often treated as illegitimate (Scott and Lyman, 1968, p. 54). Also, sometimes accounts failed to occur when prompted by the teacher. As a whole, the chapter adds to research on food in classrooms under conditions of migration by focusing on the vital role of language, and it adds to the literature on food and language socialization by demonstrating the difficulties that emerge when (what is seen as) noncompatible food understandings meet in classrooms.

11.2   Background

11.2.1   Language and Food Socialization

Language socialization studies focus on meetings between social agents with different access to ratified knowledge and power. In classrooms the social roles of teacher and student map on to an institutionally defined power structure and an epistemic order (Pace and Hemmings, 2007; Wilson and Stapleton, 2010). The relative positions of novice and expert-authority cover these dimensions. Novice-students are less culturally experienced individuals, expected to follow the teachers' directions. As expert-authorities, teachers are expected to be knowledgeable, teach, and present themselves as good examples. The positions of expert-authority and novice are interactionally achieved in different activities. In school, some activities fall within a well-defined curriculum (algebra, literacy, etc.) whereas others such as food activities concern areas that are understood as everyday concerns. Consequently, authority figures from different social domains (e.g., teacher and parent) may enter into conflictual relationships in food activities.

Within the language socialization framework, the evening meal of (middle-class) families holds a central position. This is a daily activity where experts (parents) and novices (children) engage in focused interaction, and where a range of roles, identities, values, discursive genres, and activities are made available for novices (see Aukrust and Snow, 1998; Blum-Kulka, 1997; Ochs and Taylor, 1995; Snow et al., 1990). During mealtimes across the globe, adults socialize children into understandings of food. For instance, in Japan, as food is something that often commands respect, children may be prompted to apologize to food that has been left unfinished (Burdelski, 2014). In the United States, parents consider themselves responsible for children's healthy eating habits (e.g., Ochs, Pontecorvo, and Fasulo, 1996; Paugh and Izquirdo, 2009). In Europe, although Italian parents prioritize children's socialization into food as pleasure rather than into healthy eating (Ochs et al., 1996), health does have a central position outside of the United States too, as revealed in studies from the United Kingdom (Wiggins, 2004), Sweden (Anving and Sellerberg, 2010), and non-Western societies (e.g. Riley, 2011). The parental concern with health responds to (and perhaps co-creates) dominant understandings of children's preference for unhealthy food, dispreference for vegetables, and lack of orientation to health concerns. In Swedish and US homes, family meals are exercises in delayed gratification where (unhealthy) rewards follow the consumption of obligatory (healthy) food (Aronsson and Gottzén, 2011; Ochs et al., 1996). At the Swedish middle-class table, Anving and Sellerberg (2010) observe how health orientations compete with orientations toward diversity in taste as parents educate children about a world where diversity is presented as a fact. The positions of parent and child are not pre-established but interactionally achieved, as Aronsson and Gottzén (2011) report from Sweden, and children can choose to align with either. Similarly, Yount-André (2016) discusses how a Senegalese sister and brother constructed gender and age positions through the sharing of food gifts.

Although they are ripe with conflict (Ochs and Beck, 2013, p. 49), commensal situations and meals are considered to be important vehicles of culture (Fiese, Foley, and Spagnola, 2006; Ochs et al., 2010; Ochs et al., 1996) and sites of the creation of social cohesion. In classrooms, understandings, agendas, and competences differ even more between participants than in families, yet only few school studies have examined this. Allison's (2008) study of her American son's food socialization in a Japanese kindergarten argues that school food events are regarded as essential for the creation of cultured subjects. Golden (2005) discusses Israeli teachers' work to create

Figure 11.1 *Smørrebrød* at the Great Northern Food Court, Grand Central, NYC

national alignment through eating practices among a diverse group of children. These studies, as well my own work with food socialization (Karrebæk, 2012, 2013a, 2013b), show how institutional work to socialize children and parents to particular food norms may be at the expense of intercultural considerateness. On the other hand, Burgess and Morrison (1998) reported from a socially and ethnically diverse urban UK school that some teachers were reluctant to engage with food and eating because they saw it as a sensitive issue, lacked knowledge on culturally diverse eating patterns, and were uncertain about how to handle children from low-income families in their classrooms. Other teachers regarded the topic as relatively unimportant in comparison with more traditional educational topics (literacy, algebra, etc.), because it was not part of the national curriculum and therefore did not have sufficient academic value. Also, they did not believe it would have a lasting effect.

11.2.2   A Cultural Understanding of Rye Bread

Danish rye bread differs significantly from many other (US) breads known as rye bread. It is made from sourdough, wholegrain rye flour, rye kernels, water, and salt, and it constitutes a salient contrast to light "white" yeast-based wheat bread.[1] Rye bread has been a dominant element in the Danish diet for many centuries and well into the twentieth century. Today, rye bread is praised as a gastronomic feat, even occasionally as "our national pride" (Plum, 2001, p. 147).[2] Open rye bread sandwiches, or *smørrebrød* 'butter(ed) bread,' are a traditional lunch menu item. Rye bread does come as belabored works of art but in general it is an everyday phenomenon (see Figures 11.1 and 11.4); its emblematic status is reflected by numerous cultural representations and practices. For instance, *smørrebrød* was in the top 10 in a recent poll to find the Danish national dish.[3] (See also the illustrations of contemporary [popular culture] interpretations in Figures 11.2 and 11.3).

Figure 11.2 Knitted rye bread sandwiches

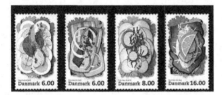

Figure 11.3 Official Danish stamps depicting *smørrebrød*

Figure 11.4 Regular school lunch box

In Denmark, rye bread is promoted as particularly healthy, as it reduces the risk of cancer and lifestyle diseases. The following quote comes from an influential Danish food entrepreneur (Figure 11.1 illustrates *smørrebrød* sold at his food court at the New York Grand Central terminal) and is typical for the promotion of rye bread, drawing on a scientifically sounding speech register:

The rye bread with all its dark, kernel-full density has been the foundation of the Danes' diet for the last 1,500 years. Despite this, newer studies of our food habits show that the consumption of rye bread has fallen steadily since the 1970s ... Grain products are also important sources of minerals, vitamin B, E and a range of antioxidants and many studies show a relation between a high consumption of whole grain products and a reduced risk of cardiovascular diseases, cancer, diabetes and obesity. (Meyer, 2010; my translation)

The health value of rye bread is also emphasized by nurses and pediatricians. They advise parents to feed their children rye bread, regardless of its strong taste. Parents are thus responsible for socializing children to acquire this taste. In summary, the institutional focus on rye bread has a particular cultural background.

11.3   Methodology

11.3.1   Data

This chapter builds on ethnographic fieldwork conducted over two years with a group of children in an urban public school in Copenhagen. The fieldwork began in week four of the first school year (kindergarten class, grade zero; starting mid-August) and lasted to the end of first grade (late June). I participated in classes, breaks, and field trips, eating my lunch next to the children, and engaging in small talk whenever possible. The data presented come from the first and most intensive year of the fieldwork, primarily because the organization of lunch changed in first grade. I give an overall introduction to lunch in grade zero below. Teachers, parents, and children agreed to participate in the study, and all participants are anonymized. I took fieldnotes and made video and audio recordings in class, in breaks and in after-school activities, resulting in more than 300 hours of audio and more than 100 hours of video recording. I also interviewed parents, teachers, and the school principal about their ideas about (ideologies of) language, bilingualism, and food, and on their school-related experiences with all of this.

Although the school principal, who was new to his post, had recently succeeded in attracting children from ethnically Danish academic families (who previously enrolled their children in private or other public schools with a better reputation), the school's student population continued to be ethnically, socially, and linguistically diverse (for other studies from the school, see Karrebæk, Madsen, and Møller, 2016).

The focal class had 23 students, aged five to seven, of a variety of backgrounds: Danish, Pakistani, Somali, Turkish, Icelandic, Chinese, Moroccan, and Syrian.[4] Some of the children oriented more easily to school-promoted norms than others, in most cases probably because school norms resembled what they knew from home. These children were advantaged with regard to the teachers' expectations and to the knowledge presupposed and communicated by the teachers. The class was taught by two female teachers, Louise and Kristine (referred to by their first names), both in their thirties, and of majority Danish background. They were formally trained in early/preschool education with supplementary courses. Louise had eight years of experience as a kindergarten class teacher; Kristine was in her second year of teaching. Of the two, Louise was the more active teacher in food socialization.

11.3.2   Method

I work within a linguistic ethnographic framework (e.g., Rampton, Maybin, and Roberts, 2015). In linguistic ethnography it is common to research one's own cultural community and question one's own cultural assumptions. I am of majority Danish background, brought up on rye bread. Language is regarded as key in the analysis of social issues, and ethnography is seen as essential for the understanding of language and discourse. To exemplify this point, we cannot know the cultural meaning of "rye bread" – or which meanings this term indexes – if we are uninformed about the local universe of understanding. We need to know that it is a daily practice for teachers to ask children about the food in their lunchboxes to appreciate what is at stake when this happens. We also need to know that rye bread is formulated as *sundt* 'healthy' and other kinds of bread as *usundt* 'unhealthy', and the social and cultural basis for such articulations. In line with the objectives of linguistic ethnography, this study compares meetings between teachers and children to general concerns in an increasingly diverse Danish society. Thereby, food is treated as a semiotic phenomenon through which belonging, appropriateness, and normalcy are negotiated, and such negotiation is done through discourse. Language socialization targets trajectories of development and change. In the present study, it is a core concern for teachers to influence the food choices of some children, and through the children to socialize their parents. They do this discursively. Language socialization also invites us to consider relations between participants and the participant roles of expert and novice, in terms of which participants are in a position to say and accomplish which actions, how they do that, and what the responses and implications are.

11.4   Food Socialization in a Kindergarten Class

In the observed classroom, food socialization occurred during different activities, yet most significantly in the course of lunch. All of the excerpts presented here come from such lunch encounters. The section opens and closes with two announcements in which the teacher, Louise, addresses the class as a group. All remaining examples illustrate a more prevalent "participation framework" (Goffman, 1981; see also Burdelski, Chapter 10 in this volume; Rymes and Leone-Pizzighella, Chapter 7 in this volume) of food socialization in the classroom, namely one-to-one encounters between teacher and child with other children as bystanders. Analytically I focus on the use of different speaker roles in the production format by teacher and student, and the parent as a conversational figure (Section 11.4.1), and on accounts (Section 11.4.2).

The children brought lunch prepared by their parents, and most of them received a pre-ordered supplementary beverage (mostly semi-skim or skim milk). Lunch usually took place in the classroom, and lasted between 30 and 45 minutes. The children ate at individual desks that they also occupied during class. The teachers had lunch with them, eating in front of the class. This way of making lunch a commensal activity validated the class as a group (Fischler, 2011). It also gave the teachers the opportunity to perform as "good examples" in addition to "experts" and "institutional authorities" through their food choices and eating behaviors. In this school, there were no official regulations concerning the contents of children's lunchboxes. Yet, the kindergarten teachers agreed that rye bread was the only bread that children should bring in their lunchboxes because rye bread is healthy and white bread is unhealthy. This message was repeated to the children daily, and to my knowledge rarely was other information regarding lunch box contents provided (but see Excerpt 11.6, line 06). In the vast majority of cases, children who brought (what was treated as) inappropriate lunch had ethnic minority backgrounds, but this was never articulated explicitly, an observation I will return to in Section 11.5.

11.4.1   Production Format and Parents as Figures

In this section I examine the way that parents are introduced as relevant participants in socializing children to normative food practices and eating habits. To initiate this theme, I show an example in which the teacher Louise articulates an understanding of rye bread as preferred and obligatory in an easily accessible manner (Excerpt 11.1). The official name of this class is *0.b*.

Excerpt 11.1 Newsletter Announcement

Month 8 into Grade 0: March 24; audio recording

01 Louise: *nu ska jeg fortælle jer noget 0.b ka I huske i går, (2.4)*
             'now let me tell something 0b do you remember yesterday, (2.4)'
02   *der havde vi alle sammen rugbrød med (1.3) hva? (.) det har jeg skrevet i*
             'we all brought rye bread (1.3) huh? (.) I've written this'
03   *et brev til jeres mor og far jeg har skrevet den på (1.4) på: computeren*
             (1.0)
             'in a letter to your mom and dad I've written it on (1.4) o:n the computer
             (1.0)'
04   *jeg (har) skrevet JUHUUUU (1.8) I GÅR HAVDE VI ALLE SAMMEN*
             RUGBRØD MED.
             'I've written HOORAYYY (.) YESTERDAY WE ALL BROUGHT RYE
             BREAD.'
05   *(0.5) vi blir (.) så (.) tæskekloge herinde.*
             '(0.5) we become (.) so (.) freaking smart in here.'

Louise's announcement demonstrates four things. First, it was somewhat extraordinary and unexpected that all class members brought rye bread for lunch, and it called for the children's attention as can be seen in Louise's pre-announcement (line 01: 'now let me tell you something'). Second, Louise presented this as good news meriting applause (line 04: 'HOORAYYY'), and her announcement simultaneously transformed the bringing of rye bread into a collective celebratory event. The similarity in lunch made a class consisting of a variety of individuals into a (homogeneous) collective. Third, the celebratory potential came from the understanding that bringing rye bread fulfilled a pre-condition for students to succeed or to 'become (.) so (.) freaking smart' (line 05). In this way Louise makes rye bread a relevant demand in the school context regardless of its peripheral status in relation to the educational subjects taught – and regardless of the many different food cultural backgrounds of the students. Fourth, rye bread was not only important to teachers and students but also to parents. Louise frames the announcement as a repetition of a message addressed to parents (lines 02–03: 'I've written this in a letter to your mom and dad'). In this case, parents were mere recipients of celebratory talk. More frequently parents were included or addressed as lunch producers, reminding them to provide children with rye bread, or even as culprits of transgressive actions such as giving the children white bread.

Parents were positioned as special but essential participants in classroom food socialization. They were "special" because they were bodily absent, but they were essential because they provided the food that children brought to school. Thereby it was necessary for the teachers to communicate with parents in order to urge children to bring specific foods. In comparison to Excerpt 11.1

above, explicit food socialization occurred primarily when teachers had noticed children eating (what was treated as) inappropriate food, mostly white bread. While some comments were aimed at encouraging individual children to think about what they consumed (a point I will return to), others were aimed at encouraging them to improve the situation by conveying food norms to their parents. I now focus on the speaker role assigned to and taken up by the child, and how the parent is positioned as a conversational figure and addressee.

Excerpt 11.2 is from the beginning of the second month of the school year. The teacher Louise has told a child (Selina) that her white bread is unhealthy and that she should only bring rye bread. Then Louise introduces Selina's mother into the discourse:

Excerpt 11.2 Remember to Tell Mommy
Beginning of month 2: September 16; audio recording. Participants: Louise (teacher), Selina (child; Moroccan background)

01 Louise: *ka du huske og sige til mor næste gang så ska du ik ha den der brød med*
            'will you remember to tell mommy next time then you are not gonna bring
            that bread'
02 Selina: *jeg havde oss brød med*
            'I also brought bread'
03 Louise: *jamen du ska <u>kun</u> ha sådan noget rugbrød med (.) ik det der brød med*
            'yeah but you are <u>only</u> gonna bring that kind of rye bread (.) not bring that
            bread'
04 Uni: *nej*
            'no'
05 Louise: *kun rugbrød*
            'only rye bread'
06   (.)
07 Selina: *jeg spiste (.) mit rugbrød*
            'I ate (.) my rye bread'
08 Louise: *ja det oss godt men du ska slet ik ha sådan noget brød med du ska ha <u>to</u>*
            rugbrød
            'yeah that's also good but you shouldn't bring that kind of bread at all you
            should bring <u>two</u> rye bread'
09   (.)
10 Selina: *det ska jeg huske og sige til mor*
            'I'll remember to tell mommy that'

Selina claims that she brought (line 02) and already finished eating her rye bread (line 07), and thereby shows awareness of the norms surrounding such type of bread. This may be an attempt at mitigating Louise's criticism. Louise insists that white bread is entirely inappropriate. She positions Selina's mother as responsible for the food and in need of being told not to give Selina 'that [white] bread' (line 01). Simultaneously Louise positions Selina as responsible for changing this situation as she "prompts" (e.g., Schieffelin, 1990) her to 'remember to tell mommy' (line 01). The lexical item 'remember' presupposes that Selina has already been informed to do so and it functions as (mild) criticism. In the prompt Louise sketches a precondition of change, namely that Selina animates Louise's implied message to her mother (i.e., "no white bread in school lunch boxes"). This is language socialization into school food norms, originating with the teacher's expert authority, directed to the child, using the child as a conduit to reach the parent. Through her partial repeat (line 10: 'I'll remember to tell mommy that'), Selina accepts her positioning as an animator of the teacher's conveyed food norm and shows alignment with it. Thereby Selina promises to be responsible for monitoring the appropriateness of her lunchbox contents.

Excerpt 11.3 illustrates the complicated patterns of distribution, transportation, and production of words and food in and in relation to the classroom. This episode occurred six months into the school year, a period during which a child (Fadime) was singled out numerous times for the contents of her lunch. Prior to the excerpt, Fadime had been observed eating white bread. This leads to rather harsh criticism from the teacher Louise, who does not just prompt Fadime to animate a message (to her parents) about bringing rye bread but also asks Fadime for her report book (i.e., a small notebook used by teachers and parents for urgent messages). The excerpt begins as Louise returns the report book to Fadime. In this excerpt, superscript letters ([a] through [d]) refer to non-verbal action in double parentheses.

Excerpt 11.3 I Did Tell Daddy

Month 7: February 2. Participants: Louise (teacher), Fadime (child, Turkish); video recording

01 Louise: [a]*nu husker du lige rugbrødet i morgen.*
'[a]now you remember the rye bread tomorrow' (([a]handing Fadime the report book))

02   (2.0) ((Louise turns away from Fadime, prepares to leave the table))

03 Fadime: [b]*det har jeg sagt til far, (.) [c]jeg har sagt det til far.*
'[b]I did tell daddy, (.) [c]I did tell daddy.' (([b]getting up, facing Louise; [c]Louise turns around, looks at Fadime))

04 Louise: [d]*nu har jeg oss skrevet det til ham.*
'[d]now I also wrote it to him.' (([d]nodding))

Louise reminds Fadime to bring rye bread 'tomorrow.' Her use of 'now' signals that Fadime has been informed previously about this expectation, and writing in the report book underscores the message that despite these prior conversations Fadime has failed to accomplish the task. In this case, Fadime is positioned as relaying the message in a more material sense, handing the father the report book. Louise does not initially involve Fadime's parents explicitly, yet Fadime introduces the father as a conversational figure. In Fadime's turn (*det har jeg sagt til far* 'I did tell daddy this'), the pronominal object *det* '(remember) to bring rye bread' is topicalized in a way that signals its importance and conveys that it is shared information. Fadime's formulation underlines that she has accomplished the expected task, namely to animate the teacher's message to her parents, and at the same time, represents Fadime as someone who suffers the consequences of others' (i.e., parents') actions. She implies that she has not failed personally and should not be criticized by the teacher. Louise does not display recognition of Fadime's discursive work. Although in other episodes Louise oriented to children as merely responsible for animating discursive content, here Louise holds Fadime responsible for the food in her lunchbox.

When teachers asked students to mediate their messages to parents, they suggested that parents were not expert authorities in relation to lunch. Children were expected to become animators of a school voice, when their food indexed a home food culture that was regarded as incongruent with food norms of the school and those of the mainstream society. Children were thereby positioned between two central authority figures: teachers and parents. Yet, the teachers did not seem to display a recognition of the difficulty of this positioning.

11.4.2   Accounts

Accounts are discursive actions that point out something as a social breach, and through this they index systems of norms, moral beliefs, and values (e.g., Sterponi, 2003). At the same time, accounts are attempts to stabilize a social situation by recategorizing the action or negotiating responsibility. In my data, teachers often prompted children to provide accounts for food in their lunchboxes (white bread) that did not adhere to expectations of what was deemed healthy (rye bread). This is demonstrated in Excerpt 11.4 from a field trip to an after-school center two months into the school year. The group was having lunch while sitting on couches and at small tables around the room. A child (Bilal) is eating a white roll when Louise approaches him.

Excerpt 11.4 Bilal's White Bread
Month 2: September 14; audio recording. Participants: Louise (teacher), Bilal (child, Moroccan)

```
01  Louise:   ↑har du ik rug↑brød med Bilal?
              '↑didn't you bring rye↑bread Bilal?'
02            (1.0)
03  Louise:   ↓har du ik rugbrød med?
              '↓didn't you bring rye bread?'
04  Louise:   hvorfor har du ik rugbrød med.
              'why didn't you bring rye bread.'
05            (3.0)
```

06 Louise: *du ska ha rugbrød med.*
            'you have to bring rye bread.'
07 Louise: ↑*ja (.) det husker du lige i morgen.*
            '↑yes (.) just remember that tomorrow.'

Louise's initial question to Bilal conveys the presupposed norm to bring rye bread (line 01). It also constructs Bilal's food choice as a deviation through the negative form *har du ik* ('didn't you'). In fact, Louise thematizes a preparatory condition for the normatively expected action of eating rye bread: one needs to bring rye bread in order to eat it, though eating it does not necessarily follow from bringing it, as we shall see later (Excerpts 11.5 and 11.6). When Bilal does not seem to answer, Louise continues with a repetition, followed by a question (line 04: 'why didn't you bring rye bread?') that invites Bilal to provide an account. Given that it is unusual in Danish society to expect young children to be involved in preparing their own lunch – as this is still somewhat early in the school year, Bilal may be unfamiliar with this type of question – it is not surprising that he does not provide an account. At the same time, Louise's question encourages Bilal to focus on what he brought in his lunchbox, and what he is currently eating, and how those two actions compare to the local food norm. Such invitations to provide accounts encouraged children to realize that they were not just food recipients, but also active participants in constructing their food choices and eating habits. Children had an opportunity and even an obligation to influence the contents of their lunchboxes and what they consumed for lunch.

Over the course of the year, the children displayed the understanding that accounts for food choices were expected. In Excerpt 11.5 we see how Merve provides an account when she is observed not eating rye bread. Notice also how the discourse structure used by the teacher is similar to the IRE (Initiation–Response–Evaluation) routines often documented in classroom discourse: the teacher asks a question looking for a specific reply, and following the student's reply provides an assessment (Mehan, 1979; see also Moore, Chapter 4 in this volume; Rymes and Leone-Pizzighella, Chapter 7 in this volume). During a routine inspection of some of the children's lunchboxes, Louise has stopped at a table.

Excerpt 11.5 Merve's Rye Bread
Month 5: January 12; audio recording. Participants: Louise (teacher), Merve (child, Turkish)

01 Louise: *hvor er dine rugbrød henne?*
            'where are your rye breads?'
02 Merve: *vi havde ik noget rugbrød.*
            'we didn't have any rye bread.'

03   Louise: *nej du ska spise dit rugbrød (.) den er usund det brød der. spis dit*
             rugbrød.
             'no you have to eat your rye bread (.) that one is unhealthy that bread. Eat
             your rye bread.'
04   Merve: *xxx usundt.*
             'xxx unhealthy.'
05   Louise: *sådan der smukke ...*
             'that's more like it beautiful ...'

In contrast to Excerpt 11.4 discussed earlier, here Louise's question to Merve
(line 01: 'where are your rye breads?') presupposes that Merve has rye bread in
her lunchbox. Again, this implicitly conveys a norm about food choices, and it
constructs the child as aware of the norm. This is five months into the school
year, and Merve seems prepared to answer the question about her food as she
immediately provides an account (line 02: 'we didn't have any rye bread [at
home]'). With her account, Merve denies Louise's presupposition that she
brought rye bread, and, as indexed by the first person inclusive pronoun 'we,'
accepts part of the responsibility. While Merve is speaking, Louise seems to
have taken a closer look at Merve's lunchbox (an action she often engaged in),
as she subsequently makes it clear that Merve has to eat her rye bread,
implying that Merve did not tell the truth and arguing that the other bread 'is
unhealthy' (line 03). When Louise finally exclaims 'that's more like it beautiful' (line 05), it is an encouraging evaluation of Merve's normatively appropriate reorientation (now eating rye bread rather than white bread). This
positive assessment includes an endearment term ('beautiful'), another symbolic encouragement of Merve's alignment with school norms.

This excerpt demonstrates how the rye bread norm was increasingly
presupposed in interactions; how it was motivated through the evaluation of
other breads as unhealthy and therefore inappropriate; and how children provided
accounts. Scott and Lyman (1968) distinguish between two types of accounts:
"justifications" where "one accepts responsibility for the fact in question but
denies the pejorative quality associated with it," and "excuses" where "one
admits that the act in question is bad, wrong or inappropriate but denies full
responsibility" (Scott and Lyman, 1968, p. 47; also Austin, 1961, p. 2). Here,
Merve presents the teacher with an excuse for the morally transgressive food
choice: this was all they had (in her family home). At the same time, she takes
part of the responsibility (through her use of pronoun 'we') and argues that she is
eating the white bread because she does not have anything else: after all, one
needs to eat lunch. Louise however does not accept this account as satisfactory.

We can compare Excerpt 11.5 both to Excerpt 11.2, in which Selina, who
had brought both white and rye bread in her lunch, explained to the teacher that
she had already finished her rye bread, and to Excerpt 11.3, in which Fadime
claimed that she had already told her father to pack rye bread. Selina's

response in Excerpt 11.2 was a justification; she implied that eating the white roll was not to be seen as a problem as she had already finished eating her rye bread. Thereby she positioned herself as complying with the local food norm. In contrast, Fadime in Excerpt 11.3 accepted the moral implications but denied responsibility and thus responded to the teacher with an excuse.

Excerpt 11.5 above has illustrated the recurrent phenomenon in the data of a child who has brought rye bread for lunch but has not eaten it. When this occurred, the child often claimed not to like rye bread, but it was not taken by the teacher as a valid account. We see this illustrated in Excerpt 11.6. The excerpt comes from an 18-minute long episode in which a child (Zaki) displays his desire to eat a wrap (i.e., white bread) brought for lunch. Before the excerpt, Louise had made Zaki put the wrap away twice in order to eat (two) rye bread sandwiches.

Excerpt 11.6 Like the Fish Sandwich
October 9. Participants: Zaki (child, Somali background), Louise (teacher); video recording

01 Louise: *Zaki har du ik mere rugbrød?*
            'Zaki don't you have more rye bread?'
02 Zaki: ((takes the wrap out of his mouth.))
03   *jeg ka ik li fiskemaden.*
            'I don't like the fish sandwich.'
04 Louise: *nej prøv og kik i pakkerne om du har nogle an↑dre rugbrødder med,*
            'no try and look into the packages if you have brought any ↑other rye breads,'
05   (2.0)
06 Louise: *den pølse du har inde den der xx rulle den er rigtig usund.*
            'that sausage you have inside that xxx wrap it's really unhealthy.'
07 Zaki: ((finds a third rye-bread sandwich which he starts to unwrap.))

Louise's question to Zaki (line 01: 'don't you have more rye bread') indexes the norm that if children have any rye bread left in their lunchboxes, they should eat it. It thus invites Zaki to eat the remaining rye bread rather than the wrap. At the same time, it leaves a conversational slot for Zaki to give an account explaining why he is eating something else. Zaki explains (for the second time; the first time is not included here) that he does not like the remaining (fish) sandwich (line 03). That is, while Zaki does have rye bread, his account implies that he should not have to eat something the child does not like. Consequently, this account is a justification in which he takes full responsibility for eating the wrap, but argues that it does not constitute a moral transgression. Louise treats this as illegitimate: individual tastes and desires are not considered a legitimate reason for not eating rye bread.

Excerpt 11.6 above, along with the others in this section, illustrates how teachers socialized the children to provide accounts and to demonstrate alignment with the school's moral regime in relation to food and eating practices. A recurring socialization message was that children have to eat even what they do not desire in order to comply with expectations.

The final example (Excerpt 11.7) illustrates a different situation: this time it is the teacher, Louise, who provides an account to the class for not bringing rye bread for lunch. At the beginning of the lunch session, Louise calls for the children's attention. Mia (introduced in line 02) is another teacher who usually brings lunch for Louise:

Excerpt 11.7 Louise's Account
March 16; audio recording. Participants: Louise (teacher), Kristine (teacher), Selma and Shabana (students) + the rest of the class

01 Louise: *jeg er nødt til lige og fortælle nu (.) der er sket noget frygteligt.*
'I just have to tell now (.) something terrible has happened.'
02 *(.) det frygtelige er (.) at Mia jo er syg i dag. (.) og hun skulle*
(.) 'the terrible thing is (.) that Mia is ill today. (.) and she was supposed'
03 *ha haft madpakke med til mig?*
'to have brought a lunch box for me?'
04 *(.)*
05 Kristine: *I ved Louises mor. (med noget I munden)*
'you know Louise's mom.'
06 Louise: jaha. ((ler))
'yeahah.'
07 Louise: *så derfor (.) så havde jeg altså ik købt noget rugbrød eller noget derhjemme*
'so that's why (.) so I hadn't bought any rye bread or anything at home'
08 *fordi jeg jo havde regnet med at Mia kom med rugbrødsmadder til mig. (.)*
'because I counted on Mia bringing rye bread sandwiches for me' (.)
09 *så jeg var nødt til at købe (noget) <u>rigtig</u> usundt mad på vej til arbejde i dag, (.)*
'so I had to buy (some) <u>really</u> unhealthy food on my way to work today,' (.)
10 *så øhm hvis det ser mærkeligt ud det jeg spiser så det altså derfor.*
'so ehm if it looks strange what I am eating then that's why.'
11 [*xxx simpelthen ik noget xxx gøre xx.*
'xxx simply nothing xxx do xxx.'
12 Selma: [*hvad er det for noget?*
'what is it?'
13 *(.)*
14 Selma: [*hvad er det for noget Louise?*
'what is it Louise?'
15 Kristine: [xxx
16 Louise: *ja det er sådan noget pizzaagtig noget jeg måtte købe på en tankstation i morges.*

'yes it's something pizzalike something I had to buy at a gas station this morning,'

17   *ikke ret spændende, ikke ret lækkert (.) men det er simpelthen derfor.*
'not very exciting, not very delicious (.) but that's simply why.'

18 Shabana: *Louise du må gerne få min meloner.*
'Louise you can have my melons,'

19 Louise: *åh du er sød (.) du er rigtig sød, jeg synes du skal gemme dem sveske,*
'oh you're so sweet (.) you're really sweet, I think you should keep them prune' ((prune = endearment term)),

20   *til din fritter eller noget*
'for your afternoon club or something'
((Several children continue to offer her vegetables and fruit from their lunchboxes.))

Here Louise demonstrates to the children a *not* good example in terms of the food she has brought for lunch, while positioning herself in relation to this transgressive food choice. This choice motivates an uninvited account, in the form of a narrative, through which Louise displays moral character and responsibility for the food she is about to eat. Louise makes clear that she shares with the children a role of food recipient (lines 02–03) (notice the joking comment in line 05 where the other teacher, Kristine, describes Mia as 'Louise's Mom'). On this day, Mia, who was ill, did not bring lunch for Louise, and Louise was out of rye bread at home. She explains that there were no healthy options at the gas station where she stopped to buy food (line 16). During this brief narrative, Louise displays her stance to the food that she bought through negative evaluative comments such as 'really unhealthy food' (line 09) and 'not very exciting, not very delicious' (line 17). Thus, she distances herself from the food, and positions herself as an accountable and morally aware social actor. At the same time, she lessens her responsibility for the unfortunate situation (e.g., 'I had to buy . . .') that justifies her problematic action: she needed to buy lunch, but there was nothing healthy to choose. After Louise's narrative account, Shabana offers her fruit to Louise. This continued with more children who shouted offers consisting of various types of fruit. By doing this, the children positioned themselves as moral subjects through having brought (an abundance of) healthy food, which they offer to share with her. This example thereby illustrates socialization into particular linguistic formats, moral regimes, and subject positions in relation to food choices.

11.5   Conclusion

Language socialization focuses on how human beings influence each other's development with long-lasting effects, how they use language to do this, and how morality, sociality, and individuality are all at stake in the process.

Teachers are expected to take on an expert role in encouraging children's acquisition of the norms and values of the community, and children are expected to accept these norms and values. Furthermore, they are expected to be moral compasses who enact and articulate what is good and to be responsible authorities, while children are expected to navigate their social worlds accordingly and to demonstrate respect. In this chapter, I have analyzed discursive encounters over lunch in a Danish kindergarten. The focus on food was productive for several reasons. First, food – including practices around and understandings of food – differs culturally, so it becomes indexical of belonging, and a way to demonstrate cultural alignment and disalignment. Second, food is generally taken as an indicator of individual and social moral inclinations. The motivations for judging food may differ. Today 'health(y)' is often treated as a self-evident, culturally neutral criterion, but it is necessary to recognize the concept's cultural embedding. Third, as in many other societies, in Denmark, kindergarten children's lunch boxes are prepared by parents and, although they were not present in the classroom, parents became relevant (imagined) participants in the lunch encounters. This relevance was occasioned by the food brought by the children, and effectuated through the discursive introductions by children and teachers. Rather than another authority in children's life, parents became a place to locate a "failed" opportunity for moral positioning. Authority is a relational notion (Wilson and Stapleton, 2010). Teacher authority is embedded in a cultural model of school and institutionally defined in relation to students, whereas parental authority is relative to children and based on a family model. Both types of authority imply expertise and experience (Pace and Hemmings, 2007). Parental authority was materialized in the lunchbox, which in return indexed home values. Thus, teachers' evaluations of the children's lunchbox were simultaneously evaluations of the parents. Children are normally expected to show gratitude for food, but this became difficult when the food was criticized by another authority. They are also expected to show respect to teachers, but this became difficult as it implied distancing from parents.

This case has a particular twist: the class was ethnically and culturally diverse, and the sub-group of students who found their parents and themselves singled out all had minority backgrounds. This was never explicitly mentioned in public, but it was difficult to overlook, and the teachers told me (in an interview) that they had decided to devote so much energy to rye bread and lunch boxes exactly because the many immigrant children could not be expected to know or respect this norm by default. The discursive practices made it clear that the children's prior understandings of good food, as they had been socialized to by their parents, needed revision. Likewise, rye bread was not talked about as "Danish food." Yet, the rye bread ideology drew on societally widespread, historically sedimented, and culturally naturalized ideas. In this sense, the teachers were animators, just like they asked the children to animate their own messages to parents. The culturally dominant character of the rye bread ideology made it less obvious that it was in fact debatable whether its enforcement was the only or even the best way to create (culturally) healthy students in a classroom characterized by diversity. Social actors are often unaware of the degree to which their food norms orient to and reproduce a national and local cultural context. Rye bread is a habit of everyday life among many Danes, and perhaps one of those habits that reproduce and flag the nation in the lives of its citizens (Billig, 1995, p. 12). Banal nationalism becomes even more visible in relation to something understood differently, an Other, and the encounters between school and family analyzed in this chapter were cultural meetings in which rye bread constructed some children as belonging, and some as Others. Rye bread reified a national tradition and insisted on similarity as a necessity in food practices; diversity could also have been explored (cf. Anving and Sellerberg, 2010).

Language socialization contributes to our understanding of classrooms by enabling us to demonstrate the fundamental role played by language, the use of which creates social positions and constraints, authority, and morality. As a case in point, I have focused on some of the discursive strategies used by teachers and children to negotiate responsibility, and on the parent as a problematic figure. The division of labor of a Speaker reflects power relations and statuses. The teacher positions herself as an expert authority by presenting directives and unconditional moral messages, and the child positions herself as a novice by aligning with and accepting them. I have no cases in which a child directly rejects or ignores the teacher's directives, although the difficulties for the teachers in making some of the children bring rye bread could be read as an implicit challenge to the dominant ideology. Language socialization highlights the minutiae of the negotiations, the multifaceted and locally constructed nature of sociality, and the cultural embedding of moral choices. All of this becomes clear not the least from data such as those analyzed here where home and school assumptions and practices differ. In reverse, classroom interaction contributes to the paradigm of language socialization by introducing complex social universes. Present and absent participants are relevant, although in different ways, and the notions of authority and expert become problematized.

NOTES

1 Similar types of rye bread are found in Finland and Northern Germany.
2 Compare this post on the US food blog *Saveur*: www.saveur.com/what-to-cook-this-weekend-danish-bread
3 Information can be found on the following website: http://mfvm.dk/nyheder/nyhed/nyhed/stegt-flaesk-er-kaaret-som-nationalret-2/
4 Some children left the class, and others joined the class over the year.

REFERENCES

Allison, A. (2008). Japanese mothers and *obentōs*: the lunch-box as ideological state apparatus. In C. Counihan and P. van Esterik (eds.), *Food and Culture: A Reader, 2nd Ed.* (pp. 221–239). New York, NY and London: Routledge.

Anving, T. and Sellerberg, A.-M. (2010). Family meals and parents' challenges. *Food, Culture & Society*, 13(2), 200–214.

Aronsson, K. and Gottzén, L. (2011). Generational positions at a family dinner: food morality and social order. *Language in Society*, 40, 405–426.

Aukrust, V. G. and Snow, C. E. (1998). Narratives and explanations during mealtime conversations in Norway and the US. *Language in Society*, 27, 221–246.

Austin, J. L. (1961). A plea for excuses: the presidential address. *Proceedings of the Aristotelian Society*, 57, 1–30.

Billig, M. (1995). *Banal Nationalism*. London: SAGE.

Blum-Kulka, S. (1997). *Dinner Talk: Cultural Patterns of Sociability and Socialization in Family Discourse*. Mahwah, NJ: Lawrence Erlbaum.

Bradby, H. (1997). Health, eating and heart attacks: Glaswegian Punjabi women's thinking about everyday food. In P. Caplan (ed.), *Food, Health, and Identity* (pp. 213–246). London: Routledge.

Burdelski, M. (2014). Early experiences with food: socializing affect and relationships in Japanese. In P. Szatrowski (ed.), *Language and Food: Verbal and Non-Verbal Experiences* (pp. 233–255). Amsterdam and Philadelphia, PA: John Benjamins.

Burgess, R. R. and Morrison, M. (1998). Ethnographies of eating in an urban primary school. In A. Murcott (ed.), *The Nation's Diet: The Social Science of Food Choice* (pp. 209–227). London: Longman.

Cekaite, A. (2012). Affective stances in teacher–novice student interactions: language, embodiment, and willingness to learn. *Language in Society*, 41, 641–670.

Cekaite, A. and Aronsson, K. (2004). Repetition and joking in children's second language conversations: playful recyclings in an immersion classroom. *Discourse Studies*, 6(3), 373–392.

Coveney, J. (2006 [2000]). *Food, Morals and Meaning: The Pleasure and Anxiety of Eating, 2nd Ed.* London: Routledge.

Fader, A. (2011). Language socialization and morality. In A. Duranti, E. Ochs, and B. B. Schieffelin, (eds.), *The Handbook of Language Socialization* (pp. 322–340). Malden, MA: Wiley-Blackwell.

Fiese, B. H, Foley, K. P., and Spagnola, M. (2006). Routines and ritual elements in family mealtimes: contexts for child well-being and family identity. *New Directions for Child and Adolescent Development*, 111, 67–89.

Fischler, C. (2011). Commensality, society and culture. *Social Science Information*, 50 (3–4), 528–548.

García-Sánchez, I. and Nazimova, K. (2017). Language socialization and immigration in Europe. In P. Duff and S. May (eds.), *Language Socialization: Encyclopedia of Language and Education* (pp. 441–456). New York, NY: Springer.

Goffman, E. (1981). *Forms of Talk*. Philadelphia, PA: University of Pennsylvania Press.

Golden, D. (2005). Nourishing the nation: the uses of food in an Israeli kindergarten. *Food and Foodways*, 13, 181–199.

Iacovetta, F. (2006). Recipes for democracy? Gender, family, and making female citizens in Cold War Canada. In A. Glasbeek (ed.), *Moral Regulation and Governance in Canada: History, Context and Critical Issues* (pp. 169–187). Toronto: Canadian Scholars' Press.

Karrebæk, M. S. (2012). "What's in your lunch-box today?": health, respectability and ethnicity in the primary classroom. *Journal of Linguistic Anthropology*, 22(1), 1–22.

Karrebæk, M. S. (2013a). Lasagne for breakfast: the respectable child and cultural norms of eating practices in a Danish kindergarten classroom. *Food, Culture, and Society*, 16(1), 85–106.

Karrebæk, M. S. (2013b). Rye bread and halal: enregisterment of food practices in the primary classroom. *Language and Communication*, 34, 17–34.

Karrebæk, M. S., Madsen, L. M., and Møller, J. S. (2016). Introduction to everyday languaging: collaborative research on the language use of children and youth. In L. M. Madsen, M. S. Karrebæk, and J. S. Møller (eds.), *Everyday Languaging: Collaborative Research on the Language Use of Children and Youth* (pp. 1–18). Berlin and Boston, MA: Mouton de Gruyter.

Margetts, B. M., Martinez, J. A., Saba, A., Holm, L., and Kearney, M. (1997). Definitions of 'healthy' eating: a pan-EU survey of consumer attitudes to food, nutrition and health. *European Journal of Clinical Nutrition*, 51(2), 23–29.

Mehan, H. (1979). "What time is it, Denise?": asking known information questions in classroom discourse. *Theory into Practice*, 18(4), 285–294.

Meyer, C. (2010). *Meyers bageri*. København: Lindhardt and Ringhof.

Ochs, E. and Beck, M. (2013). Dinner. In E. Ochs and T. Kremer-Sadlik (eds.), *Fast-Forward Family: Home, Work, and Relationships in Middle-Class America* (pp. 48–66). Berkeley, CA: University of California Press.

Ochs, E., Shohet, M., Campos, B., and Beck, M. (2010). Coming together at dinner: a study of working families. In K. Cjrostemsem and B. Schneider (eds.), *Workplace Flexibility: Realigning 20th-Century Jobs for a 21st-Century Workforce* (pp. 57–70). Ithaca, NY: Cornell University Press.

Ochs, E. and Taylor, C. (1995). The "father knows best" dynamic in dinnertime narratives. In K. Hall and M. Bucholtz (eds.) *Gender Articulated: Language and the Socially Constructed Self* (pp. 97–120). New York, NY: Routledge.

Ochs, E., Pontecorvo, C., and Fasulo, A. (1996). Socializing taste. *Ethnos*, 61(1–2), 7–46.

Pace. J. and Hemmings, A. (2007). Understanding authority in classrooms: a review of theory, ideology, and research. *Review of Educational Research*, 77, 4–27.

Pallotti, G. (2002). Borrowing words: appropriations in child second language discourse. In J. Leather and J. van Dam (eds.), *The Ecology of Language Acquisition* (pp. 183–202). Amsterdam: Kluwer.

Paugh, A. and Izquierdo, C. (2009). Why is this a battle every night? Negotiating food and eating in American dinnertime interaction. *Journal of Linguistic Anthropology*, 19(2), 185–204.

Plum, C. (2001) *Et ordentligt brød*. København: Gyldendal.

Rampton, B., Maybin, J., and Roberts, C. (2015). Methodological foundations in linguistic ethnography. In J. Snell, S. Shaw, and F. Copland (eds.), *Linguistic Ethnography: Interdisciplinary Explorations* (pp. 14–50). London: Palgrave Advances Series.

Riley, K. (2011). Learning to exchange words for food in the Marquesas. In L. Coleman (ed.), *Food: Ethnographic Encounters* (pp. 111–125). Oxford: Berg Publishers.

Schieffelin, B. B. (1990). *The Give and Take of Everyday Life: Language Socialization of Kaluli Children*. Cambridge: Cambridge University Press.

Scott, M. B. and Lymann, S. M. (1968). Accounts. *American Sociological Review*, 33 (1), 46–62.

Simovska, V. (2007). The changing meanings of participation in school-based health education and health promotion: the participants' voices. *Health Education Research*, 22(6), 864–878.

Snow C. E, Perlmann, R. Y., Berko, J. G., and Hooshyar, N. (1990). Developmental perspectives on politeness: sources of children's knowledge. *Journal of Pragmatics*, 14(2), 289–305.

Sterponi, L. (2003). Account episodes in family discourse: the making of morality in everyday interaction. *Discourse Studies*, 5(1), 79–100.

Wiggins, S. (2004). Good for 'you': generic and individual healthy eating advice in family mealtimes. *Journal of Health Psychology*, 9, 535–548.

Wilson, J. and Stapleton, K. (2010). Authority. In J. Jaspers, E.-O. Östman, and J. Verschuren (eds.), *Society and Language Use* (pp. 79–70). Amsterdam and Philadelphia, PA: John Benjamins Publishing.

Wortham, S. (2006): *Learning Identity: The Joint Emergence of Social Identification and Academic Learning*. New York, NY: Cambridge University Press.

Yount-André, C. (2016). Snack sharing and the moral metalanguage of exchange: children's reproduction of rank-based distribution in Senegal. *Journal of Linguistic Anthropology*, 26(1), 41–61.

Part IV

Conclusion

12 Language Socialization in Classrooms
Findings, Issues, and Possibilities

Patricia A. Duff

12.1 Language Socialization: Shifting Sites, Populations, and Foci in Recent Years

First-generation language socialization research conducted by linguistic anthropologists, sociolinguists, and psychologists, as demonstrated by scholars featured in the seminal volume edited by Schieffelin and Ochs (1986), typically took place in homes and other informal settings. There they observed young children's interactions with siblings, peers, caregivers, and parents, the types of activities community members engaged in, and the prompts and sometimes rebukes produced by interlocutors to help socialize the youngsters into expected ways of performing and into valued cultural and linguistic knowledge and dispositions. In such spaces, the children were party to mundane or routine language and activities – games, conversations, calling out or repeating routines, teasing and shaming practices, and narratives – each culturally significant and complex in its own way. By participating in such sociocultural practices, children learned a great deal about interactional pragmatics, grammatical systems, suitable displays of affect and politeness, the role of nonlinguistic or paralinguistic semiosis, and about other aspects of their cultures and their roles, identities, and status (e.g., sense of legitimacy, belonging) within their social groups.

Although some of the first-wave language socialization studies (e.g., Heath, 1982, 1986; Philips, 1983; Watson-Gegeo, 1992; Watson-Gegeo and Gegeo, 1994) also examined *classroom* cultures and socialization, participation patterns, and interactional routines found within them and looked at the practices of *older children*, such studies were more the exception than the norm (see review by Garrett and Baquedano-López, 2002). One reason was that much of the earlier research examined infants and very young children (from birth to age five, but typically under three years of age) not yet attending school, with attention paid to oral language especially, a focus that has continued in early childhood language socialization research worldwide (e.g., chapters in Duranti, Ochs, and Schieffelin, 2011). Another reason is that the language socialization researchers themselves were not typically affiliated with schools, colleges, or faculties of education at their own universities and their audiences tended not to be educators primarily or at all. Their interests and fieldwork involved, to use a current phrase, languages and socialization "in the wild" – in naturalistic, informal learning contexts – often in distant parts of the world such as on islands in the Pacific. Most of the scholars, furthermore, were first-language (L1) acquisition researchers (e.g., Slobin, 1985) whose interests had shifted from functional grammar systems to socialization into communicative competence and local cultural systems. Parallel work by scholars more embedded in the field of education and in classrooms (e.g., Cazden, 1988; Erickson, 1982; Mehan, 1979), not framed as language socialization but very much concerned with the same processes, was taking place at about the same time.

12.2   Language Socialization in Formal Educational Contexts and "Contact Zones"

In the intervening decades, as former (graduate) students of language socialization have themselves entered a variety of educational spaces, research has flourished on first language (L1), second language (L2), and multilingual socialization into and through *formal educational processes and practices* as well as informal ones (see, e.g., chapters in Duff and May, 2017; plus review articles by Duff, 2010a, 2010b; Duff and Anderson, 2015; Duff and Talmy, 2011). Research is now increasingly situated in schools, universities, workplaces, and virtual spaces across the lifespan (Bayley and Schecter, 2003; Duff and May, 2017) or even across generations (Heath, 2012). Sometimes the research takes place concurrently or sequentially in and across multiple sites (e.g., Lee and Bucholtz, 2015; Räisänen, 2016), examining participants' distributed networks and *trajectories of socialization* (Wortham, 2005, 2006) or, as Jaffe (Chapter 5 in this volume) illustrates, "trajectories of texts and oral practices" themselves. Although situated in schools, the majority of studies in this volume, consistent with earlier language socialization research, deal with relatively young children (e.g., under age 12); the exceptions are the two studies with adolescent learners (Klein, Chapter 3; Rymes and Leone-Pizzighella, Chapter 7) and one with university students (Friedman, Chapter 8). I return to this point in the final section.

Increasingly, unlike most of the first-wave language socialization research, these chapters demonstrate clearly how students are negotiating *multiple* languages, norms, roles, ideologies, identities, curricula, and/or ethnolinguistic communities at the *same time*, sometimes taking up expected practices and values, sometimes resisting or subverting them in creative ways, and sometimes being prevented from participating in expected ways despite institutional norms, hopes, and efforts (García-Sánchez, Chapter 2 in this volume; see also Duff, 1995, 1996). Students experience weekend community heritage-language schooling in which affinities with home languages, histories, and cultures are being fostered, for example, while at the same time engaging in public schooling into and through the societally dominant language; or they experience secular schooling during the week and religious schooling (Sikhism, Orthodox Christianity) on weekends. Another possible disjunction is that they receive education through two languages (e.g., Hindi and English), involving sacred and other school registers in a postcolonial context (Bhatta-charya and Sterponi, Chapter 9 in this volume); or, to give another example, they may have food practices and preferences at home (e.g., white bread) that are disallowed at school (Karrebæk, Chapter 11 in this volume). In each context, different literacy practices, forms of embodiment, language varieties and registers, subjectivities, and ideologies may be invoked or indexed. To borrow a term from Pratt (1991) commonly used in research in writing studies (also cited by García-Sánchez, Chapter 2 in this volume), students, instructors, families, and administrators may find themselves in various kinds of "contact zones," where it can be challenging to learn to "play the game":

Despite whatever conflicts or systematic social differences might be in play, it is assumed that all participants are engaged in the same game and that the game is the same for all players. Often it is. But of course it often is not, as, for example, when speakers are from different classes or cultures, or one party is exercising authority and another is submitting to it or questioning it. (Pratt, 1991, p. 38)

To make matters more complicated, the "rules" and "games" may be changing (or in flux), in ways both big and small, in response to shifting demographics, critical incidents, educational policies and reforms (e.g., Duff, 1993), and other issues that arise in such contact zones (e.g., social conflict, exclusionary practices) that may require active intervention. Or the rules and games may be different for different subgroups of participants or in different social spaces or even in different enactments of the same speech event (e.g., Duff, 2009). Rymes and Leone-Pizzighella (Chapter 7 in this volume) note how the ground rules for producing and interpreting behaviors differ across the spaces and activity settings within a school.

The so-called games (a metaphor also favored by Wittgenstein (1953) in relation to language) often have very high stakes attached to them: inclusion and acceptance within cultures, on the one hand, or exclusion, derision, or persecution, on the other, to cite possible endpoints on a continuum; or even questions about the sustainability of the language being taught, in contexts of language shift where heritage languages become endangered (Jaffe, Chapter 5 in this volume). Furthermore, as early language socialization research posited and continues to emphasize (e.g., Ochs, 1986; Ochs and Schieffelin, 2011, 2017), newcomers or novices are also *active agents* of socialization and change who can disrupt or challenge the status quo when it does not seem to accommodate them or their interests, aspirations, or communicative repertoires, as can the "oldtimers" or more experienced and authoritative community members in their midst. Indeed, there may be serious "unintended consequences" in such contact zones associated with both acts of resistance and intervention (García-Sánchez, Chapter 2 in this volume).

The theoretical foundations of language socialization research both in and out of classrooms are well documented by each of the chapter authors as well as by the volume co-editors, Burdelski and Howard, in their introduction (Chapter 1). Expositions of these foundations are also found in various handbooks and encyclopedias on language socialization (e.g., Duff and Hornberger, 2008; Duff and May, 2017; Duranti, Ochs, and Schieffelin, 2011) as well as in numerous stand-alone review articles (e.g., Duff, 2010b; Garrett and Baquedano-López, 2002; Zuengler and Cole, 2005; Ochs and Schieffelin, 2011, 2017). Therefore, this commentary chapter will not revisit this theoretical terrain. Instead, my focus is how the current generation of classroom-oriented socialization research, as exemplified by the studies in this volume, is changing our understandings of language socialization and pedagogies in school/university contexts. Naturally, one edited volume cannot include the myriad situations in which language socialization takes place in and out of classrooms and the different possible foci: food, language, fitness or physical comportment, generic literary practices, and so on. Therefore, in the final section below I consider other "contact zones" and populations that might be included in future research and publications.

12.3   Interdisciplinary and Institutional Networks in Language Socialization Research

The authors of the 11 chapters, as noted in the introduction by Burdelski and Howard, are located institutionally in several countries and in various kinds of university programs and administrative units, which is not unusual within this field of study: in the United States, Denmark, Sweden, and Japan; and in child studies (Cekaite), anthropology (García-Sánchez), (educational) linguistics (Rymes and Leone-Pizzighella, Jaffe, Klein), Nordic Studies and linguistics (Karrebæk), Japanese linguistics and liberal arts (Burdelski), second language studies (Friedman), and education (Moore, Bhattacharya and Sterponi), or combinations of these fields and cross-appointments in anthropology and linguistics, for example. This range of affiliations reveals the rich interdisciplinarity of language socialization research and of the scholars themselves, even among scholars conducting studies in, or surrounding, *classrooms*.

Despite their different institutional and national affiliations, however, many of the authors *do* share a common academic genealogy (one that I, too, proudly share): prior academic socialization into applied linguistics and/or linguistic anthropology and especially into language socialization research at the University of California, Los Angeles (UCLA). It is therefore not surprising that the chapters approach their studies in quite similar theoretical ways by citing much of the same foundational literature even when examining quite disparate language socialization processes and topics in their respective studies. Each chapter, without exception, reports succinctly on ethnographic research conducted with careful attention to broader social, historical, and cultural contexts, and employs a discursive (and often visual) analysis of interactional data for a more micro-analytic perspective of indexical and ideological processes. Several of the authors do not share the same institutional history, although in some cases they have collaborated with (former or current) UCLA colleagues. Nevertheless, they follow the same general theoretical and methodological approaches (considered normative by various other, although not all, language socialization scholars as well; e.g., Garrett, 2017; Kulick and Schieffelin, 2004; but see Duff and Talmy, 2011, for another perspective). That shared history means that, although each study is situated in a different sociocultural, multilingual, and educational context, there is a high degree of compatibility and consistency across the set, which creates obvious thematic cohesion.

12.4   The Focus of Socialization in (and out of) Classrooms: Beyond Language

Through a wide variety of routine activities, verbal and nonverbal, and embodied actions such as throwing balls to partners or receiving graduation certificates from a principal, we observe attempts to socialize students (and others) into particular ideologies or values, dispositions, affective and epistemic stances, types of voice, identities, and morality, using various participation frameworks. Together, the studies constitute a very fertile cross-section of contemporary educationally oriented language socialization research because of the different contact zones examined and the different means and objects of socialization and types of interaction that the authors have chosen to focus on. Although some of the activities examined were associated with religious schooling and history education in diaspora heritage-language contexts (e.g., Klein and Moore, Chapters 3 and 4 in this volume), most pertained to secular education. The studies in this volume make an important and timely contribution to our understanding of contemporary schooling and multilingual enculturation from early experiences in preschools, to elementary and secondary schools, and on to graduate school. They provide optimism for dynamic ways in which newcomers can be supported in their language and literacy learning, but also provide glimpses into some very worrisome sociocultural and interactional practices and discourse.

Geographically, the studies add to the existing literature on language socialization by investigating, in one volume, education in Corsica (Jaffe), Denmark

(Karrebæk), India (Bhattacharya and Sterponi), Spain (García-Sánchez), and Sweden (Cekaite), in addition to the studies situated in the United States. This last cluster of studies is far from homogeneous, however, and it too covers a wide assortment of languages and educational settings: English in a high school (Rymes and Leone-Pizzighella) and a graduate degree program (Friedman), Japanese in a preschool heritage-language program (Burdelski), and English (and some Punjabi formulaic speech) and Russian in religious weekend schools (Klein and Moore, respectively).

Prominent in the authors' accounts are issues connected with means of inculcating heritage, migration, social memory and collective history, community-building, belonging (or exclusion), and citizenship through particular socializing practices in the various contexts (particularly in diaspora contexts); these same themes are taken up in much current theorizing and scholarship in applied linguistics more generally (e.g., Duff, 2015). The concept of *diaspora* itself is interrogated (see Klein, Chapter 3 in this volume) as more an aspirational stance than reference to an actual community. Klein and the participants in her study reveal how an ethnic group such as Sikh immigrants in California have in the past (in the Punjab) been, and are still, at risk due to dangerous and discriminatory perceptions of them in the dominant local community (e.g., that they might be Middle Eastern terrorists), stances that students in the observed *gurdwara* history classes were being socialized to confront peacefully and with pride in their heritage and spirituality.

The learning and use of language(s) is not (necessarily) itself the primary focus of these studies, despite employing the shared conceptual framework of "language socialization." Indeed, in some of the chapters larger circulating discourses, such as "tolerance," were being both socialized and contested (García-Sánchez, Chapter 2); in fact, there were often *unspoken* or *unspeakable* political and moral stances and ideologies at play, thus explicit language use regarding linguistic practices was not always the means by which socialization took place. The discussion in that study of activities in which minority students of Moroccan ancestry in a Spanish school were visibly and vocally shunned by local Spanish students – and even within a program aimed at creating greater inclusion and tolerance – revealed disturbing and seemingly entrenched trends of just the opposite: social exclusion, ostracism, and blatant discrimination. The visual depictions and narratives of ball-throw turn-taking, a paired dance practice fiasco, and rejection of a Moroccan girl joining other girls' jump-rope game were striking.

Sometimes, in other language socialization studies not in this book, there are contradictions between explicit ideologies and actual practices, even by teachers or parents, for example in proclaiming but then contravening a monolingual classroom norm (Guardado, 2009; Mökkönen, 2012); or providing remedial education practices or accommodations that actually undermine students' educational engagements and futures (Talmy, 2008); or, in Karre-bæk's study (Chapter 11 of this volume), the teacher's constant reminders to students to bring rye-bread sandwiches as the only sanctioned form of lunch at the school, but then her admission to her class of eating a piece of gas-station-bought pizza after running out of rye bread at home.

In some chapters, the language being taught (e.g., Russian as a heritage language in a Russian Orthodox Church program in California) *is* inextricably linked to, and explicitly taught in concert with, notions of (Russian) culture, history, identity, affect, and (Orthodox Christian) religious/cultural affiliation (Moore, Chapter 4). Learning the Russian lexical items for various church-related referents, such as *priest, deacon, armlets* (part of their ceremonial robes), or *incense*, was emphasized in such cases. So, too, was learning to express a strong affective, spiritual stance *in Russian* by means of positive assessments, or aligning one's stance with that of the teacher toward those same revered religious individuals and objects.

Positive alignments and affective stances and "keys" (such as humorous language play and lighthearted teasing) are sometimes inculcated in studies focusing on language learning. This was observed, for example, in Jaffe's study of teachers' practices of socializing students into paired Corsican poetry improvisations (*chjam'è rispondi*), or joking exchanges, as part of larger Corsican language revitalization efforts. The Corsican language – as exempli-fied by the development of this particular genre – is both an important means and end of teachers' socialization of children. Peer and teacher assessments in Jaffe's study were also part of the process of judging the aesthetic qualities of students' candidate lines of poetry in Corsican (e.g., based on content, rhyme, meter, grammatical accuracy) and the process of collaboratively constructing other, possibly better lines. This process entailed explicit socialization by teachers or, in other words, the apprenticeship of young students into the identities of emerging poets and speakers of Corsican through analysis of the merits of particular generic forms, giving the students a sense of agency and ownership over the resulting poems. What is more, the multimodal, embodied, collective process of generating the poetry, with appropriate scaffolding, connected children at schools located in different parts of Corsica. They otherwise would have limited contact or limited opportunity to use Corsican (not to mention playful poetic genres) with one another. This connection (initially achieved electronically) then gave them a wider sense of audience and community as they subsequently performed and published these poetic texts in more public forums at a museum and at poetry festivals.

In Moore's study, as in Jaffe's, the learning, production, and cherishing of the heritage language (Russian and Corsican, respectively), as well as strong affective connection to the culture and Russian community, was a critical goal of the socialization interactions. Burdelski's study, discussed further below, was also situated in a heritage-language program, but did not discuss this form of affective cultural or linguistic engagement, but rather focused more on a sense of duty to perform certain ritual actions appropriately.

The use of specific linguistic devices, such as indexical epistemic stance-markers, modal verbs, and pronouns, as well as analogies with other persecuted or minoritized groups (e.g., Jewish, Latinx, African American in Klein's chapter), or hypothetical events (e.g., welcoming a newcomer to the Church in Moore's chapter), was found to create a sense of common history and purpose in relation to social justice and spirituality (Klein), even if the purpose was not to teach the grammatical forms themselves (e.g., to students who were already highly proficient in English, the primary language of instruction).

The linguistic focus of Cekaite's study (Chapter 6) of socialization into Swedish as an additional language for newcomer immigrant children was *vocabulary* – both forms and explanations – which became affective stance displays and opportunities for alignment. One example was the word *längtar* ('long for,' e.g., summer); another being *tjata* ('nags,' i.e., to nag a parent to get a pet). Explanation of such terms through a series of interactions with the children allowed the teacher and students to align both their understanding of the term and the cultural context, or their current "lifeworlds" (i.e., the significance and pleasures of summer in a Nordic country such as Sweden; egalitarian relations between children and parents). The use of hypothetical situations, participant examples, embedded quotation, and repetition, noted in other chapters as well (e.g., Moore's), was an integral part of the teacher's socialization strategy for providing a fuller range of sociocultural and semantic associations with the new expressions.

Thus, students and their interlocutors in these studies, as in other related work, were being socialized into cultural activities and routines, into the (celebrated) local habitus, and into prevailing values that had a special status, history, and significance in those sites. Sometimes the school-based linguistic and cultural processes represented tensions – between home-language/culture norms (and communities) and those at school, themes also examined in some first-generation L1 socialization research (see, e.g., review in Duff, 2008). Such disjunctions can become quite pronounced in heritage-language programs in the United States (see He, 2011, 2015) and in studies of immigrant students' engagements with dominant societal norms such as Danish (Karrebæk) and Swedish (Cekaite) in Europe, as well as in contexts of language revitalization (e.g., in Corsica; Jaffe). Educators, such as those cited by Klein, and students from diverse backgrounds often seek to find "common ground" (see Cekaite) across such differences or creative "third spaces" (Bhabha, 2004; Gutiérrez, 2008; Gutiérrez, Baquedano-López, and Tejeda, 1999) constituting meaningful, syncretic habituses.

Rymes and Leone-Pizzighella (Chapter 7) proposed the musical metaphor *contrapuntal* to describe ways in which different voices, registers, identities, and stance-displays often co-exist in classroom discourse. In their research, in a high school honors class in the United States in which *Hamlet* was being discussed, they conceptualized two parallel melodic lines, one representing official instructional discourse (i.e., expected Initiation–Response–Evaluation slot-filling), and the other, unsanctioned side sequences produced by students that nonetheless displayed certain kinds of engagement with the course material, but also different student identities and forms of intersubjectivity. These distinct discursive "lines," they noted, also represented different communicative repertoires. Following Goffman (1961), they described these unofficial, sidebar-like discussions as *underlife* interactions or activities and pointed out that "[p]art of the student socialization process, then, is about knowing how and when to participate in various lines of contrapuntal talk" (p. 139, this volume). My own reading of their examples is that they illustrate different ways of engaging with register within the confines of IRE sequences: The teacher displayed a casual, informal register drawing on analogies with students heading to college, for example, who are being given useful advice by a parent, while paraphrasing key concepts from lines of *Hamlet* in vernacular English. But different students, in their responses to the teacher's initiation prompts, enacted different registers even within the official IRE frame, which then indexed different identities or stances as students (i.e., serious students of Shakespeare, etc.). The teacher himself performed a particular type of teacher identity too (which the authors casually described as "chill"). In the study overall, though, language (or even register) was not the main goal of socialization so much as it was ways of having students relate to the content meaningfully and for the teacher to successfully engage them and their attention.

Friedman (Chapter 8) examined academic and professional socialization in a very different context from the other studies. Her participants were mature, multilingual students in an American university graduate program for teachers of English. This student group included both native and nonnative speakers of English (and experienced teachers in the case of the latter), who were often positioned as such (NS vs. NNS, or American vs. international) through institutional discourse and professional ideologies circulating more broadly, as well as in their own teachers' comments and assumptions. Friedman analyzed epistemic authority, status, and stance-taking in relation to metalinguistic knowledge of English grammar, for example, but also highlighted the positioning of the focal participants by teachers into one of these two social/ epistemic categories, and thus their likelihood of performing certain tasks easily or effectively (e.g., identifying and labeling grammatical errors, such as *non-restrictive relative clause pronouns*). Both data extracts she included required that students identify errors in published written texts using particular labels. However, the status of NS vs. NNS in undertaking the tasks was foreshadowed by the teachers in each case in terms of their likely success. These processes therefore reproduced existing dichotomies about professional attributes of the two groups and thus their suitability to perform particular metalinguistic tasks, thereby contributing to further native-speakerism in TESOL, in Friedman's assessment.

As in much earlier research on language socialization and some of the other chapters in this volume, Bhattacharya and Sterponi (Chapter 9) identified a salient cultural and pedagogical activity – the Morning Assembly – as the locus for socialization into linguistic practices, subjectivities, and morality in a school in northern India. The Morning Assembly is a ritualized, multi-genre, multimodal, communicative event comprising song, prayer, chant, recitation, meditation, lecture, with strict control of students' body positioning. The authors interpreted the ritual Pledge recitation as part of the Morning Assembly, for example, as a "textual technology that interpellates children into subjecthood predicated on reverence for adults and relatedness with all fellow Indians" (p. 189). It thus served to unite the children (in their choral recitation) and also promised deference to authority figures. Although different in form and imbued with spiritual content, the Morning Assembly seemed to share some functions with the ubiquitous forms of recitation observed in Hungarian public schools in my own research (Duff, 1993), emphasizing social control, authority (in texts/teachers' lectures) and cultural reproduction. In comparing modern government-prescribed teacher–student relationships and "bookish" curriculum with the traditional curriculum based on deference and obedience to a guru's teaching and meditation (among other practices), the authors suggested that in this site it was the latter that was privileged. They asserted that this traditional orientation to teaching/learning would ultimately have negative academic and socio-economic consequences for the (underprivileged) students in the school – a strong claim, to be sure.

The theme of *embodiment* in communication and socialization, and the discipline of body movement and comportment or *kata* 'form' was also taken up by Burdelski (Chapter 10), in the context of a Japanese heritage-language preschool graduation ceremony in the United States. He noted that certain carefully trained bodily actions or states, like language, serve as important indexes in relation to the sociocultural world, and that in the Japanese context these embodied practices are socialized through careful preparation and rehearsal. (As a former practitioner of *Shotokan karate*, I am personally familiar with this keen emphasis on precise *form/kata* through modeling, repetition, correction, and performance.) The embodied presentation of the graduation certificate by the "school principal" (played by a teacher during the rehearsal) received by each student in turn was Burdelski's focus, which involved coordinated speech acts, movements, and actions such as bowing and extending hands in a particular sequence, and stepping forward and then back, to receive the important document. Children were socialized by admonishments not to create embarrassment by failing (morally) to comply with norms, by observation and modeling, by "hands-on" (haptic) and other non-verbal instruction (pointing, gaze) and by being given ample feedback or correction. This "meta-corporeal" discourse reflected deep cultural ideologies of public self-presentation, deference, conformity, correctness, and precisely controlled movements associated with specific formal rituals.

The final study, in terms of chapter sequence in this volume, by Karrebæk (Chapter 11), discusses language and food socialization in the context of a Danish kindergarten with children coming from diverse backgrounds. Just as conformity to prescribed, ritual physical postures and movements (*kata*) was socialized and enforced in the Japanese language program Burdelski researched, conformity regarding healthy food choices – specifically rye bread sandwiches – was socialized and policed in the Danish kindergarten classroom examined by Karrebæk on moral (health) grounds primarily. The central focus of food socialization in the study, *rye bread*, is considered a cultural and dietary food staple in Denmark, and a "semiotic phenomenon" (index of belonging, being health-conscious, following rules) in these spaces as well. Children and their parents were both held morally responsible and criticized for non-compliance with the rye bread dictum (when children brought white bread or buns). During their lunch breaks, which took place in classrooms and were supervised by teachers, the children's food (lunchbox) selections were therefore assessed according to ideologies about health and wellbeing, within the Danish cultural frame of reference: "no white bread in school lunch boxes." This food-oriented research, in sum, builds on an important early, and continuing, strand of language socialization research connected with dinnertime discourse, including discourse surrounding food and foodways. Here, though, the children who did not bring rye bread were being socialized, in turn, to socialize their own (immigrant) parents to prepare rye bread (two slices) for each lunch and to remind them repeatedly (otherwise the children would be singled out for unwanted attention). It is not clear from the chapter, however, what the researcher's own stance is as to what could easily be construed as hegemonic, nationalistic practices and ideologies regarding families' personal food choices, which for me, at least, was very surprising (despite my own fondness for rye bread).

12.5   Reflections on Some Common Themes

In addition to the common structure and framing of each of the chapters reporting on empirical research, in terms of theory and methodology, many of them deal with issues that commonly arise in regimented, conservative, hierarchical institutions such as schools and universities, and all the more when diversity is a significant factor and there are perceived and actual divisions in status between major groups (e.g., Moroccan vs. Spanish; NS vs. NNS; visible minority vs. White) that serve to position one or the other group as illegitimate, unknowing, or undesirable (as dance partners, for example). Beyond linguistic forms and indexical social meanings, socialization in these studies often focused on such notions as authority, epistemic stance/status, legitimacy, and affect and how these were inculcated, negotiated, and taken up. Several of the chapters made explicit reference to social justice concerns (vis-à-vis tracking in schools, or expectations of complete deference to authority). Others, conversely, highlighted the creative capacity of participants to collaboratively bring to life curricular and linguistic elements (such as poetic genres) that are otherwise at risk of disappearing from local cultures with complete language shift.

In very few cases do we see actual evidence of the *outcomes* of socialization activities beyond the immediate lessons in which students were observed through the entire cycle of a project, for example (Jaffe's study being one exception; Burdelski also mentioned briefly that the children had successfully performed their required actions when receiving their diplomas at the actual graduation ceremony a month later). Yet the richness and poignancy of the socialization events, no matter how mundane or brief they might appear on the surface, was persuasively argued. Teachers were observed trying to bring the curriculum to life through various modes and means, even when trying to just animate simple phrases, such as *priest* or *long for*, or more complex ones, such as *"Neither a borrower nor a lender be."*

The authors have done a commendable job of drawing unique insights from their studies and also bringing in various interdisciplinary theoretical perspectives, constructs and, in some cases, metaphors. Some researchers' relationships and histories with the study sites, populations, and teaching foci were made explicit through reflections on their involvement and positionality. This relationship and background was less clear in other cases, apart from the researchers' explanations of longitudinal engagements with their sites as part of larger projects. In two studies, the authors reported on collaborating with the teachers through different kinds of planned interventions over an extended time in order to make what they believed to be important contributions to curriculum and pedagogy, e.g., in relation to poetry teaching/performance (Jaffe) or "Citizen Sociolinguistics" (Rymes and Leone-Pizzighella). It is less clear what roles the other researchers might have played in their contexts, or how they viewed socialization events as they unfolded, apart from being relatively detached but sympathetic ethnographic observers and analysts with an interest in the communities being studied.

12.6 Conclusion

As I noted earlier, most of the studies reported on here involved young children, some of whom were engaged in relatively low-level language or literacy tasks (for those focusing on language teaching and learning, e.g., meanings of phrases) or bodily movements (e.g., receiving a certificate appropriately) or bringing and eating particular food products for lunch. This is not to say that the socialization processes and identity work are not complicated and linked to many kinds of ideologies. The authors have demonstrated just how multifaceted these processes are. (Another edited volume containing studies of classroom language socialization, by Barnard and Torres-Guzman (2009), also dealt primarily with elementary school children.)

However, a growing body of language socialization research is now taking place both inside and outside of classrooms, in face-to-face and online or blended learning environments, and with older children and adults of all ages engaging in various forms of (multi)literacies, often in transnational situations (Duff and Anderson, 2015; Duff, Zappa-Hollman, and Surtees, in press). Some of that research, described as *academic discourse socialization*, aims to track students across courses or sites through their distributed social and semiotic networks, as they negotiate different languages, genres, registers, and identities in the process (e.g., working outside of class with group members in Japanese and inside class in English to complete and then present project work; Duff and Kobayashi, 2010). This emerging body of language socialization research sometimes provides explicit critiques of prevailing discourses or ideologies (e.g., neoliberalism, in the context of international education, or English as a global language). Future language socialization research in (or connected with) classroom learning is likely to address populations across an even wider spectrum of ages, stages, and disciplines, charting trajectories of socialization across other combinations of languages in creative ways, and confronting problematic or conflictual ideologies related to language forms, food choices, embodied experience, and other topics (e.g., "voice" in academic writing). For now, the field is greatly enriched by this highly original volume and the unique contributions it offers other researchers, scholars, and educators. It is my sincere hope, and belief, that the collection will inspire other language and literacy socialization research internationally in contexts as compelling, textured, and multiscalar as those featured here (Duff, 2019).

REFERENCES

Barnard, R. and Torres-Guzmán, M. (eds.) (2009). *Creating Communities of Learning in Schools: International Case Studies and Perspectives.* Clevedon, UK: Multilingual Matters.

Bayley, R. and Schecter, S. (eds.) (2003). *Language Socialization in Bilingual and Multilingual Societies.* Clevedon, UK: Multilingual Matters.

Bhabha, H. K. (2004). *The Location of Culture.* Abingdon, UK: Routledge.

Cazden, C. (1988). *Classroom Discourse: The Language of Teaching and Learning.* Portsmouth, NH: Heinemann.

Duff, P. A. (1993). "Changing times, changing minds: language socialization in Hungarian-English schools." Unpublished doctoral dissertation, University of California, Los Angeles.

Duff, P. A. (1995). An ethnography of communication in immersion classrooms in Hungary. *TESOL Quarterly,* 29, 505–537.

Duff, P. A. (1996). Different languages, different practices: socialization of discourse competence in dual language school classrooms in Hungary. In K. Bailey and D. Nunan (eds.), *Voices from the Language Classroom: Qualitative Research in Second Language Education* (pp. 407–433). New York, NY: Cambridge University Press.

Duff, P. A. (2008). Language socialization, participation and identity: ethnographic approaches. In M. Martin-Jones, A-M de Mejia, and N. Hornberger (eds.), *Encyclopedia of Language and Education, 2nd Ed., Vol. 3: Discourse and Education* (pp. 107–119). New York, NY: Springer.

Duff, P. A. (2009). Language socialization in a Canadian secondary school: talking about current events. In R. Barnard and M. Torres-Guzman (eds.), *Creating Communities of Learning in Schools* (pp. 165–185). Clevedon, UK: Multilingual Matters.

Duff, P. A. (2010a). Language socialization into academic discourse communities. *Annual Review of Applied Linguistics,* 30, 169–192.

Duff, P. A. (2010b). Language socialization. In N. H. Hornberger and S. McKay (eds.), *Sociolinguistics and Language Education: New Perspectives on Language and Education* (pp. 427–454). Bristol, UK: Multilingual Matters.

Duff, P. A. (2015). Transnationalism, multilingualism, and identity. *Annual Review of Applied Linguistics,* 35, 57–80.

Duff, P. A. (2019). Social dimensions and processes in second language acquisition: multilingual socialization in transnational contexts. *Modern Language Journal,* 103 (Supplement 2019), 6–22.

Duff, P. A. and Anderson, T. (2015). Academic language and literacy socialization for second language students. In N. Markee (ed.), *The Handbook of Classroom Discourse and Interaction* (pp. 337–352). Malden, MA: Wiley.

Duff, P. A. and Hornberger, N. H. (2008). *Language Socialization: Encyclopedia of Language and Education, Vol. 8.* New York, NY: Springer.

Duff, P. A. and Kobayashi, M. (2010). The intersection of social, cognitive, and cultural processes in language learning: a second language socialization approach. In R. Batstone (Ed.), *Sociocognitive Perspectives on Language Use and Language Learning* (pp. 75–93). Oxford: Oxford University Press.

Duff, P. A. and May, S. (2017). *Language Socialization: Encyclopedia of Language and Education* (3rd ed.). Cham, Switzerland: Springer.

Duff, P. and Talmy, S. (2011). Language socialization approaches to second language acquisition: social, cultural, and linguistic development in additional languages. In D. Atkinson (ed.), *Alternative Approaches to SLA* (pp. 95–116). London: Routledge.

Duff, P., Zappa-Hollman, S., and Surtees, V. (in press). Research on language and literacy socialization at Canadian universities. *Canadian Modern Language Review*, 74(4).

Duranti, A., Ochs, E., and Schieffelin, B. B. (eds.) (2011). *The Handbook of Language Socialization*. Malden, MA: Wiley-Blackwell.

Erickson, F. (1982). Classroom discourse as improvisation: relationships between academic task structure and social participation structure in lessons. In L. C. Wilkinson (ed.), *Communicating in the Classroom* (pp. 153–181). New York, NY: Academic Press.

Garrett, P. B. (2017). Researching language socialization. In K. King, Y. L. Lai, and S. May (eds.), *Research Methods in Language and Education* (pp. 283–295). *Encyclopedia of Language and Education* (3rd ed.). Cham, Switzerland: Springer.

Garrett, P. B. and Baquedano-López, P. (2002). Language socialization: Reproduction and continuity, transformation and change. *Annual Review of Anthropology*, 31, 339–361.

Goffman, E. (1961). *Asylums: Essays on the Social Situation of Mental Patients and Other Inmates*. New York, NY: Anchor Books.

Guardado, M. (2009). Speaking Spanish like a boy scout: language socialization, resistance, and reproduction in a heritage language Scout troop. *Canadian Modern Language Review*, 66, 101–129.

Gutiérrez, K. (2008). Developing a sociocritical literacy in the third space. *Reading Research Quarterly*, 43(2), 148–164.

Gutiérrez, K., Baquedano-López, P., and Tejeda, C. (1999). Rethinking diversity: hybridity and hybrid language practices in the third space. *Mind, Culture, and Activity*, 6, 286–303.

He, A. (2011). Heritage language socialization. In A. Duranti, E. Ochs, and B. B. Schieffelin (eds.), *The Handbook of Language Socialization* (pp. 587–609). Malden, MA: Wiley-Blackwell.

He, A. (2015). Literacy, creativity, and continuity: a language socialization perspective on heritage language classroom interaction. In N. Markee (ed.), *The Handbook of Classroom Discourse and Interaction* (pp. 304–318). Malden, MA: Wiley-Blackwell.

Heath, S. B. (1982). *Ways with Words: Language, Life and Work in Communities and Classrooms*. Cambridge: Cambridge University Press.

Heath, S. B. (2012). *Words at Work and Play: Three Decades in Family and Community Life*. Cambridge: Cambridge University Press.

Heath, S. B. (1986). What no bedtime story means. In B. B. Schieffelin and E. Ochs (eds.), *Language Socialization across Cultures* (pp. 97–124). Cambridge: Cambridge University Press. [Reprinted from *Language in Society*, 11, 49–76].

Kulick, D. and Schieffelin, B. B. (2004). Language socialization. In A. Duranti (ed.), *A Companion to Linguistic Anthropology* (pp. 349–368). Malden, MA: Blackwell.

Lee, J. S. and Bucholtz, M. (2015). Language socialization across learning spaces. In N. Markee (ed.), *The Handbook of Classroom Discourse and Interaction* (pp. 319–336). Malden, MA: Wiley Blackwell.

Mehan, H. (1979). *Learning Lessons: Social Organization in the Classroom*. Cambridge, MA: Harvard University Press.

Mökkönen, A. C. (2012). Social organization through teacher-talk: subteaching, socialization and the normative use of language in a multilingual primary class. *Linguistics and Education*, 23, 310–322.

Ochs, E. (1986). Introduction. In B. B. Schieffelin and E. Ochs (eds.), *Language Socialization across Cultures* (pp. 1–13). Cambridge: Cambridge University Press.

Ochs, E. and Schieffelin, B. B. (2011). The theory of language socialization. In A. Duranti, E. Ochs, and B. B. Schieffelin (eds.), *The Handbook of Language Socialization* (pp. 1–21). Malden, MA: Wiley Blackwell.

Ochs, E. and Schieffelin, B. B. (2017). Language socialization: an historical overview. In P. A. Duff and S. May (eds.), *Language Socialization* (pp. 3–16). *Encyclopedia of Language Education* (3rd ed.). Cham, Switzerland: Springer.

Philips, S. U. (1983). *The Invisible Culture: Communication in Classroom and Community on the Warm Springs Indian Reservation*. New York, NY: Longman.

Pratt, M. L. (1991). Arts of the contact zone. *Profession*, 33–40.

Räisänen, T. (2016). Finnish engineers' trajectories of socialisation into global working life: from language learners to BELF users and the emergence of a Finnish way of speaking English. In F. Dervin and P. Holmes (eds.), *The Cultural and Intercultural Dimensions of English as a Lingua Franca* (pp. 157–179). Bristol, UK: Multilingual Matters.

Schieffelin, B. B. and Ochs, E. (1986). Language socialization. *Annual Review of Anthropology*, 15(1), 163–246.

Schieffelin, B. B. and Ochs, E. (eds.). (1986). *Language Socialization across Cultures*. New York, NY: Cambridge University Press.

Slobin, D. I. (ed.). (1985). *The Crosslinguistic Study of Language Acquisition, Vol. 1: The Data*. Hillsdale, NJ: Lawrence Erlbaum.

Talmy, S. (2008). The cultural productions of the ESL student at Tradewinds High: contingency, multidirectionality, and identity in L2 socialization. *Applied Linguistics*, 29(4), 619–644.

Watson-Gegeo, K. A. (1992). Thick explanation in the ethnographic study of child socialization and development: a longitudinal study of the problem of schooling for Kwara'ae (Solomon Islands) children. In W. A. Corsaro and P. J. Miller (eds.), *The Production and Reproduction of Children's Worlds: Interpretive Methodologies for the Study of Childhood Socialization* (pp. 51–66). San Francisco, CA: Jossey-Bass.

Watson-Gegeo, K. A. and Gegeo, D. W. (1994). Keeping culture out of the classroom in rural Solomon Islands schools: a critical analysis. *Educational Foundations*, 8 (2), 27–55.

Wittgenstein, L. (1953). *Philosophical Investigations*. Oxford: Basil Blackwell.

Wortham, S. (2005). Socialization beyond the speech event. *Journal of Linguistic Anthropology*, 15, 95–112.

Wortham, S. (2006). *Learning Identity: The Joint Emergence of Social Identification and Academic Learning*. New York, NY: Cambridge University Press.

Zuengler, J. and Cole, K. (2005). Language socialization and L2 learning. In E. Hinkel (ed.), *Handbook of Research in Second Language Teaching and Learning* (pp. 301–316). Mahwah, NJ: Lawrence Erlbaum Associates.

Index

academic discourse socialization, 261
accommodation, 3–5, 115, 254
accounts, 9, 18, 214, 225, 235–240
acquisition, 1, 3, 9, 219
  culture, 3, 241
  language, 3–4, 51, 100, 107, 129, 250
    L2 (second language),
      158, 163, 167
active watching, 215, *See also* observation
activity
  as focus of LS research, 15
  goal of, 37, 39–40, 44
  literacy. *See* literacy activity
  official vs. unofficial, 133
  reading. *See* reading
  situated interactive, 208
  social. *See* social, activity
addressee, 13, 15, 215, 233, *See also*
    participation framework
aesthetic
  See esthetic
affect, 85, 94–95, 108–109, 118, 249, 260,
    See also emotion; feelings; stance,
    affective
  intensifier, 77, 79, 83–84
  specifier, 77, 79, 83–84
affective stance. *See* stance, affective
Africa, 115, 204, 207
African American, 64, 256, *See also* Black
agency, 12–13, 65, 99, 109, 115, 120,
    126–127, 159–160, 251, 255
alignment
  affective, 41
  student displays of, 17, 59, 76, 80–81, 118,
    126, 171–172, 234, 237
  teacher displays of, 12, 59, 81
Althusser, L., 10, 18, 183, 189
ambiguity, 171, *See also* indirectness
America
  Central, 52
  North, 6, 160
  South, 52, 164

American, 161–162, 166, 174, 226, 257
  Anglo-, 5
  Jewish, 59
  society, 49–50, 52, 60, 63, 66
  student, 168–169, 171, 173
  White middle-class (WMCA), 3
analogy, 137, 147, 256–257
ancient truths, 181
Anderson, B., 49, 58
animator, 13–14, 126, 145, 171, 215, 225,
    234–235, 242, *See also* production
    format
answer, 14, 145, *See also* IRE;
    question–answer sequence
  correct/right, 134–135, 154
  incorrect/wrong, 79, 154
apprenticeship, 93–94, 96–97, 99–100,
    255
Arabic, 51–52, 207
arts, 8, 17, 33–37, 40, 42–44, 132, 140, 155,
    202–203
  martial, 203
ascription, 12, 119, 124, 126, 129, 159–162,
    166–167, 169, 171–172, 174, *See also*
    positioning
Asia, 115, 164
Asian, 140, 160
assertion, 63, 84, 170, 196
assessment, 7, 9–10, 58, 61, 63, 77–84, 164,
    171, 206, 214, 224, 236–237, 255,
    See also evaluation; moral, assessment;
    praise
  definition of, 72
asymmetrical relationship, 12, 35
attention, 18, 44, 60, 117, 151, 186, 201–204,
    206, 218–219, 232, 239, 257, *See also*
    orientation
attitude, 10, 52, 55, 61, 65, 71–72, 112
audience, 96–97, 100, 107, 109, 135–136, 162,
    203, 206, 208, 210, 215, 255
authenticity, 11, 59, 93, 95, 100–101, 109
  vs. inauthenticity, 59, 93

Printed in the United States
by Baker & Taylor Publisher Services